Julie Andrews

Also by Robert Windeler

Sweetheart: The Story of Mary Pickford

The Films of Shirley Temple

Burt Lancaster

The Party Book
(with Milton Williams)

Sing a Pretty Song...
(with Edie Adams)

Vanishing Values

Links with a Past

The Quotable Golfer

Julie Andrews

A Life on Stage and Screen

• • • • • • • • • • • •

Robert Windeler

A Birch Lane Press Book
Published by Carol Publishing Group

A Birch Lane Press Book
Published by Carol Publishing Group
Birch Lane Press is a registered trademark of Carol Communications, Inc.

Editorial, sales and distribution, rights and permissions inquiries should be
addressed to Carol Publishing Group, 120 Enterprise Avenue, Secaucus, N.J.
07094

In Canada: Canadian Manda Group, One Atlantic Avenue, Suite 105, Toronto,
Ontario, M6K 3E7

Carol Publishing Group books may be purchased in bulk at special discounts
for sales promotion, fund-raising, or educational purposes. Special editions can
be created to specifications. For details, contact Special Sales Department,
Carol Publishing Group, 120 Enterprise Avenue, Secaucus, N.J. 07094.

Manufactured in the United States of America
10   9   8   7   6   5   4   3   2   1

Library of Congress Cataloging-in-Publication Data

Windeler, Robert.
    Julie Andrews : a life on stage and screen / Robert Windeler.
        p.   cm.
    "A Birch Lane Press book."
    ISBN 1-55972-391-2 (hardcover)
    1. Andrews, Julie.   2. Motion picture actors and actresses—Great
Britain—Biography.   3. Singers—Great Britain—Biography.
I. Title.
PN2598.A65W32   1997
791.43′028′092—dc21
[B]   97-5932
                                                             CIP

For Edie Adams

My friend who always inspires me to believe "It's Possible"

Contents

Acknowledgments

My chronicling of this subject can now be measured in decades, in three different books, in the 1970s, 1980s and now in 1997. I first met Julie Andrews half a lifetime ago, and it's been a fascinating privilege to relive my own life as I have reassessed hers. Time Inc.'s Richard Burgheim was there at the beginning, at the top of Coldwater Canyon, and I'm thankful for his encouragement and friendship during my *Time* and *People* years, and since. Many other important friendships have spanned the whole time period, and I appreciate especially the constant support of Robert Beardsley, Dorothy Nielsen, Stephen Paley, and Joyce Jillson.

For early insights into Julie Andrews, I remain grateful to Carol Burnett, John Calley, Blake Edwards, James Garner, Elsie Giorgi, Tammy Grimes, George Roy Hill, André Previn, Martin Ransohoff, Max Von Sydow, Robert Wise, and the late Rex Harrison and Alan Jay Lerner.

For their sustained enthusiasm and interest, Julie's loyal fans, such as Kathy Mervine, Sharon Murphy, Terry Nelson, Robert Corbell, and Marie-Jeanne van Hovell, are a remarkable group, and I am grateful for their long-standing kindness to me.

I especially thank Tom Wilson, who again gave a selfless assist with photographs. Curt Gunther was there at the outset, with his camera. Roy Moseley nicely provided the vaudeville context of Julie's early days in Britain. And Critt Davis filled in the photographic gaps at the end.

Allan J. Wilson has now been an editor of mine for twenty years and I deeply appreciate his patience, persistence, knowledge, and love of the theater and movies—and his sense of humor.

As always, libraries were essential, including that of the British Film Institute in London, the New York Public Library for the Performing Arts at Lincoln Center, and—particularly—the Margaret Herrick Library of the Academy of Motion Picture Arts and Sciences in Beverly Hills.

Most of all, I am grateful to Judith Crist, who first showed me, at Columbia University, how to forge a profession and even to live a life incorporating my passion for movies and the theater—and the late Richard Clurman of *Time*, who first allowed me to do it for real.

Julie Andrews

Prologue

On Monday, May 6, 1996, the American Theatre Wing and the League of American Theatres and Producers announced their nominations for the Antoinette Perry (Tony) Awards for the 1995–96 Broadway season. Conspicuously absent from the list of best musical nominees were the two big-budget stage shows that, coincidentally, had been based on movie hits of the 1980s: *Big* and *Victor/Victoria*. The struggling *Big*, which cost $10.3 million to mount—and would lose its entire investment when it closed six months into its run—managed to garner a total of five nominations; for score, libretto, choreography, leading actress, and featured actor. But the $8.5 million *Victor/Victoria*, which was running close to capacity, netted just one Tony nominee.

Alphabetically first among the candidates for Best Actress in a Musical was Julie Andrews, the title star of *Victor/Victoria*. She first had been nominated in this category almost forty years before, for her role as Eliza Doolittle in *My Fair Lady*, and had been named again in 1961, for the part of Queen Guinevere in *Camelot*. The first time she lost to Judy Holliday in *Bells Are Ringing*, the second to Elizabeth Seal in *Irma La Douce*. Andrews would have won the Tony just for showing up at the awards in 1996—not so much for her singing and acting in *Victor/Victoria* as for her entire body of work on stage and in movies, television, and recordings over the previous five decades.

Two days after the Tony nominations were announced, the Wednesday matinee audience rose to its feet to give *Victor/Victoria* and Julie their 318th standing ovation in 318 performances at the

3

Marquis Theatre. After the sustained applause, she held up her hand. In the other hand she held some papers. Still in her glittering finale costume, Andrews, standing center stage in front of the rest of the cast, asked the audience to be seated. "I would like to share something with you," she said, as the previously invited local, national and international press, and television cameras gathered at the front of the orchestra. She paid tribute to the other Tony nominees, but added, "flattered as I am, and honored to be also nominated, I have to say how deeply sad I am to be the only nominee in this extraordinarily gifted company.

"*Victor/Victoria* is a collaboration—between [*sic*] designers, choreographer, director, cast and crew—an extremely happy and successful collaboration, which makes it especially sad that so many of my colleagues have been ignored by this year's nominating process. I could not have done all this alone. I have searched my conscience and my heart. Sadly, I cannot accept this nomination, and prefer to stand instead with the egregiously overlooked...." She gestured to the cast standing behind her, and named the principal performers, designers, and composers, the late Henry Mancini and Frank Wildhorn, and lyricist Leslie Bricusse. Andrews spoke of "the seventy-five other members of the *Victor/Victoria* family...We stand together in celebration of our show and of audiences like you, who stand for us."

Julie did not mention by name her husband of twenty-seven years, Blake Edwards, who had written, produced, and directed the musical *Victor/Victoria*, which had been adapted from his 1982 movie of the same name in which she also starred. Blake and Andrews were also principal investors (along with the rock group Aerosmith) in the show, which marked Blake's Broadway debut in any capacity, and Julie's first return to the Broadway stage since she had closed in *Camelot*. With so many jobs on the production and so much at stake, Edwards was clearly the most overlooked of all of the *Victor/Victoria* company, whether "egregiously" or not.

When the musical opened in New York in October of 1995, the reviews had been mixed to negative for the material and its staging, at the same time almost unanimously glowing of Andrews. The healthy box office advance and ongoing ticket sales were not harmed by the critics nor by word of mouth. No theater parties were canceled. Julie's fans had waited thirty-three years to see her back on Broadway, even if it was as a down-on-her-luck opera singer in 1930s Paris pretending to be a female impersonater in a nightclub, a portrayal they had already seen in the movie. Some critical objections centered on the banality of Mancini's music and especially on Bricusse's lyrics (only four songs had been retained from the motion picture; the rest were new). Other caveats concerned the fact that Blake Edwards, a stage novice who had written and directed seven of his wife's seventeen movies, had not really rethought *Victor/Victoria* for the theater. The movie had been "with music"; its song and dance numbers were performed only in a nightclub context. In any stage musical the songs, even those sung in a cabaret, should either advance the plot or help to define a character. Often the numbers in *Victor/Victoria* did not really accomplish either of those things.

Reaction to the Andrews Tony bombshell was also decidedly mixed. "This public sulking makes you look like just another Broadway prima donna," wrote New York *Daily News* drama critic Howard Kissell. "Get over it," *Esquire* told her in print. *Time* listed Julie's press conference ninth among "The Worst Public Performance of 1996." "Not saying thank you is one of our least favorite things," the magazine began. "Her sincerity would have played out a little better if somebody hadn't tipped off the TV news crews who came rushing into the theater thirty minutes before curtain time."

But some admirers hailed Julie's stand as an act of bravery, and the next day her dressing room was filled with more flowers than on her opening night. The tabloid *New York Post* front headline screamed "Mary Poppins Hoppin' Mad!" That newspaper's theater and dance critic, Clive Barnes, while "shocked to putrefaction" over some of the Tony nominees, claimed the list didn't make him like *Victor/Victoria* any better. Ticket sales for the show leaped 30 percent the week after the Andrews outburst.

Julie Andrews was a woman with a careerlong goody-two-shoes image, try as she might to change it, and, even more important, a lifelong desire to please and a fear of offending. Thus she seemed unlikely casting for the role of a defiant Broadway rebel. "It was, on the one hand, the easiest decision I ever had to make," she told Peter Marks of *The New York Times*. "On the other hand, I was quaking in my boots. My biggest worry was that I was going to hurt someone or something that I hadn't considered. Then, when I really, really thought about it, I really couldn't hurt anybody. It just felt right. It came from my heart, that's all I can say."

Julie's mother, a performer herself, told her daughter that while she must always do her best when she performed, once the curtain came down she had no further obligation to the audience. This, in part, explained Julie's quixotic attitude toward signing autographs and receiving admirers, among other things. Julie's constant search since childhood had been for a stable family life, and this search extended to creating a happy working environment on the set or backstage. She always went to great lengths to keep casts and crews content and in her corner. Pouring tea for them was just a symbol of her concern. So those who knew Julie well were not surprised that she had chosen the folks backstage over the theater establishment and its rituals.

As usual, her coworkers returned her affection. After the Sunday matinee on May 12, 1996, the entire company of *Victor/Victoria*, including ushers and box-office personnel, gathered in the wings as Julie's costar Michael Nouri read his tribute reflecting the group's feelings:

"Once in a while, if we're lucky, someone comes along to remind us of the better parts of ourselves, someone who reflects the nobler aspects of who we are, someone who through courageous example demonstrates that when you are willing to stand alone for what you know is right, you find out who your friends are. Standing alone, yet now surrounded by your true friends, you know that you need never again stand alone. Your reward is beyond any award, beyond any earthly measure, your reward for being true to yourself is being surrounded by what you truly are."

The company presented Julie with a $2,000 silver Tiffany bowl engraved with the words "Jooles, you are our crowning jewel. With endless love and admiration, your *Victor/Victoria* Family." The crew mounted a five-foot replica of the Tony Award medallion, depicting the masks of comedy and drama, on Julie's dressing room wall. The logo had been stolen from the previous year's ceremony.

Although her name remained on the ballot, Julie did not win the 1996 Tony for Best Actress in a Musical (Donna Murphy won for *The King and I*). Tony Awards host Nathan Lane cracked that if Andrews had won the honor it would have been accepted by "a very grateful Susan Lucci," the star of the soap opera *All My Children* and a seventeen-time Emmy loser. Julie did not perform at or even attend the Tony ceremonies, which she had thrice co-hosted in three different decades: in 1970, with Anthony Quayle; in 1984, with Robert Preston; and in 1991, with Jeremy Irons. Because of the controversy, the *Victor/Victoria* box office surged yet again the day after the Tony Awards telecast.

Over the course of her five-decade career, Andrews had seen more hits and flops, and perhaps more emotional peaks and valleys, than most actors and entertainers. As the star of the movie *The Sound of Music*, she understood better than most that the public's response to a piece can be diametrically opposite to that of the "experts." As a woman, she had come to understand that her show business career was not her whole identity, it was merely what she did for a living, though it happened to be out in public. Her family came first and her art would speak for itself.

"In the long run," Julie said, "it is a person's *body of work* that matters. If it is honest, with an integrity about it, and people sense a love of work in it, those are the things that last and that one is remembered for, possibly."

On February 3, 1997, Andrews was inducted into the Theater Hall of Fame, whose members are elected by America's drama critics and drama editors. Entering the Hall of Fame with her were actors Eileen Atkins and Brian Bedford, costume designers Florence Klotz and Irene Sharaff, critic Richard Coe, and comedienne Nancy Walker. Julie joined such previously inducted colleagues as Rodgers and Hammerstein, Lerner and Loewe, Maxwell Anderson, Richard Burton, Gower Champion, Carol Channing, Cy Feuer, Joel

Grey, Rex Harrison, Moss Hart, Danny Kaye, Gene Kelly, Angela Lansbury, Beatrice Lillie, Howard Lindsay, Christopher Plummer, Robert Preston, Gene Saks, Stephen Sondheim, Dorothy Stickney, Peggy Wood—and Tony Walton.

The next night, Julie returned to *Victor/Victoria* after a four-week vacation, mostly at her home in Gstaad, Switzerland. Her "dear chum" Liza Minnelli had taken over the dual role, playing to a somewhat different but equally enthusiastic audience. Julie was committed to remaining with her show until it turned a profit, or at least through June 1 of 1997. That was about a year later than the originally hoped-for target: up to the time of the Tony Awards of 1997 rather than the Tony Awards of 1996.

In October 1997, Julie would turn sixty-two and celebrate the fiftieth anniversary of her solo professional debut, at the age of twelve, in the revue *Starlight Roof* at the London Hippodrome.

Having started so young, Julie Andrews became a star before she became a person. Eventually she learned how to be both. This is the story of her sixty-two year life and her fifty-year career.

1

Bandy Legs, Buck Teeth, and a Freak Voice

Julia Elizabeth Wells was born on October 1, 1935, in Walton-on-Thames, Surrey, eighteen miles south of London. She was named after her two grandmothers, Julia Morris and Elizabeth Wells, though it was not long before she became known as Julie.

Her father, Edward C. "Ted" Wells, was a teacher of woodworking and metalcrafting in a state school in Ockley, Surrey. Her mother, Barbara Morris Wells, who also was born in Walton-on-Thames, gave piano lessons and was a part-time pianist for an evening dancing school run by her sister, Joan Morris. Joan lived with the Wellses in their modest but not poverty-stricken circumstances. Joan Morris's dance classes, which cost one shilling for half an hour, were held in a building that served as a private preparatory school by day. When Barbara Wells played the piano for the classes, she wheeled along her infant daughter in a baby carriage. Thus Julie heard music and saw dancing long before she was walking or talking.

"My mum, when she was younger, had been a very promising concert pianist," Julie said, "but her parents died when they were young, and she had to quit studying to raise her younger sister." It was that same sister, Joan Morris, who gave Julie her first parts on stage. When she was two, Julie appeared in the dancing school's pageant in the non-speaking role of a fairy. The next year she had her first singing and speaking part as Nod in the school's production of *Wynken, Blinken, and Nod*. Ted Wells built the set, a children's nursery, and Barbara Wells played the piano accompaniment as usual. Little Julie wore white pajamas with flaps in the rear with one of the two buttons deliberately undone to show a pair of pink tights underneath. While she was singing her Nod part of the title song in a childish but on-pitch treble, the other flap button worked loose, leaving her exposed in back. "My second cousin twice removed (another actor in the play) dashed to my rescue," she recalled, "but it was only natural that I should go on."

Just before Great Britain entered World War II, in the summer of 1939, when Julie was not quite four, Barbara Wells took a job as a pianist for a variety show, *The Dazzle Company*, at a seaside music hall in Bognor Regis. Also on the bill, as a last-minute substitute act, was "The Canadian Troubador, Songs and a Guitar." The songs were sung in a rich tenor voice and the guitar was played by Ted Andrews, a Canadian who had emigrated to England as a vaudeville entertainer. By summer's end, Ted Andrews and Barbara Wells had become a double act.

None of the principals ever spoke about what happened next. Julie said later, "I don't remember anything because I was kept in the dark about it all." But war did break out when Hitler invaded Poland in September and Bognor Regis emptied. The younger men of the cast and crew of *The Dazzle Company* were drafted. Barbara Wells and Ted Andrews joined an Entertainments National Services Association company (ENSA, similar to the American USO) to entertain the troops. Aunt Joan Morris took care of Julie and her brother John; the two children were later evacuated to a riding school in the Kentish countryside.

Ted Wells first helped with the evacuation of schoolchildren in Surrey, then worked in a war factory in Hinchley Wood. There he met Winifred, a hairdresser training to operate a lathe. As Ted and Barbara Wells grew further apart, Barbara and Ted Andrews grew closer together and the Wellses were divorced. Barbara then married Ted Andrews, and Ted Wells married his Win.

Although it was unusual for the time, Ted Wells was awarded custody of both Julie and her younger brother but he voluntarily returned his daughter to her mother. He had decided that "with war work taking up so much of my time, I could not do my duty as a father to both children." His other considerations, he recalled, were that a growing girl needs a mother's influence, and that Barbara and Ted Andrews "being in the theater themselves were better equipped than I to pay for her training." Wells added that he had determined from his children's earliest theatricals that Julie belonged on the stage, although he did not particularly approve of it as a lifestyle.

The divorce and subsequent custody arrangements were accomplished amicably, at least on the surface. Partially because she and John were at the riding school (where they were allowed to ride the ponies), that when her parents parted, Julie hardly realized it. "There were no fights, no loud scenes, thank God. The next thing I knew, a personality as colorful and noisy as show business itself—another Ted—came into my life. He thundered across my childhood."

So did World War II, in the most literal sense. "I was lucky because we weren't hit, but it was scary at times," she remembered. "Sometimes I think I've almost forgotten those childhood memories, and then I go to an utterly beautiful land like Hawaii, and the banging comes back to me all at once." On the set of *Darling Lili* in 1968, an actor fired a gun containing blanks, and Julie turned a terrified white. She continued to hate sudden violent noises, a fear that her 1960s analysis sessions traced to a specific blitz during the War.

"When I was told that John would be staying with Daddy and I would be staying with Mummy and that because of her work we had to leave Walton and live in London I began to feel that my world was breaking up," Julie wrote in an autobiography in *Woman's Magazine* when she was twenty-two.

Julie was five or six when she went to live with her mother and new stepfather, whom she had disliked on first meeting. "My mum wanted me to call him 'Uncle Ted,' which I was opposed to instantly," she said. "To avoid muddling I did end up calling him 'Pop' and my real father, 'Dad' or 'Daddy.'"

Ted and Barbara were not yet well known and only doing war work for ENSA, which didn't pay very much. So at first the new Andrews family (Julie's surname was legally changed later, when she joined the act) was "very poor, living in a tiny flat in Mornington Crescent, right opposite a very large cigarette factory in one of the bleaker parts of northwest London. After the green and leafy lanes of Walton I simply hated it. That was a very black period in my life. I hated my new home and the huge man who seemed to fill it. His huge voice, singing arias as he shaved, literally made the tooth mugs jump on the bathroom shelves. I half longed for, half dreaded my visits to Daddy, because when the time came to say goodbye I felt so sad at leaving him. Yet I couldn't have borne the thought of not going back to Mummy."

Soon Ted and Barbara Andrews began to achieve greater success as a supporting act in the music halls. "We were never top of the bill," Mrs. Andrews recalled. "After all, we were musical and not comedy, and the comedians got the best billing. But we were the second feature, a good supporting act with a drawing room set and ballads—nice family-type entertainment."

Ted, Barbara, and Julie moved to a larger apartment in a nicer part of London, in Clarendon Street, Victoria. The new Andrews flat was on the ground floor and the building provided two air-raid shelters in the basement. Joan Morris lived in a small flat nearby while her new husband, Bill Wilby, was a Royal Air Force prisoner of war. Julie remembered helping her aunt send letters to "Dinglebell" as she and her new half-brother Donald called him because they couldn't say "Uncle Bill."

By the time Julie was eight, the family again had moved up in the world, to a rented house in Beckenham, Kent. The area's inhabitants tended to ignore most official air-raid warnings and go into shelters only when they actually saw German airplanes and "doodlebugs" (flying bombs) virtually overhead. Julie was outfitted with opera glasses and a whistle with which to watch for doodlebugs and warn the neighbors. Ted Andrews often led a cappella community singing in the shelters during the air raids. One night Julie suddenly joined in the singing, soaring an octave, or sometimes two, above the general pitch.

"In all fairness, I truthfully do not know whether I started in show business because of my parents, or circumstances or what," Julie said. "But I was under everyone's feet. My stepfather, not knowing what to do with me—and I think in an attempt to get closer to me—sent me off to a singing teacher."

A specialist confirmed that the self-described bandy-legged, buck-toothed child possessed "an enormous, belting, freak voice with a range of four octaves and some fierce high notes. I sounded like an immature Yma Sumac," Julie recalled, referring to the lynx-eyed Peruvian-born singer with a five-octave range whose first heyday was the 1940s but who enjoyed a major revival among twentysomethings in the 1990s, appearing at such unlikely venues as West Hollywood's The House of Blues. "Once, to the amazement of me and all the dogs in the area, I actually hit a C above top C," Julie remembered.

Since Julie's larynx was fully developed, singing would do her no harm, the doctor decided. Ted Andrews was delighted with his stepdaughter's newly discovered talent, and he literally forced her to develop it. When she was eleven, he sent her off to his own voice teacher, Madame Lilian Stiles-Allen, who lived near Leeds, in Yorkshire. She had been a renowned concert singer and was a "wonderful woman" who stayed with Julie as friend and coach until long after Julie had become a superstar. "It's thanks to her that I didn't do more damage to my voice with all that singing when I was young and, later, in *My Fair Lady*," Julie recalled. "I used to watch her give lessons to all her other pupils, then I would take lessons twice a day. She had an enormous influence on me. She was my third mother."

In fact, when Barbara Andrews was pregnant with Julie's younger half-brother Christopher, the eleven-year-old girl took the two-hundred mile train trip alone to Leeds to spend four or five days at a time with Mme. Stiles-Allen. The teacher stressed, among other things, perfect diction, describing singing as musical speech. She also instilled in Julie the belief that "a voice is a gift, given to you to care for and use. If you work hard and with humility, one day you may be able to bring pleasure to many people. And in giving pleasure you yourself will gain great joy."

Ted Andrews pushed his stepdaughter hard. To avoid over-straining her voice, Julie was "made to practice singing only a half an hour a day, but it seemed much longer than that. And none of the other girls I knew had to practice singing at all. I loathed singing and resented my stepfather. He acutely embarrassed and upset me by asking me to perform. But he was a very good disciplinarian, and later I was grateful that he had made me take singing lessons. It gave me an identity which later became very necessary. Without it I would have been ten times more mixed up than I was."

Julie occasionally attended the Cone-Ripman School in London, which taught acting and ballet in the morning and the more conventional subjects in the afternoon. Her aunt Joan taught there between sessions of her own dancing school; classes had become erratic because of World War II. Toward the end of the war, during school holdiays—when there was school—Julie was taken to whatever city her mother and stepfather were working in. Otherwise she stayed at home with a housekeeper.

"I enjoyed school," she said, "and like any other small girl I wanted to be just exactly the same as everyone else. No matter how hard Mummy tried to make this come true for me, I *was* different. I had two fathers, my parents were in show business, and I went to a different town each holiday-time. The girls I envied most were good at games; I was awful."

But Julie kept practicing, and developed such perfect pitch that fifty years later musicians would still marvel at her voice. "I'm firmly convinced that one can *develop* perfect pitch," she said. "You don't have to be born with it. I was one of those child brat-prodigies, and for my age I had an immensely powerful voice. It was to everyone's great surprise that it was there; there were no vocal musicians in my family." Those who did not know that Ted Andrews was not Julie's biological father just assumed that she had inherited her talent from him.

In 1945, when Julie was ten, the war ended. The next year the Andrews family moved back to Walton-on-Thames and bought a house called The Old Meuse. Barbara Andrews later discovered that her mother, Julia Morris, had worked in that same house as a maid. Barbara continued to live there, by herself, long after her only daughter became famous, and even after her second husband, Ted Andrews, died of a stroke in 1966. The house was demolished in 1973 to build a series of Old Meuse Townhouses.

"I came from a long line of below-stairs maids and gardeners— good old peasant stock," Julie told Jonathan Van Meter of *Vanity Fair* in 1995. "My mother and her sister made a quantum leap out of that life. Then I made another quantum leap."

Julie continued to practice and would sometimes sing for friends, depending on her mood. "Then came the day I was told I must go to bed in the afternoon because I was going to be allowed to sing with Mummy and Pop in the evening," she recalled. "I had to stand on a beer crate to reach the microphone to sing my solo. It was such immense fun that I did it several times more, during school vacations, on an odd Tuesday night when it was not desperately important. My mother played the piano, my stepfather sang, and once in a while I joined him in a duet. It must have been ghastly, but it seemed to go down all right."

Ted and Barbara Andrews had to get permission from theater managers for Julie to appear in these unbilled "surprise bits" in their act. When so allowed, Julie would join Ted in a sentimental standard such as "Come to the Fair." "Some of the managers wouldn't take a chance on a rather ugly ten-year-old child," Julie said. "They thought my parents were quite out of their minds. But the ones that did take a chance were very nice."

There had been some family discussion of Julie's enrolling in the Royal Academy of Dramatic Art in London, but, as Barbara

Andrews explained, "we decided that a little toughening up as far as the theater was concerned would be good. So we took her into our act. Let's face it, it didn't hurt the act either."

The highlight of this triple act came on December 5, 1946, when eleven-year-old Julie joined Ted and Barbara at a royal command performance at London's Stage Door Canteen, where servicemen had been entertained during World War II. Julie got to sing her big solo, the Polonaise from *Mignon,* in front of Queen Elizabeth, who would later become the Queen Mother and Princess Margaret. "I was too excited for stage fright, and I got my notes out without mistakes," Julie recalled. But when she was presented to the Queen in a receiving line after the performance, "my knees almost buckled; all I could think about was whether I should curtsy both before and after meeting the Queen."

"You sang beautifully, Julie, and we all enjoyed it very much," said Queen Elizabeth.

"I was in heaven," Julie remembered.

After two years of Julie's occasional beer-box appearances with her parents, capped by this unexpected treat (Julie hadn't known she was going to sing for royalty until it happened, and they hadn't asked for her by name—yet), Ted Andrews decided that she was ready for a career of her own. Julie remembered herself at the age of twelve as a "hideous child, with pigtails, crooked teeth, very bad legs" and eyes that at times moved quite independently of one another. She had freckles and had inherited her mother's swooped nose and protruding jawline. But she also remembered her step-father as "a whiz at selling anything."

One day in October 1947, just after Julie turned twelve, Ted Andrews was playing golf with Val Parnell, the managing director of Moss Empires, the largest booking firm in England and the owners of the London Palladium, London Hippodrome, and theaters all over the provinces. Andrews persuaded Parnell to come home with him to hear his stepdaughter sing. At the time, Julie was playing in a tree with her half-brother Donald. Ted went "out to the garden and yanked this scruffy kid wearing a smudged smock into the house to sing an aria," she recalled. Again, it was "I Am Titania" from

Mignon. After singing for Parnell, she returned to playing in the tree.

Parnell was impressed enough to sign Julie for *Starlight Roof,* a revue that he was just about to open at the London Hippodrome starring comedians Vic Oliver and Fred Emney, singer Pat Kirkwood, and featuring Wally Boag, who made animal sculptures out of balloons. Instead of her usual Polonaise from *Mignon,* Parnell assigned Julie the much tamer "Skater's Waltz." But the night before the October 23rd opening, he decided that the naive girl singing the simple song did not match the theme of his sophisticated review and he fired her.

"My mother and my agent descended on him and said, 'you've got to give this girl her big break,' and all that sort of awful nonsense," Julie remembered. Parnell relented on the afternoon of the opening, though he asked her to sing Titania's aria from *Mignon* instead, which Julie remembered as "a song ten times more difficult than the one I'd started out with."

Fortunately, she knew the aria by heart from all the times she sang it, and that night she and the song were a success; the twelve-year-old reached the F above high C with ease. Julie got all the notices the next day. She was signed as a regular.

At each performance, she would sit with her mother in the audience until it was time for her number. Boag would have just finished creating his balloon animals and asked if there was a boy or girl in the audience who wanted to come up to the stage and get one of the animals. It was always Julie who got the balloon animal. She exchanged a few lines of dialogue with Boag and star host Vic Oliver, sang her aria, took a bow, then walked back down into the audience and out of the theater without waiting to take a curtain call with the rest of the cast. (Performers under the age of fifteen were prohibited by the London County Council from working in the theater after ten P.M.) "I only had that one song," she said, "but fortunately it stopped the show."

For this solo professional debut Julie Andrews, in pigtails, earned fifty pounds (then about $200) a week. Her salary was paid to her mother and stepfather. All Julie got was a raise in her allowance from two to five shillings (from about forty cents to a dollar) a week; the rest went into a trust fund. That December, Barbara and Ted turned down an offer for Julie to perform in a Christmas pantomime for a salary of one hundred pounds ($400) weekly, insisting that she be neither spoiled nor overworked.

Parnell introduced Julie to the Grade brothers, Lew and Leslie, who were already among London's top bookers of music hall acts. The Grades were then too busy to take her on, so Parnell put her together with Charles Tucker, a well-liked agent-impresario of the second tier who became her agent/manager until 1965. She called him Uncle Charlie, and loved to visit his "cozy office, right at the top of a tall building overlooking Piccadilly Circus." He would always inspect her fingernails.

"Sometimes as we walked down Piccadilly," Julie remembered, "I would point to a beautiful car or a lovely frock in a window, and Uncle Charles would say, 'You'll be able to buy things like that one day. You're going to be a big star.' And I would giggle, 'Don't be silly, Uncle.'"

With Tucker in charge of her career, "the buck teeth were seen to immediately," Andrews recalled. There was little that could be done about Julie's bandy legs, but she corrected her lazy right eye by using the exercises developed by Dr. William H. Bates. "First I had to practice how to use my eyes, then I had to practice how to breathe," she remembered. "I was always practicing something. The eye practice was fun when Mummy did it with me to music, but otherwise it was a dreadful bore. Everyone said I would have to wear corrective glasses but Mummy was determined I should be spared this."

Julie settled into a year-long run at the Hippodrome, feeling that she was getting by on her "freak" singing. "I knew no other profession, no other life," she recalled. "I didn't know that it was not good for a twelve-year-old girl to be singing in a sophisticated review. I just thought I was the luckiest girl alive."

In December of 1947, Julie had her first and only screen test. It was filmed in black and white at Metro-Goldwyn-Mayer in London for the American producer Joseph Pasternak. Her mother Barbara played the piano, and Julie was decked out in ribbons and curls and a little-girl dress. Her weight was given as seventy-nine pounds, her height 4'10½". "They tried to make me look like a child star," she remembered, "but with my teeth and legs I didn't look like much of anything." The studio did not sign her, and until she actually appeared in her first movie, *Mary Poppins*, seventeen years later, Julie Andrews was deemed unfilmable, at least for the big screen.

"Of course we never dreamed of film," Barbara Andrews said on a visit to the set of *Little Miss Marker*, her daughter's eleventh movie, in 1979. "Julie used to complain bitterly about her nose and her jaw. But for a plain little girl I think she has some rare qualities, something that's not necessarily beauty, but a wonderful warm quality that is somehow luminous."

Her run in *Starlight Roof* led to Julie's being requested to appear at a Royal Command Variety Performance at the London Palladium on November 1, 1948, a month to the day after her thirteenth birthday. Danny Kaye, a court favorite from America, was the headliner. The bill also included Hollywood's dancing Nicholas Brothers and a male impersonator, Ella Shields, who sang "Burlington Bertie from Bow," a song that July later sang on her 1962 record album *Don't Go Into the Lion's Cage Tonight*, and again as Gertrude Lawrence in the movie *Star!* "Who knows," Julie said in 1995 about Ella Shields, "she could have been the lady that set me on the road to *Victor/Victoria.*"

Danny Kaye agreed to give a press conference and sit for photographs with some of the other acts on the bill. Julie, not having heard about the picture-taking, arrived for the press conference in jodhpurs, straight from horseback riding in the country. "I looked absolutely ridiculous, with this huge toothy smile," she remembered, "and they plunked me on his lap," while Kaye, in his Burberry trench coat and cap looked a bit like Sherlock Holmes.

As the photographers' flashbulbs exploded around them, Danny tried for a sense of rapport by chatting with the girl he had just met. He asked Julie what she would be singing that night. As she recounted it for Martin Gottfried's biography of Danny Kaye,

Nobody's Fool, she replied, "Oh, I don't think you would know it; it's a rather obscure song." When Danny smilingly pressed her, Julie answered, hesitantly, "It's the 'Polonaise' from *Mignon.*"

"Oh!" she recalled his saying, "the one that goes da-da-DUM-da-da." He hummed through to the end. "He knew it quite familiarly and I was astounded—truly impressed. He was divine. He could not have been more gentle, more kind, more truly interested. I sort of instantly fell in love."

Then she went off to change into her performance costume, "a white dress with a pink underlay—sort of chiffony or Georgette—with puffy shoulders. The whole idea was to make me look [even] younger than I was."

Julie was described in the official advance announcement for the royal command performance as "a thirteen-year-old coloratura soprano with the voice of an adult," and in the program as "our youngest operatic soprano." She was the youngest performer ever chosen to perform for royalty at the Palladium. Again Queen Elizabeth and Princess Margaret attended the concert, this time along with King George VI, Princess Elizabeth (later Queen Elizabeth II), and her husband, the Duke of Edinburgh. Ninth on the bill, Julie yet again sang her "bastardized" aria from *Mignon,* on which "I had nearly busted a gut taking a top F nightly for a year" in the revue. (She had never missed that F during the run, but occasionally did later.) After she led the company in a rousing rendition of "God Save the King," Julie was presented to the King and Queen, the Princesses Margaret and Elizabeth, and the Duke of Edinburgh.

Once her year in *Starlight Roof* was over (the show continued to run but the London County Council prohibited minors under the age of fifteen from working for more than twelve months in the same show), Julie began to tour music halls all over Britain. Sometimes she appeared with Ted and Barbara, who by now had acquired a trailer. With two young children in tow, it was easier to drive and sleep in the trailer than to go by train and search for family "digs." More often Julie went out as a solo act, for which she was paid seventy-five pounds ($350) a week. Either way, she figured, "this was the daughter of Ted and Barbara Andrews that everyone had come to see. My mother and stepfather had become big stars and I was, in effect, part of the act."

Julie also followed Ted and Barbara into radio and television, making her radio debut in 1946. She sang a duet with her stepfather on the BBC variety show *Monday Night at Eight*. On October 8, 1949, a week after her fourteenth birthday, Julie joined legendary World War II singer Vera Lynn and music hall comic Stanley Holloway on a BBC-TV program called *Radiolympia Showtime*. Seventeen years later, Holloway would play Julie's father in *My Fair Lady*.

Julie's schooling, which had been sporadic at best, was abandoned entirely in favor of a governess and chaperone, who taught her for four hours a day until Julie was fifteen, when she stopped her formal learning altogether. "I bitterly regret not having had more education," she said. "I envy my children when they go to college." A Miss Knight (Julie never knew her first name) was the traveling tutor when Julie went "on the halls" in vaudeville, in which "I mostly sang bastardized versions of operatic arias." After she was no longer required to take along a teacher, "there was always someone like Alfred Marks or Max Wall to look after Julie," Barbara Andrews remembered. But Julie also went home to Walton on Sundays, so her life was both rigorous and sheltered.

Barbara Andrews at first did all the dealing with reporters, who usually asked questions such as "How much money does little Julie make?" Even little Julie didn't know the answer to that until she was almost seventeen and firmly in the 150-pounds-weekly ($600) bracket. "I had very little publicity," she recalled, "and applause was never to be overestimated. My mother helped me to keep a fairly level head, raising me strictly but fairly." (For instance, Barbara would not let Julie open her own fan mail at the theater. It had to be brought home for Barbara to review first.)

Being in vaudeville, which was "on its last legs when I came on the scene," and going on the road alone "was good training for me, and I suppose it paved the way for what was to come. I wouldn't change much if I could go back and do it all over. But I wouldn't raise my own children that way. Being in show business is unnatural for a child, and I'm not sure being an actor or actress, even as an adult, is the best thing in the world. Why are there so many performers going to psychiatrists? That should tell you something about the pressures and problems."

Julie toured the length and breadth of Great Britain "endlessly, it seems. It was lonely, and sometimes the towns were awfully bare and unpleasant. The worst things were Saturday night second house in a rough town like Glasgow, Cardiff, or Liverpool, when you got all the rowdy people in and it was terrifying to stand up on stage. I didn't like it much, but it was good for me—a toughener-upper. Having survived the variety years, nothing else ever seemed so bad."

In her vaudeville appearances, she was "kept in short, short dresses, patent-leather shoes and ankle socks, trying desperately to look ten years younger, [yet] growing a bosom and feeling wretched about that." At the same time, in her middle teens, "I was struggling to find out who I was and what I was doing," performing "below-par stuff and knowing that it was below-par stuff."

Julie found Christmastime pantomimes, holiday fairy tales in song, to be much more fun than touring in vaudeville. In pantomimes, in which she performed from the ages of thirteen through eighteen, Julie wore elegant costumes and "was always the principal girl who was rather wet and makes goo-goo eyes at Our Hero and gets him in the end." That principal "boy," such as the prince in *Cinderella*, was always played by another female. Often an older female character, such as the wicked stepmother, was played by an older man in drag. Danny LaRue was the most famous of these actors, and did later play the wicked stepmother in *Cinderella*. The pantomimes were always interspersed with popular songs not necessarily tied to the plot, including audience sing-alongs, and equally unrelated vaudeville acts.

When she was thirteen, Julie auditioned for Emile Littler, who was presenting the London Casino's Christmas pantomime, *Humpty Dumpty*. After Julie sang, Littler said to Barbara, "Her voice is out of this world, but what on earth are we going to do about her feet—they're enormous." (By this time, she had achieved her adult size eight As.) Still, he hired her to appear, in curled-up gnome shoes to make the least of her feet, as the title character, which of course was an egg.

She felt this was very Freudian, since it was during the run of *Humpty Dumpty* that Julie met Tony Walton, who was fourteen. He also lived in Walton-on-Thames, but they never had met. Seeing her in Humpty Dumpty was when "I first laid eyes on her in the flesh," Walton recalled. "When the egg fell from the wall there was this enchanting little girl with chocolate makeup all over her legs, which I found extremely seductive."

Tony and Julie found themselves on the same train back to Walton from London, where he asked for her autograph. "He had seen the show, and we started talking," Julie said. "When we got off the train I asked her where she lived," he remembered, "and she said, 'On the other side of the tracks.'" The next day Tony went to the theater and asked Julie for photographs. He and his brother found out where she lived and began visiting her at the Old Meuse. "He wrote to me from school," she said, "and sent me sweet and wonderful drawings he had done. We became sort of mates. We saw each other at vacation times, whenever we could. That's the way it began, I guess."

Humpty Dumpty was unusual for a seasonal show in that it ran for a full year. During the run Julie acquired a Welsh corgi and named him Humpty. The Christmas she was fifteen she played the title role in *Little Red Riding Hood* in Nottingham. Whenever Red Riding Hood was afraid she burst into song, including the recent seasonal hit "Rudolph the Red-Nosed Reindeer." She had celebrated her fifteenth birthday (at the BBC's Paris Casino studio) by reportedly exclaiming "At last I am free from the London County Council." Now she could have an adult career. There was a second liberation party at the Old Meuse.

Little Red Riding Hood earned Julie enough money to buy her mother and stepfather a Hillman Minx with a radio in it (the radio was a big deal in Britain in 1950, since in many ways it was still the Post-War era). "They called it 'Julie's car' and proceeded to drive it for the next three years," she remembered.

That same year, Julie began appearing on the popular weekly

BBC radio program *Educating Archie*. Archie, whose last name coincidentally was Andrews, was the ventriloquist's dummy manipulated by the comedy show's host, Peter Brough. Comedians Benny Hill and Max Bygraves were also regulars on the show. During her "song spot" Julie would sing such standards as "The Blue Danube Waltz."

The Christmas she was sixteen, she returned to Eugene Littler and the London Casino to portray the principal girl in the pantomime *Aladdin*, Princess Balroulbadour. Julie recalled, "Now I was so *tall* that the principal boy had to wear four-inch heels." The title part of Aladdin was played by Jean (later Jeannie) Carson, who had also been on the *Starlight Roof* bill with Julie and would have a successful career on early American television. For the Christmas season of 1952–53, Julie played Princess Bettina in *Jack and the Beanstalk*, at the Coventry Hippodrome, for which she was paid a record 250 pounds ($1000) a week.

In the spring of 1952 Julie had rejoined Ted and Barbara Andrews briefly in a vaudeville show at London's Victoria Palace. Sophie Tucker, the aging American "Last of the Red-Hot Mamas," and a young Joan Collins were also in the lineup. But as Julie's career expanded, Ted's and Barbara's began to slip. Even when they played together, the billing was reversed forever. Instead of reading "Ted and Barbara Andrews with Julie Andrews," the marquee, posters, and advertisements now read "Julie Andrews with Ted and Barbara Andrews." Even as separate acts, Julie was playing the best of the remaining music halls while her parents were appearing in the second-rank venues. One summer at the blue-collar seaside resort of Blackpool, Barbara recalled, "We were on the pier and she was at the big theater in town—really a step above us."

Ted and Barbara played less and less frequently and finally retired from show business altogether. Ted did take a sales job for a time. But soon Julie, who was regularly making between 100 and 125 pounds ($400 and $500) weekly, began to support the family, including her younger half-brothers Donald and Christopher, even putting one of them through school. "It's something we never spoke of," she said, "but I can see now that it hurt terribly. If I hadn't been around, I suppose they'd have found a way to support themselves. The ability to be the breadwinner came pretty naturally to me. We needed money, and I was able to manage it. It kept us going."

"Weird and plenty seedy" was the way Tony Walton later described Julie's situation with her four dependents. "From age thirteen on Julie was head of the family, and it was a grade-B movie existence. Right up until *Camelot* she had a guilt feeling about taking it easy."

When the reversal of fortune occurred and Julie was the star and her parents were has-beens, Walton remembered, "her stepdad was going through some drinking problems. He had a tendency to break up the house now and then." "She was an unhappy girl," agreed Tancred Aegius, the boy next door in Walton-on-Thames who was briefly Julie's boyfriend when she was seventeen. "Her mother and stepfather were always drunk—on liquor that she had paid for. It was sad."

"It's only in retrospect that one realizes one was ever unhappy or uncomfortable," Julie said in 1995. She was always reluctant to talk about her mother and stepfather's drinking problems while they were living. "I was not abused," she said in a *Vanity Fair* interview in 1995. "I came close to being abused."

In 1990, she told Glenn Plaskin of the *New York Daily News* "my parents were both alcoholics." But to Mike Wallace on *60 Minutes*, in 1995, she hedged a bit about her mother: "She was eventually, probably, a co-dependent alcoholic."

From her earliest years, to cover the truth of her home life, Julie wrote phony diaries filled, in Tony's words, "with fanciful images of what a beautiful, happy family she had, how lucky she was, how perfect and magical her home life was, and what a glamorous existence she led."

"As a young girl she bottled up her feelings, like the trouper she is," her real father, Ted Wells, said in later years, "and got on with the business of living. But then, nearly a quarter of a century later, all the pent-up unhappiness of that period suddenly caught up with her, so she sought the advice of a psychoanalyst."

Ted Wells, who died in 1990 at the age of eighty-five, saved a story that Julie had written when she was about five. It read as follows: "Wuns the wos a mother and father. The motheer wanted a little girl and boy. It was Crisms, the night Santer Claus hee came to bring the two babis. Wen the mother woke up she was so pleased she loot for them and they live hapleevrovter."

"To be truthful, at the time I think I thought I was happy," Julie said. "Children bounce back rather quickly from all their troubles. At any rate I would go around saying how happy—how desperately happy—I was. I fancy I was protesting too much."

Although she had some friends her own age in Walton, Julie was, by her own description precocious and a loner. "I enjoyed the company of older people." She spent a good deal of her free time with Ted Wells, partly because she wanted to and partly because he had had liberal visitation rights written into the custody agreement when he had returned her to her mother. Julie couldn't always decide with which parent she wanted to live.

"I guess I mostly wanted to be with my mother because she seemed to lead a rather colorful existence," Julie recalled. "She supplied the rougher, bawdier side of my life. My real father filled in the love of the countryside, outdoor sports, reading. When I was with him we led a quiet, more relaxed life. My stepmother was a wonderful woman, but I must admit I found it hard to live with my stepfather."

Still, for public consumption, she idealized Ted Andrews, and made the most of his and her mother's less-than-voluntary retirement: "He has such a lovely voice; I'd rather listen to it any anything. He used to sing ballads like 'Love, Could I Only Tell Thee How Dear Thou Art to Me.' Mummy always wanted to be just Mummy, so Pop gave up show business."

Whatever the truth of their relationship, Ted Andrews and his stepdaughter shared a profession, one that, in the most literal sense, he had given her: singing for an audience. His past and her future met on the night in 1952 when they went (with Charles Tucker and Barbara) to see Mary Martin in the West End production of the latest Rodgers and Hammerstein hit musical, *South*

Pacific, the first big musical Julie had ever seen. It was at the Theatre Royal, Drury Lane, and Ted put on a dinner jacket to make it a really special occasion. "Afterwards, I talked about how wonderful the music was. And Charles Tucker said, 'Some day, Julie, Rodgers and Hammerstein will be writing songs for you.'"

2

America and *The Boy Friend*

The day came when Charles Tucker and Barbara Andrews finally had to concede that Julie, in her late teens, was not only no longer a little girl but that she couldn't even pass for one. Tucker, with Barbara's blessing, hired Pauline Grant, a ballet teacher, who taught Julie to dance and also took over the whole responsibility for her dress, demeanor, and appearance. Julie's transformation from an ugly duckling into a swan under Grant's direction was dramatic: suddenly British women's magazines featured Julie in stories on makeup tips and clothes. She also became more attractive to both herself and to the opposite sex.

She even fell in love for the first time, temporarily abandoning Tony Walton in favor of a Danish acrobat, Freddie, from one of her shows. "He was so good looking, and such a wonderful acrobat," she recalled. "He was always hanging upside down from something or standing on his head. Donald and Chris, my brothers, were entranced with him, too. But Tony, and the rest of our gang, were shocked at my traitorous behavior."

Despite Julie's flirtation with Freddie and a few other minor dalliances, Tony remained a steadfast friend, still writing to her on the road and signing his letters with "love" or "all my love," while when she wrote back, she signed merely with "best wishes." His drawings accompanying the letters now consisted mostly of ideas for stage sets and costumes. Unusually, the late spring and early summer she was seventeen Julie was at home in Walton-on-Thames for two months. So was Tony, having finished boarding school and not yet off to national service.

"That was my idyllic summer," she said. "Everyone was within reach and everything seemed to go right. I'd never had so much time with the family before. Mummy and Pop were now always at home. One warm and sunny afternoon Tony and I went picnicking. We found a shady spot by the river under a tree. For once he was not talking about the theater. I was not bantering with him. We just lay flat on our backs gazing up at the sky through the leaves. Then, for the first time, he kissed me. I knew there was now a new seriousness, something more than a childhood friendship."

Her vacation over, Julie toured for three months in the late summer and early autumn of 1953, to Birmingham, Brighton, and Glasgow, in *Cap and Belles*, a revue. In it she not only sang "My Heart Is Singing" but danced with a corps de ballet and wore her first off-the-shoulder dress on stage. Julie turned eighteen, on October 1, 1953.

Work still followed upon work, and "I couldn't think of anything else I could do or wanted to do." Julie's last appearance in a pantomime, in the title role of *Cinderella*, came over Christmas of 1953 and into February of 1954, at the London Palladium (with Max Bygraves as Buttons and Adele Dixon as the "principal boy," the Prince). This was the top of the heap for pantomime, and proved to be Julie's greatest London success to date.

Next, in 1954, she played a Tennessee belle in a play with music, *Mountain Fire*, in Leeds, Yorkshire. "It was an incredible disaster," she recalled. "The story was all about Sodom and Gomorrah and bootleg whisky and Lot's wife's turning to a pillar of salt. I can't tell you what went on. You've never heard a worse Southern accent than mine. In the play I got pregnant by a traveling salesman. Thank God the miserable thing closed before we got to London."

Mountain Fire proved to be as much responsible as *Cinderella* for sending Julie to America, where she heard a real Southern accent for the first time and "nearly died of shame." But for most of

1954, she wasn't pondering an adult performing career in England, much less thinking of traveling to the United States. "All the time I was growing up I knew I could sing," she said, "and I thought that was rather good. But I didn't ever dream I would be singing after my childhood. When I thought of the future I thought of meeting all sorts of attractive boys, and eventually settling down with one who often, in my imagination, had a strong resemblance to Tony, getting my own home, and having a family, with five children, at least. I used to think: 'What am I going to do when I grow up?'"

As it turned out, she did not marry the boyfriend but starred in *The Boy Friend*. Sandy Wilson wrote the libretto, music, and lyrics for this affectionate lampoon of the silly songs and stage plots of the 1920s. Wilson's music deliberately evoked that of Noel Coward, Jerome Kern, and Richard Rodgers. The title song was an answering echo to Rodgers and Hart's "The Girl Friend"; "A Room in Blooms-bury" was consciously inspired by Coward's "A Room With a View." *The Boy Friend* began as a ninety-minute piece that ran for three weeks at London's Players Club in the spring of 1953. It was so successful that Wilson expanded it to a three-act production for a six-week run at the club that fall. From there the show transferred to the suburban Embassy Theatre, then to Wyndham's Theatre in the West End in early 1954, becoming a rare homegrown musical comedy hit, running for 2,084 performances.

The American producers Cy Feuer and Ernest Martin bought the rights to *The Boy Friend* for a Broadway opening that same September. It was still too early in the London run to transfer any of the original cast to America, but Feuer and Martin, author Sandy Wilson, the show's director, Vida Hope, and the choreographer, John Heawood, were determined to retain the flavor of the West End production. "We wanted as many English actors as possible," Feuer recalled, "because we wanted to reproduce it on Broadway as close as possible to the original." Anne Rogers had scored a personal triumph in creating the leading role of sweet Polly Browne, the English heiress at an exclusive school for perfect young ladies on the French Riviera. The major casting problem was replacing Rogers for what was expected to be an extended New York run.

Vida Hope had seen Julie's *Cinderella* the previous Christmas season and Sandy Wilson remembered her *Starlight Roof* appearance six years earlier, when "still a small girl in a party frock and large white shoes, she had filled the theater with a soprano of astonishing range and purity." Hope and Feuer took a train to Leeds to see Julie in *Mountain Fire*. The American producer was horrified by her atrocious Southern dialect and even worse, her breaking off her dialogue to begin a gratuitous song *after* which the leading man and the orchestra came in. But Feuer also recalled that "her pitch was perfect and her voice delightful."

Julie was invited to audition for *The Boy Friend* at the London Coliseum. Wilson remembered that her mother Barbara, "a rather forceful lady with red hair came with her and sat in the pit to accompany her." Heawood, the choreographer, called Julie's audition "pure *Gypsy*. We asked her to dance and Barbara stood up and said, 'Go on, Julie, show them your tap.' Julie, being very modest, said, 'I don't think I can.' But she did, and at the end of this very difficult audition Vida whispered to me, 'That's it. We've found her.'"

Ted, Barbara, and Charles Tucker were all for Julie accepting the role of Polly Browne on Broadway and could not understand her hesitation, since even she admitted that the part was "one of the most exciting chances a girl of eighteen could have." But her first thought was, "Oh good Christ, the idea of leaving my home and family—I couldn't do it. I had toured on my own all through England, but suddenly the idea of two years in American was too much. I did what I always did when I had a tough decision to make: I asked my Dad, my real Dad, the wisest and dearest man I knew. He advised me to see America while I had the chance ('it will open up your head'), and pointed out that the show might not be a hit and last only three months—or three weeks. I decided to go if I could get them to agree to a one-year contract [instead of the standard two-year commitment for a lead role in a Broadway musical]. Charles Tucker did get them to agree to a one-year contract and an increase in salary as well. It was the first time I really put my food down on something. I wouldn't have earned enough to bring my family over, and they certainly couldn't afford it, so one year was it."

"Her parents had to sign her over to us because of her age,"
Feuer recalled, "but I was struck by her maturity. Most performers
at that age are very amateurish, but even then she had great
equanimity and poise. She didn't rattle. She had a very good
dramatic ability even then; she was an insinctive actress."

Before *The Boy Friend* troupe left for the United States, Sandy
Wilson took his new leading lady out to dinner. With Vida Hope, her
husband, and Neil McCallum, an actor and Julie's current admirer,
they went to the Royal Court Theatre Club, which was then a
restaurant-cabaret. "Throughout the evening I was struck again by
Julie's perfect behavior: a combination of school-girlish innocence
and a control and poise far in advance of her years," Wilson wrote
in his autobiography *I Could Be Happy.*

> As I watched her and listened to her, I wondered if we might
> be about to assist at the birth of a new star, someone as
> remarkable in her way as Gertrude Lawrence. Then, in a
> moment of insight unusual for me, I realized that this girl
> would be a star anyway, with or without our assistance. It
> was nothing that she said or did, and she certainly betrayed
> no symptoms of egotism or ambition; she simply had about
> her an unmistakable air of cool, clear-cut determination.
> For Julie, I could tell, it was going to be the top or nothing.

Julie and her company (which also included Millicent Martin
and Moyna MacGill, Angela Lansbury's mother, as Lady Brockhurst,
the title boyfriend's mother) boarded the plane together in London.
Julie felt as though she were "moving in a nightmare from which I
couldn't wake up. I was frightened and homesick. I felt the plainest,
drabbest girl in the whole bunch. As the plane took off I left all my
heart behind. I sat through the flight all night, numb with misery.
The other girls were laughing and chattering." Julie sat next to
Dilys Lay, an outgoing, red-headed comedienne who was playing
Dulcie, another teenaged flapper in *The Boy Friend.* (Her big
number was "It's Never Too Late to Fall in Love.")

The Boy Friend troupe arrived in New York tired and cramped
at seven one morning in August of 1954, during an immense heat

wave. "We were all sweltering in our autumn suits," Julie recalled. Julie was met by Lou Wilson, her new American agent. He drove her and Dilys from Idlewild (later John F. Kennedy) Airport, across Queens and through the Midtown Tunnel into Manhattan. "I gazed about me unbelievingly," she remembered. "Every great road carried four lanes of traffic. The hundreds of cars were all big, luxurious, and brightly colored, not black and gray like ours, and went at such speed that it was like watching multi-colored spangles flashing past your eyes."

Julie's first American home was the seedy Piccadilly Hotel on West 45th Street near Broadway, on the same block as the Royale Theatre, where *The Boy Friend* would be playing. Only the hotel's name was English. "I had one stuffy room with a tiny window," she recalled. The express elevator to her thirtieth-floor aerie gave her a sick feeling, which was not helped by moving back and forth between high humidity and air conditioning. Even for someone who had known early poverty and tacky English music halls, this was hardly an adequate stopping place.

Once the show opened, Julie and Dilys agreed to share an apartment. Julie, who was acquiring the first roommate of her life, at the time termed the bed-sitter "a modest suite in the modest Park Chambers Hotel on Sixth Avenue (which down at our end, near Central Park, you might call New York's Bloomsbury)." The apartment had a bedroom, a living room and a stand-up kitchenette. The rent, $275 a month, was anything but modest for the West Side of New York in the mid-1950s.

"It made a horrible hole in our budget," Julie said, "and I had no sense of money or of taking care of myself." Since two months' rent was payable in advance, the pair had to get an advance on their $100-weekly rehearsal salaries just to get into the apartment. Almost two-thirds of Julie's $400-a-week salary during the actual run of the show went for taxes, Charles Tucker's commission, and family support. Much of what was left over she spent on trans-Atlantic telephone calls to Walton-on-Thames, during which Julie's half-brother Donald would kick her corgi, Hump, to get him to bark into the telephone.

More than forty years later, Julie recalled herself and Dilys as "the oddest but ultimately most satisfying coupling, because where I was painfully shy and would never have ventured out, she was this extrovert that wasn't afraid of anything." Dilys agreed: "Julie was a very private person whereas I effervesced all over the place. I don't think I went to bed for four months. Her heart was always in England."

At the rooms in "Bloomsbury," Dilys did the cooking while Julie did the shopping, the washing up, and made endless pots of tea. They later acquired a maid. And they learned to cook American-style in an electric broiler. For Christmas, the girls gave one another a dachsund, which they named Melanie. One of their many male admirers gave them a television set, and watching Charlie Chan mysteries and old English movies on *The Late Show* quickly replaced their going out to midnight showings of feature films. "We have a sworn pact in blood not to wait up for *The Late* Late *Show*," Julie told an interviewer. "It makes the management quite queasy if we don't sleep enough."

Julie didn't like New York at first: "it was too large, too humid, too noisy, too crowded, too expensive. I was frightened of it." Other negatives included "soggy tea bags and ghastly water." But plusses included such "poppets" as "New York cab drivers, the second teller from the left at Manufacturers Trust Company, and other people you like in spite of everything."

She also liked Dixieland jazz, bandleader Benny Goodman, and the East Side of Manhattan, "so neat and uncluttered and clean, and every girl is as attractive as [Princess] Margaret Rose." Then there were the nightclubs—The Latin Quarter (where Mae West was holding forth) and The Stork Club—and the restaurant "21." She loved American drug stores, which were so much more comprehensive than the English chemists' shops. Also, "cream cheese and jelly sandwiches, your wonderful milkshakes—ruinous but marvelous—and your beer, fine for me, light (as the commercials say), but I'm afraid an Englishman wouldn't like it." She also enjoyed shopping for full nylon petticoats, not yet available in England.

Dilys and Julie found differences between English and American men besides their taste in beer. "A British friend asks you where you would like to go," said Julie, "but an American says you're going *here* or *there.*"

"Usually both," added Dilys, "with Americans one does get around a bit."

The two teenagers went out often, at first with young Englishmen from the Old Vic company which was also performing in New York, later with "some American chaps" the girls had met in the course of the run. "Johnny Ray and Frank Sinatra, dreamy," Julie said of two contemporary singers she had seen. "Our dates were annoyed. They forgot we watch other performers with a professional air."

Professionally, things were not quite so cozy or so much fun. Because a totally new company had been created for *The Boy Friend* on Broadway, there were a full six weeks of rehearsals and previews, rather than out-of-town tryouts, before the show opened on the last day of September. The hours frequently ran from 10 A.M. to 4 A.M. the next morning. "And not a minute is wasted," Julie wrote home. "It's detail, detail all the way. Every gesture, every line, is gone over, again and again. But it's fun and a terrific experience. If I miss anything at all, it's not backstage but at the front of the house. Theaters here haven't got the regal atmosphere and character that they have in London. You get the impression that the people who designed them had only one idea: to pack in as many customers as possible."

The production of *The Boy Friend* at Wyndham's Theatre had cost about $8,000 to mount; the Broadway version would cost around $240,000. Despite the producer's protestations of fidelity to the original—they had filmed a London performance in order to copy the costumes, scenery, and props down to the minutest detail—what had been an intimate show, even in the West End, was being transformed into a big Broadway musical. Sandy Wilson and Vida Hope became increasingly unhappy with the more fulsome orchestrations, faster pacing, and over-the-top stylization of their light parodic pastiche.

Cast members were fired, replaced, and rearranged. Feuer and

Martin then fired Hope as director, although her name remained on
the show's credits in perpetuity, and Feuer took over the direction
of *The Boy Friend* himself. The show's composer and creator,
Sandy Wilson, was barred from the theater (along with Hope) until
opening night—Feuer actually hired private detectives to keep
them away. One musical number, crucial to the delicate structure of
the love story (Polly falls in love with a messenger boy, named Tony,
who turns out to be as rich as she) was cut: "It's Nicer in Nice,"
resurfaced in most revivals of *The Boy Friend*, but it was never
heard in the first Broadway production. Nor is it on the original
New York cast album.

Julie just barely survived the creative turmoil, as did choreographer John Heawood. But he recalled that, at one point, "they
wanted the understudy to replace her. She was a woman of about
thirty-five, who sang very nicely and moved like a Churchill tank."

The vaudeville bits in the show were no problem for Julie.
During the first duet between Julie and John Hewer as Tony, "I
Could Be Happy With You," he lifted her onto a footstool, where she
whistled one whole chorus of the song while he did his soft-shoe
specialty. But acting was another matter altogether.

"She was extraordinarily shy, not only socially and in life
offstage," Tony Walton recalled, "but also in terms of how little she
knew of conventional acting techniques. She was never trained, but
the moment she got before an audience she was home—that's what
she knew."

"Julie was used to standing up there playing those perky little
girls—playing herself," Dilys remembered. "Suddenly she was being
asked to play a girl who is lost, who is lonely, who thinks nobody
loves her except for her money, who is *in* love. It's a long journey she
was asked to take at age eighteen."

"I was awful," Julie admitted. "I had to learn a whole new style
of acting for this show—my own style was rather quiet. During
previews I never played it the same way twice, and hence never got
the same reaction from the audience." Feuer, as the director, took
Julie outside by the theater's fire escape the day of the opening. "He

sat me down and said, 'You were simply lousy last night. You're trying to be clever and it's dead. You're way, way out and sending it up rotten.' He really let me have it. He said, 'Believe everything you say—*be* Polly. If you do that, you'll be a success. If you don't, you'll be a disaster.' Thanks to Cy and his advice I *was* Polly. I did it because I was told to do it."

Feuer, years later, refused to talk about what he did to help Julie and others in the cast who were foundering. "It would be very unbecoming of me and I couldn't teach Julie very much. Dramatically she had it all along. She performed far beyond the ability of anyone that age. She was a marvelous person to work with, a very sweet person. She did everything you asked without complaint, and was a lot of fun. There's some kind of bubble inside her. She was just everything you could ask for in a performer, and always on time for rehearsals and performances."

Opening night at the Royale Theatre found most people in the audience and the critics enthralled with the show and with Julie as Polly Browne. *The New York Times* drama critic Brooks Atkinson, then the doyen of "the Seven Butchers of Broadway," called *The Boy Friend* "a delightful burlesque…of the standard musical play of the twenties…extremely well done in manuscript as well as on stage. [Wilson] has written book, songs, and lyrics with satirical inventiveness; and someone has directed it with great ironic skill. It is hard to say which is funnier: the material or the performance."

Atkinson called Dilys Lay "a miniature Beatrice Lillie," but wrote, "It is probably Julie Andrews, as the heroine, who gives *The Boy Friend* its special quality. She burlesques the insipidity of the part. She keeps the romance very sad. Her hesitating gestures and her wistful shy mannerisms are very comic. But, by golly, there is more than irony in her performance. There is something genuine in it, too. I was happier than she was when she found Prince Charming in the last buttery scene."

In the *Herald-Tribune*, Walter Kerr said *The Boy Friend* "isn't really a parody at all. It's a romantic adolescent's love-letter to a girl in a cloche hat." As the girl, "Miss Andrews is perfect. With

trembling upper lip, a blonde marcel, the largest amount of blue eye-
shadow I have seen anywhere, and hands clasped winsomely just
above her right knee, she breathes lunatic sincerity."

The "Seven Butchers of Broadway," the seven daily newspaper
drama critics, gave *The Boy Friend* six raves and one favorable
review. Only Henry Hewes, writing in the high-brow magazine the
Saturday Review, dissented, but only on the grounds that show had
not traveled well: "What Feuer and Martin have done to this show is
make a fast, raucous burlesque out of a carefree valentine [but] very
possibly only those looking for an old sweetheart will find *The Boy
Friend* a loud-mouthed date who, unlike his British cousin, *knows*
he is being the life of the party."

At the box office *The Boy Friend* was an unqualified hit,
beginning the next morning, October 1, 1954, Julie's nineteenth
birthday. She celebrated, surrounded by floral tributes, with a
room-service breakfast of bacon and eggs in bed while writing a
ten-page letter to her mother about both the show's and her
opening-night triumph. Barbara Andrews soon flew over to New
York to share in Julie's success in *The Boy Friend.* Left behind in
Walton-on-Thames was the stepfather who had insisted on Julie's
singing lessons.

Nonetheless, Julie's onstage delivery of such songs as "I Could
Be Happy With You," "A Room in Bloomsbury," "Poor Little
Pierette" and the title song, "The Boy Friend," more than justified
Ted Andrews's long-standing faith in her talent.

Feuer explained Julie's success in *The Boy Friend* as the result
of a combination of attributes, only one of which was her voice.
"This girl is tall, she has large features, which are great for the
stage: you can see her a mile away. People like that take light. They
don't disappear into the scenery. Taken singly, those features may
not be much, but the way they're put together they turn out to be
attractive. She is a kind of built-in leading lady, has a kind of built-
in dignity and a kind of built-in musical know-how."

In November 1954, Julie was awarded featured billing by Feuer
and Martin, the only member of either the New York or London cast
so honored. The first evening her name was up in lights, Julie

arrived at the theater in a taxi, trying hard to keep her face turned away from the Royale marquee that read

THE BOY FRIEND
SMASH HIT MUSICAL COMEDY
WITH JULIE ANDREWS

Finally she looked, and said softly, "Ah there it is," and the man who was in the cab with her said, "Sure enough, her eyes were shining."

The following April, she returned from her first American baseball game at the Brooklyn Dodgers' stadium at Ebbets Field, to find that she and John Hewer, who played the other romantic lead, the messenger boy, had been promoted even further, to above-the-title stars, "in recognition for their contribution," said Feuer and Martin. The Royale marquee now read

JULIE ANDREWS   JOHN HEWER
IN
THE BOY FRIEND
SMASH HIT MUSICAL COMEDY

Other honors came her way that spring, such as one of the twelve Theater World Awards for promising new personalities. The other winners that season included Barbara Cook for *Plain and Fancy*, Anthony Perkins for *Tea and Sympathy*, and Christopher Plummer for *The Dark is Light Enough*. Julie also won a Donaldson Award for outstanding female Broadway debut. (*The Boy Friend* was shut out at the 1955 Tony Awards, which celebrated *The Pajama Game* as Best Musical and honored such other shows as *Peter Pan, Fanny, House of Flowers*, and *The Saint of Bleecker Street*.)

Julie pronounced herself thrilled with her accolades and recognition, but she remained somewhat reticent. "Here you make a star out of practically nothing too quickly," she noted at the time. "In England you have to prove yourself over a long period in a variety of roles. We adopt more of a wait-and-see attitude there. Here, one has one hit and, whoosh! Well, I'm English and I'm waiting and seeing."

Just as she was achieving star billing, at the mid-point of her year in *The Boy Friend*, Julie got one of the more famous telephone calls in show business history. Dick Lamarr, who worked for Alan Jay Lerner and Frederick Loewe, telephoned to ask routinely when she would be available again. She had been suggested for the lead in the musical version of George Bernard Shaw's play *Pygmalion* that Lerner and Loewe had written. "When I told him I would be free in August he almost fell off the other end of the phone," she remembered. "They had assumed I had a two-year contract like everyone else. Because I thought I'd get homesick, I was free at just the right time."

Julie auditioned for Lerner, the lyricist-adaptor, and Loewe, the composer, for the role of Eliza Doolittle, the Cockney flower girl who becomes a lady under the tutelage of Professor Henry Higgins. She read a Cockney dialogue scene, sang a few songs and listened while Loewe played and sang "Wouldn't It Be Loverly," and "I Could Have Danced All Night." Entranced, she asked Loewe to play them again. This time, she sang along: "I just couldn't resist the music." Lerner and Loewe complimented her voice but did not yet offer her the role.

She also auditioned for Richard Rodgers, who was casting his and Oscar Hammerstein's *Pipe Dream*. After telling Rodgers about seeing *South Pacific*, Julie sang songs from another Rodgers and Hammerstein hit, *The King and I*. Rodgers would have liked to hire her on the spot, but knowing that she was a serious contender for the Lerner and Loewe musical, "Dick was absolutely wonderful about it and said *Pygmalion* would be the wiser move," she recalled. (The title *My Fair Lady* had not yet been decided upon.) "I got the *Pygmalion* part and things went on from there."

But no matter how many good things happened to her, Julie was still homesick. Every Saturday night as she left the Royale Theatre after the week's last performance, she marked the week off the stage-door calendar, counting down the time until she could go back to England. She even resumed writing to Tony Walton, whom she had kissed off for an older man before leaving London, and from whom she hadn't heard a word since she'd been in New York.

Tony wrote back, cautiously at first, signing "all the best." Then he began to send sketches again, and his regular letters "sent the weeks by swiftly," she said.

"I knew then that no matter whether we decided we were in love with each other again or not, I should never again be so careless of a friendship that had grown up with me—a friendship I knew now would always be mine even if we both married someone else."

Finally, the day came. Julie left New York for her three-month holiday in Walton-on-Thames on her twentieth birthday, October 1, 1955. In November, however, her long vacation was interrupted by the offer of two weeks in Hollywood to play opposite Bing Crosby in a filmed ninety-minute musical version of Maxwell Anderson's *High Tor* for CBS television.

This was to be the network's first non-live entertainment special, and the first-ever made-for-television movie, according to *The Guinness Book of World Records*. CBS spent more than $300,000 on the show, a record TV budget at that time. Much of the money went to the plaster re-creation of the mist-wrapped craggy mountain at RKO-Pathe Studio in Hollywood. (A second-unit crew did go to New York state to climb the real High Tor for some authentic long shots.)

High Tor also provided Julie some important firsts: her American television debut, her first work in front of a movie camera, and her first trip to Hollywood. She loved it in the daytime, "it was all new and exciting," she said, but the nights were lonely, since she knew no one in town.

Crosby, who greeted her on the set in an orange jacket and Panama hat, had some professional misgivings about the production. "I've been in lots of features," he said, "but nothing like this. Can you imagine, we're shooting this in twelve days? At a major studio it would take thirty days, at least."

He played the lead role of a contemporary young idealist, Van Van Dorn, who owns the historic High Tor mountain along the Hudson River in the Dutch-settled area of lower New York State. He loves the ghost of a Dutch girl, Lise, who has been dead for three hundred years (played by Julie). Nancy Olson, best remembered as

Betty Shafer in the 1950 movie version of *Sunset Boulevard,* played Van Dorn's real-life fiancée. Olson was also the current Mrs. Alan Jay Lerner, and would remain so through the making of *My Fair Lady.*

Anderson's original play *High Tor,* though sometimes bitter, had been low-key, touching, and fantastic in the purest sense. Anderson, who had adapted his play with John Monks, Jr. and director James Neilson, were going for "more warmth and heart," in the musical version, and leaving out all the bitterness. Arthur Schwartz, who also produced *High Tor,* wrote six songs for which Anderson wrote the lyrics.

The key premise of both the original play and the musical version was that the love between Van and Lise—a love spanning three centuries—was doomed. This notion was summed up in one scene in which they looked dreamily over Long Island Sound at the stars. Julie as Lise asked, "See the great gulf that lies between the heavy red star down in the west and the star that comes with the morning? There's that much lies between us."

Julie found Crosby "the most relaxed and experienced actor I had ever worked with," adding, "I was the most tense and inexperienced singer he had ever worked with. But he would deliberately ruin a scene himself if I wasn't doing it well, so that an expensive re-take could not be blamed on me. When I left Hollywood to go home again I wore a wonderful farewell present from Bing: a heavy gold, pearl-encrusted pendant ring. It was inscribed: 'Julie, thanks, Bing.'"

High Tor aired just five nights before *My Fair Lady* opened in New York, in March of 1956. It took every bit of the four months between filming and airing to edit *High Tor.* Despite her co-star Crosby, this first appearance before movie cameras was not a distinguished one for Julie, although it did her no particular harm. The big singing role was Crosby's, and he was wrong for the part. The whole static "special," supposedly outdoors, looked more like the studio set quickie that it really was. And that crucial scene between the man of the 1950s and the girl of the 1650s lacked feeling.

Looking back, ten years later, after even she would have to admit that her stardom had been secured by two more Broadway hits and four successful movies, Julie said, "The year I spent in *The Boy Friend* was one of the best of my life. I learned a lot about timing and comedy from American audiences. I used to be a slow learner, and it was a marvelous experience to learn on the job and get away with it."

Even more important, "I realize now that the high point of my life was coming to America. I was very aware, even at the time, of having some door open somewhere and passing through it. I was on my own, and standing on my own two feet for the first time. I was having to function as an independent person, where before I'd been a guarded child."

3

Broadway's Fair Lady

After an Old Meuse family Christmas, "with the tree touching the ceiling in the hall, and all the colored fairy lights on the drive," Julie had to face the fact that she was leaving Walton-on-Thames for America again on New Year's Day, 1956. This time there could be no half-commitment if the show was a hit. She was contracted for a possible two-year run, and there would be "no point in trying to cross off one hundred and four weeks on a calendar." But this time, too, "Mum" would be there to lend moral support on opening night in New York.

"I had given Julie a copy of the play to think about over the vacation," Alan Jay Lerner recalled, "and told her that we would see her when rehearsals began. Her first tryouts had not been very good. Julie had no sense of being a star, none of that sense of obligation a star has toward a play. The others, Rex Harrison [Professor Higgins] and Stanley Holloway [Alfred Doolittle, Eliza's father], turned up several weeks ahead to talk over their parts. Not Julie. She sent us a letter saying that she would arrive from London the day rehearsals began, not before, because she had promised to take her two little brothers to a pantomime. It was so different, so unbelievably unprofessional, that we were amused rather than annoyed."

Another reason for Julie's delay might have been sheer terror.

The twenty-year-old performer regarded this *Pygmalion* musical as "a monstrous task. Shaw simply terrified me. The singing part was the only thing I thought I might somehow do. When it came to acting, I was simply awful at first, and terrified of Rex Harrison. It was obvious that I needed a lot of attention."

Lerner and Loewe had hired Julie for her "dazzling array of gifts," as Lerner wrote in his autobiography, *The Street Where I Live,* and only after the partners had gone to see *The Boy Friend,* along with their producer Herman Levin. "Julie had a charming soprano voice, so flexible she could sing light opera and popular with equal ease; probably the most immaculate diction of any soprano in memory; she danced; she moved with grace; whatever she had to say in *The Boy Friend* she did with conviction and style; and physically she was as pretty as any eye might decide her to be." But even after she was hired, Lerner had to wonder, "Could she play Eliza Doolittle?"

Shaw had described Eliza, in his stage directions, as "perhaps eighteen, perhaps twenty, hardly older." Lerner's libretto had kept that conception. Yet Julie was to be the first actress of that age to play the part. Mrs. Patrick Campbell, for whom Shaw originally wrote *Pygmalion,* was forty-nine when she appeared in the premiere in London, in 1914. Lynn Fontanne was thirty-nine when she played Eliza for the Theatre Guild in New York in 1926. Gertrude Lawrence was forty-four when she played the Cockney flower girl on Broadway in 1945. And Julie Harris was well into her thirties when she starred in *Pygmalion* on television.

Wendy Hiller, in the 1938 motion picture *Pygmalion,* directed by Anthony Asquith, was the definitive Eliza, so far as *My Fair Lady* was concerned. Lerner had screened the movie several times in preparing to write his libretto, even appropriating the film's embassy ball scene and more upbeat ending rather than using the original play's more ambiguous one. Julie also saw the movie, in which Leslie Howard played Henry Higgins, "countless times, and bawled every time." Wendy Hiller was already an accomplished actress of twenty-six when she portrayed Eliza.

Lerner, in writing the libretto, had been faithful to the spirit of

Shaw's play. Although he added new scenes—at the Ascot Races, "on the street where you live" outside the Higgins house, at the ball—it was nearly impossible to tell where he had invented dialogue. When he did, it was Shavian in spirit. The only serious plot change from *Pygmalion* was the softer ending (Shaw's epilogue contended that Eliza would marry Freddy) and most of Shaw's piercing social commentary on England's rigid class distinctions remained intact.

Moss Hart, the director of *My Fair Lady*, met Julie for the first time at the first rehearsal, January 3, 1956. "She was charming," he remembered, "but it seemed to me she didn't have a clue about playing Eliza. About the fifth day I got really terrified that she was not going to make it." Julie told friends that she *thought* she knew what her director wanted, but that every time she tried to do it "something comes up in front of me and I'm like a crab clawing at a glass wall with Moss on the other side."

Rex Harrison recounted that in rehearsals Julie "burst out laughing at every scene I played. It was a form of nerves, I think. She was really only a kid and it must have been a frightening experience for her. I always asked her why she laughed, and she never did tell me." (In later years, Julie did not remember the laughing.) On the third Friday of rehearsals, Harrison stormed out of the theater, threatening, "If this bitch is here on Monday, I'm quitting the show."

Hart cancelled general rehearsals for the entire weekend and spent the two days alone with Julie at the New Amsterdam Theatre, trying to develop her performance. She called it "the now-famous, dreaded weekend," and he termed it "the days of terror. It was the sort of thing you couldn't do in front of a company without destroying a human being. We met in this silent, lonely, dark theater and I told her, 'This is stolen time, time I can't really afford. So there can be no time for politeness, and you mustn't take offense, because there aren't any second chances in the theater. There isn't time to do the whole Actors' Studio bit. We have to start from the first line and go over the play line by line.' With someone not gifted, this would have meant nothing, this rehearsal in depth."

Miles Krueger, then a Lerner employee and later the founder and head of the Institute of the American Musical, was an unseen eyewitness to the first hour or so of the process. "I watched as Moss Hart went through the script, line by line, explaining every joke to Julie Andrews," Krueger recalled. "If you've ever had to explain a joke to somebody who didn't get it, that's difficult enough. But to have to explain an entire script—Lerner out of Shaw—to some-one....Andrews had it all in there, way down deep somewhere, because it was like lifting the veils. And two days later, when rehearsals resumed, Julie Andrews was, full-blown, the Julie Andrews we know today—that uninhibited, wonderful comedienne who can give so much and do screwball things, do everything. Moss Hart was the Pygmalion of *My Fair Lady*. I watched him, before my very eyes, create a performer named Julie Andrews."

"Moss was like a Svengali," the newly-embodied Trilby/Galatea agreed. "I was too shy, too gauche and too full of insecurities in those years to have a clear picture of what Eliza should be." Both days of the weekend, from 2 P.M. to 6 P.M. and again from 8 P.M. to 11 P.M. (the mornings had to be devoted to costume fittings for Julie), "we sweated it out. He bullied and pleaded, coaxed and cajoled. He *was* Eliza Doolittle sometimes." Hart told Andrews such things as: "You're playing this like a Girl Guide"; "You haven't any idea of how to play that"; "You're not *thinking*, you're just oozing out the scene"; or "You're gabbling."

"He made me *be* Eliza," Julie acknowledged.

"Those two days made the difference," Hart conceded. "She was neither affronted nor hurt. She was delighted. We were both absolutely exhausted, but she made it. She has that terrible English strength that makes you wonder why they lost India."

"Come Monday—though I probably dropped halfway back again through sheer nerves at facing the company—he had really given me an insight as to how the part should be played," Julie recalled. When the full company rehearsal finished, "Rex Harrison looked at me and said in frank and complimentary astonishment, 'My word, you *have* improved.' And then, almost excitedly, 'I say, do you think we could go over that scene once again, because I've got an idea that when Eliza says this Higgins would…' He was talking to me as though I were an actress—a *real* actress."

Moss Hart was "a dear man, but at the time he made me infuriated, and scared and mad and frightened and in awe and full of an inferiority complex. While knowing I could do it, he worked and worked on me. I really did need a strong guiding hand. It was such a big musical and I had so little courage. I didn't know what Eliza should be—a whiny girl or a gutsy girl, a weak character or a strong one. Moss supplied the route, the direction, and as the nights went by I absorbed Eliza more and more."

Frequently Julie and her "Svengali" would take fifteen-minute refresher sessions in the powder room at the Mark Helliger Theatre, while the rest of the cast continued rehearsals on stage. Yet, for the next three and a half years (two years on Broadway and eighteen months in London) of eight performances a week, Julie "was never really sure, on any given night, that I had enough strength to do the whole thing flat out. I found it an enormous weight every night. I can't remember a single performance when I didn't wonder to myself: 'Am I going to get through it tonight?' or think, 'I'll have to save myself a little in this song so that I have enough voice left for my next number.' It was such an enormous show—the screaming, the singing purely, the singing 'on the chest,' the great dramatic requirements."

With no battery microphones for performers to wear back then, with only well-placed microphones on stage, "at times I went through hell," Andrews recalled before opening in *Victor/Victoria* in 1995. "I did have vocal problems from time to time. That's my greatest fear today. If I have worries about my performance now it's, 'Oh, God, I don't want to disappoint an audience tonight. I want to be fresh and great.'"

Harrison remembered that it was hard, at first, for Julie to do the long Shaw dialogue scenes, "but she certainly overcame that quickly. The other thing that she found difficult, and Audrey [Hepburn, in the movie version of *My Fair Lady*] did too, was to get the gutter quality in Liza. That's a very exacting thing."

Julie took great delight in the fact that she learned her Cockney dialect from an American, Alfred Dixon, a former actor who had been teaching pronunciation for twenty-five years. Dixon had catalogued, he said, all the world's inflections of speech, which made him as close a vocational cousin to Henry Higgins as could be found. At first the Cockney speech used in *My Fair Lady* proved too authentic for American audiences and had to be toned down considerably. "The trouble with the dialect," Julie recalled, "was that it varied slightly between men and women, and between that in use today and in the period of the play, which is Edwardian. In those days men were different: their voices were deep and low, and the women's were shriller and sort of high."

In Shaw's original *Pygmalion* script, the only part written phonetically was at the very beginning, when the posh layabout Freddy Eynsford-Hill, looking for a taxi for his mother and sister outside Covent Garden, knocks Eliza's flowers into a puddle. Liza says to Mrs. Eynsford-Hill: "Ow eez ye-ooa san, is 'e? Wal, fewd dan y'de-ooty bawmz a mather should eed now bettrn to spawl a pore gel's flahrzn than ran away athat pyin. Will ye-oo py me f'tehm?" ("Oh, he's your son is he? Well, if you had done your duty by him as a mother should he'd know better than to spoil a poor girl's flowers and then run away without paying. Will you pay me for them?") Julie had to learn the pronunciation of the rest of Shaw's Cockney lines from Dixon. Her own favorite was "Oi woodn't 'ave et it, only oi'm too lidy-loike to take it aout of me maght." ("I wouldn't have eaten it, but I'm too ladylike to take it out of my mouth.")

Despite his new-found respect for his co-star's acting, Harrison remained irascible throughout rehearsals, mostly because of his insecurity about his singing and his fear of being drowned out by the orchestra. Although biographer Philip Hoare said that Noel Coward had first been offered the role of Higgins, Lerner and Loewe had not really written Higgins's songs until after Harrison was signed, and then they wrote to the musical limitations of his voice. Still, Harrison complained to Lerner that the lyrics to his opening number, "Why Can't the English?" made him sound too much like a road-company Noel Coward. Lerner agreed that the internal rhyme scheme might be a bit too Cowardy. Thus he changed "In Norway there are legions of literate Norwegians" to "This verbal class distinction by now should be antique."

Harrison also loudly objected to standing on the stage doing nothing but watching while Julie sang Eliza's big denoument liberation number, "Without You." "I am not going to stand up there and make a cunt of myself while this young girl sings a song at me," he said.

The creative team, especially Hart, decided to ignore this problem, even skipping rehearsing the song altogether, until other problems were straightened out. First came the show's title, which became crucial when advertising had to be ordered and programs printed for the first week of tryouts in New Haven, Connecticut. With no working title other than "the musical *Pygmalion*," Lerner and Loewe originally had considered *Liza* or *Lady Liza*, but since Harrison had top billing these were rejected. So was *Come to the Ball*, which was also the name of Rex's big waltz number in the first act. The creators finally compromised at the last minute, because they had to, on the least objectionable option: *My Fair Lady*. It was a title that they had earlier discarded because, in Lerner's words, "it sounded too much like an operetta." Even now, they thought they would change it on the road. *My Fair Lady* did not derive from any line of dialogue or lyric in the musical. It came from the nursery rhyme "London Bridge is Falling Down," and provided eternal proof that a great show can survive a lousy title.

One problem that *My Fair Lady* never had, unlike most other musicals-in-the-making, was finances. A single backer, the Columbia Broadcasting System, put up the show's entire $400,000 budget. Goddard Lieberson, president of the company's Columbia Records division, thus wisely acquired the rights to the original cast album. Whatever problems the production was having, music and lyrics mostly were not among them. To all advance ears, Loewe's score and Lerner's lyrics soared on the first hearing. Julie was to sing no fewer than nine of the show's songs, including "Wouldn't It Be Loverly," "Say a Prayer for Me Tonight," "I Could Have Danced All Night," "Show Me," and "Just You Wait."

With a solid budget, the producers could afford to hire the best. Lerner and Loewe convinced Cecil Beaton, who "designed the Edwardian era or the Edwardian era designed him," according to Lerner, to design only the costumes for the 1912 period piece. Beaton usually liked to take charge of the overall design of a show, including sets. But, with Beaton's blessing, Oliver Smith, who had done the sets for Lerner and Loewe's *Brigadoon* and *Paint Your Wagon*, was the only choice for set designer. A changing style in American musical comedy had rendered the overt "big ballet" choreography of Agnes de Mille somewhat obsolete, so Hanya Holm was hired to integrate movement into the musical that may have more spoken dialogue than any other.

Every little detail was attended to. CBS, for purposes of authenticity, made a recording of the bells of St. Paul's Cathedral in London as a sound effect. The church bells would strike the second quarter during the Covent Garden opening scene, when Higgins studies Eliza's Cockney speech.

Stanley Holloway, whose big numbers were "With a Little Bit of Luck" and "Get Me to the Church on Time," said he could not survive rehearsals without his "cuppa" tea. So whatever else was brewing, he and the other English principals, including Harrison, Robert Coote as Colonel Pickering, and Cathleen Nesbitt as Henry's mother, Mrs. Higgins, took their tea break every day at four. Producer Herman Levin saw that proper English biscuits were always served. "Julie had become the little mother," Lerner recalled, "and brewed tea for all her countrymen while rehearsals halted for half an hour."

The veteran music hall entertainer Holloway was miffed that Hart was spending so many evenings working with Harrison on his performance and that the director had devoted a whole weekend to Andrews. Holloway called his agent and threatened to quit the show. Hart cajoled, "Now look, Stanley, I am rehearsing a girl who has never played a major role in her life and an actor who has never sung on stage in his life. You have done both. If you feel neglected, it is a compliment." Holloway laughed and stayed in the cast.

The first week of out-of-town tryouts in New Haven produced

some major problems. Only on the train up to Connecticut from Grand Central Station had Hart persuaded Harrison to try out an alternate staging for Julie's "Without You" solo. "The song is going to be sung," Hart said to Harrison, "don't make any mistake about that....Now, you can walk offstage while it's being sung, and walk back on again when it's over, but you will look like the biggest horse's ass in the history of the theater." To pacify the star, Lerner and Loewe composed a coda for the song. Higgins bursts in at the end of Liza's song and says "I did it! I did it! I said I'd make a woman and indeed I did. Liza, you're magnificent." Since the lines stepped on a big Eliza and Julie moment, and redirected all the attention back to Higgins and Harrison, he loved the change. It stayed in and he stayed on stage.

But a bigger problem loomed. The first New Haven performance was set for Saturday night, February 4, 1956, in front of a full house consisting of local patrons and hordes of theater people coming up from New York. Harrison and the rest of the cast had just rehearsed with the full thirty-two piece orchestra (and the complete or-chestrations by Robert Russell Bennett and Phil Lang) for the first time the night before and Harrison was panicked. "I don't think I've been as frightened before or since in my life," he wrote in his autobiography *Rex*. So despite what conductor and musical direc-tor Fran Allers remembered as "a very solid rehearsal" on Saturday afternoon, afterwards, around five o'clock, Harrison announced that he could not perform that night and that he needed all of Sunday just to get ready for Monday night's show. Worse, he ordered that the performance be cancelled because of "technical difficulties."

"He just went to pieces and locked himself up in the dressing room," Nancy Olson recalled. "He was terrified." Kitty Carlisle (Mrs. Moss) Hart remembered her husband's telling her that Har-rison raged, "I never liked musical com, and I won't do musical com."

In the meantime, a severe snowstorm had started falling on New Haven. Some determined ticket holders had already left their homes in the suburbs for dinner before the theater and the New

Yorkers were all on the train. Despite frequent announcements of the cancellation on local radio stations amid the weather reports, it was likely that almost a full house would show up. The Shubert's manager refused to go along with the fictional reason for cancellation. His loyalty was to his audience and he was going to tell them that Rex Harrison simply refused to go on. An hour before curtain time, Harrison relented. (His agent had arrived from New York and threatened the end of Rex's career.)

The theater filled up and the curtain went up on the first performance of *My Fair Lady* only a little late, at 8:40 P.M. (8:30 P.M. being the usual curtain time then). "From the moment the curtain rose I felt that we were on a winner," Holloway recalled. "You could sense the cordiality coming up from the audience in waves. There was an electricity in the atmosphere. You realized that everything was falling into place."

Not so oddly, there *were* some technical difficulties—the set revolves were too slow and a few rising or falling curtains got caught on scenery. The first act was twenty-five minutes too long. Two pre-ball songs failed totally with the audience: "Come to the Ball," which was supposed to have been Harrison's big number in waltz-time, and Julie's "Say a Prayer for Me Tonight." But the Liza-Higgins-Pickering trio, "The Rain in Spain," quite literally stopped the show. Julie, as a veteran vaudevillian, knew just what to do about that. She said, "Come on, boys," to Harrison and Coote and then escorted them downstage for an unscheduled little bow. In later performances, when "The Rain in Spain" stopped the show, it was Harrison who controlled any impromptu bows.

"The second act played beautifully," Lerner wrote in his autobiography, "but more important, the total effect was stunning and when the curtain came down the audience stood up and cheered."

The fixes came fast in the next few days in New Haven. "Come to the Ball" and "Say a Prayer for Me" were dropped, which left Julie "only" eight songs in the show. " 'Say a Prayer...'was *my* song, and I was sad when they cut it," she said. Loewe recalled, "It was a charming song and Julie Andrews did it beautifully. But it laid an egg, and we threw it out the very next night." Lerner and Loewe employed "Say a Prayer for Me" to better effect in a similar context in their next collaboration, the 1958 movie *Gigi*, where it was sung by Leslie Caron. (Oddly, Julie did not include the song on her all-Alan Jay Lerner recording, *Here I'll Stay*, in 1996.)

By the time the company opened its final four weeks of out-of-town previews at the Erlanger Theatre in Philadelphia, on February 15, 1956, the show was virtually frozen. The word was out that *My Fair Lady* was the next big hit and that Julie Andrews was the next big Broadway star. Rex Harrison was rumored to be magnificent in his first musical, having conquered the role in New Haven. Audiences and reviewers were moved to superlatives. During the Philadelphia run, Andrews, Harrison, Lerner, Loewe, Hart, and Levin were besieged by New York friends for opening night tickets at the rate of ten requests for each seat in the theater. It got so bad that Julie and Rex left word with the hotel operators that no long-distance calls were to be put through to their rooms. She was reminded of her "waiting and seeing" stance about stardom after her triumph in *The Boy Friend*, and asked if she had yet changed her mind. "No," she answered, "because we still haven't opened in New York."

Barbara Andrews was among the glittering premiere audience who did get into the Mark Hellinger Theatre on the evening of March 15, 1956. Julie had bought her mother a Dior gown and rented her a mink coat for the occasion. "Opening night of *My Fair Lady* in New York was the greatest night of my life," Barbara Andrews declared. "Apart from the night I had Julie. That first transformation from the guttersnipe Eliza to her appearance at the Ascot races! And when she came down [the staircase] in white, with the feather!" Barbara's pride in her daughter's performance was underscored by tumultuous ovations after every song. "As the cheering and the applause roared over us," Julie remembered, "I knew I had gained my first knowledge of that great joy in pleasing an audience."

There was no opening night party *per se*, and the Lerners, Harts, and Liebersons, with Rex Harrison, repaired to a private dining room at *21*. Only Andrews and Loewe, among the principals, felt confident enough to show up at Sardi's for the traditional first-night supper, standing ovation, and wait for the reviews. "When I saw the big sheaf of newspapers coming in, my heart dropped," she remembered. "But the reviews, they were wonderful. I went right home and put through a call to London to my father. It was eight-thirty in the morning over there, but I don't think he had slept much during the night."

The critics were literally unanimous in their praise of both the musical and Julie. Walter Kerr wrote in the *New York Herald-Tribune*, "Miss Andrews descended a staircase looking like all the glamour of the theater summed up in an instant." Brooks Atkinson, in *The New York Times*, called the show "wonderful....To Shaw's agile intelligence it adds the warmth, loveliness, and excitement of a memorable theater frolic." Julie, he wrote, "does a magnificent job. The transformation from street-corner drab to lady is both touching and beautiful. Miss Andrews acts her part triumphantly."

A long line began to form at the theater box office the day after the opening, and for the next six and a half years (2,717 performances), *My Fair Lady* shattered all existing Broadway attendance and revenue records.

My Fair Lady was sold out for every performance of the two years that Andrews and Harrison performed in it. Eighteen months after the opening it was still impossible to get tickets for six months in the future.

The Broadway original cast album, which was recorded and released before the end of March, actually outgrossed the show in its first year of release, with one million copies sold for approximately five million dollars. In London these records were legally unobtainable, but copies smuggled in by airline and ship employees fetched the equivalent of fifty dollars each. It was the number one album for fifteen weeks on the *Billboard* magazine charts. *My Fair Lady* quickly became the bestselling cast album of all time, and remained so for almost two decades. In 1997, *My Fair Lady* still holds the record for the number of weeks as a Top 40 album, 292.

The fifty-four minute Columbia recording was done in fourteen hours at a converted Gothic church studio on East 30th Street in

Manhattan, on a Sunday, ten days after the opening of the show. Lerner rewrote and rearranged lyrics. "For God's sake, get me to the church on time" became "Be sure and get me to the church on time" to ensure that the record could be played on radio and television. This prompted Stanley Holloway, whose number it was, to mock "Be Shaw, be George Bernard Shaw to get me to the church on time." Loewe and Franz Allers, who at one point was conducting with one hand and holding up his trousers with the other, changed tempos and orchestrations. Some instrumentalists were awarded their own microphones. Lieberson supervised both studio and control room, where Loewe was pounding a wooden shelf and shouting such lines as "Hit the D! Hit the D! and "Cymbals, cymbals, cymbals."

The session started at 10 A.M. with Holloway and chorus singing "With a Little Bit of Luck," which he accompanied with gestures and soft-shoe routines. Julie, accompanied by her mother, arrived just after lunch, and by the time she had sung two of her eight songs, "Show Me" and "Wouldn't It Be Loverly?" she remarked that her nerves were raw. Harrison, in a green vest, arrived at 3:45 P.M. and talked "You Did It" with Robert Coote. Julie's "I Could Have Danced All Night" came next, and then dinner. Andrews, Harrison, and Coote performed their dance steps for "The Rain in Spain" to enhance the mood, although sound effects rendered them unnecessary to the recording.

A barefoot Harrison played the violin with the orchestra during songs sung by others, but he reluctantly gave up his chair when the time came to do "I've Grown Accustomed to Her Face." Julie and Harrison did their duet—"Without You"—as Allers asked for "two minutes of silent prayer, please." Rex's "Why Can't the English?" and "I'm an Ordinary Man," and Julie's "Just You Wait" finished the recording session just after midnight. The drums were so strong during "Just You Wait" that she began imitating a drum majorette at her microphone. Within thirty-six hours of the end of the session, the first pressings were being produced to fill advance orders for 100,000 records. (The album jackets had been printed for two weeks.)

My Fair Lady won the New York Drama Critics Circle Award, the Outer Critics Circle Award, and the Tony Award as Best Musical. Tonys also went to Harrison as Best Actor in a Musical, Lerner as author and lyricist, Loewe as composer, Hart as director, Levin as producer, Oliver Smith for his sets, Cecil Beaton for his costumes, and Fran Allers as conductor and musical director. Julie lost as Best Actress in a Musical to Judy Holliday for *Bells Are Ringing*. (Ethel Merman was the third nominee, for *Happy Hunting*.) Hanya Holm lost the choreography Tony to Michael Kidd, for *L'il Abner*. (Kidd had been interviewed for *My Fair Lady*.) Julie did win the New York Drama Critics Award for Best Actress in a Musical.

The movie rights were sold to Warner Brothers for $5.5 million, a record then and a price unsurpassed for at least twenty-five years. An American touring company of the show, the London production, and various foreign language versions of *My Fair Lady* brought the property's gross receipts to more than $100 million in just a few years.

Julie, a major reason for *My Fair Lady*'s success, was now inundated with offers to better her already quite respectable $2,000-a-week salary. She became the first international musical theater leading lady since Gertrude Lawrence had arrived in New York in 1924 and sung "Limehouse Blues" in *Charlot's Revue*. A parade of celebrities saw the show and visited Julie's dressing room, including Marlene Dietrich, Noel Coward, Ingrid Bergman, and Danny Kaye, who remembered her sitting on his lap eight years before.

Coward wrote in his diary that *My Fair Lady* was "quite enchanting from every point of view. Rex Harrison and Julie Andrews were wonderful, score and lyrics excellent, decor and dresses lovely, and the whole thing beautifully presented."

"Toast of the town," Julie said of herself, with some sarcasm, at the time. "I haven't had much time to be toasted very much. I receive a great many invitations but I can accept only a few. I dare not go out before a matinee, and the next day I am recuperating from two shows. People expect so much more of you after something like this—more letters, more effort, more entrances. Then, if you don't produce, they think you've gone big-headed."

One of the things people most expected from Julie was tickets to *My Fair Lady*. But she couldn't get them, not even for her "discoverer" Vida Hope. "I know she didn't believe me," Julie said. "Nobody does. I don't know where everybody comes from."

During the rehearsal period, Julie had moved back into a modest suite at the modest Park Chambers, by herself this time. It was the first time she had ever lived alone, and she pronounced it "not so terrifying as I had imagined." After *My Fair Lady* opened, she moved to "a minute flat in the east sixties with a sweet little patio in the back and a proper cooking range." Mornings she slept in until 11 A.M. or 12 noon, trying to rest nine and a half hours a night. She rented studio space in which to practice her singing for an hour a day. And now she eschewed the American cheeseburgers she had come to love in order to keep her flower-girl figure.

Homesick for the English spring, she bought daffodils from the flower man outside her subway stop as a pale reminder of the clumps of daffodils outside her window in Walton-on-Thames. She sent Dictaphone "letters" back home every week, and found that the best thing about her new affluence was that she could afford to fly family members to New York for visits. Julie decided that in any future career she would live in England and spend three or four months of the year in the United States working, preferably in the American autumn. But she preferred her homeland because "I like the smallness of England; it's all so vast over here, it really knocks you off your feet."

Tony Walton arrived in New York in April of 1956, just a month after the opening of *My Fair Lady*, to study scenic design. Julie spent much of her free time with him, and he called for her at the theater after every performance. They picnicked in the country whenever possible, and took an out-of-season winter vacation in Bear Mountain, New York (after turning down invitations to Nassau, Jamaica, and Bermuda) in 1957, during her week off from *My Fair Lady*. On many nights after the show, they went to the Windsor Pharmacy at 58th Street and Sixth Avenue for a "Windsor Special," which Julie described as a "a banana thing with wads of coconut." (In 1997, the Windsor Pharmacy was still there, but the soda fountain was long gone.)

Denying that she and Tony were engaged (as her mother and stepfather were having to do in London), Julie nevertheless publicly acknowledged him as her boyfriend. For her twenty-first birthday, October 1, 1956, he gave her a brooch in the shape of a laurel leaf that she wore on everything. The future course of the romance had been decided, but they were delaying a formal engagement because Julie was committed to playing Eliza in London for eighteen months after her two years on Broadway, and Tony had to study for and pass his examinations for the scenic design union in New York. Julie depended on Tony to be another Svengali. "She has no conception of her capabilities," he said at the time. "It's all there— just needs a bit of dragging out."

Charles Tucker gave Julie her first fur coat for that twenty-first birthday, a black Alaska sealskin with which to combat the New York winters. But now that she could afford just about anything she wanted, Julie seemed to have lost a good deal of her former acquisitiveness. "Every time I'm tempted by something elaborate," she said, "I hear Mummy saying: 'Simplicity, simplicity.'"

Although she was still intermittently insecure in the show ("I still feel unsure sometimes, as though I've tackled something miles above me"), Julie had long since ceased to be a problem child for the cast and management of *My Fair Lady*. Moss Hart said that she reminded him of Gertrude Lawrence, whom he had directed in *Lady in the Dark*. Hart also said of Julie, "She has this curious kind of glacial calm, as though she came down from Everest every day to play the show, instead of from a hotel room." Stanley Holloway said, "This child isn't spoiled one bit by success—it's hardly believeable in an age where teenagers are so worldly. I'm lucky to have her for a stage daughter. She *might* have been a scene stealer."

Even Rex Harrison, who used to amuse himself by trying to rattle her, changing around bits of stage business, finally gave in to her surface calm. (The rest of the cast called her "The Rock" because she would stand stoically by while Rex pulled his pranks.)

She did have some trouble dancing with him ("He's left-handed and hence left-footed and starts the waltz from the left side—it can be confusing") and throwing his slippers at him towad the end of the show.

"He was quirky, selfish, charming, dashing, and brilliant," Julie said of Rex almost forty years later. "I would learn so much just standing on stage and watching him. However mad one got at him for the odd bit of selfishness, he cut the mustard so brilliantly every single night that one forgave him."

"She is absolutely the same offstage as on," Harrison said in 1966. "She is marvelously even, her performance doesn't vary; it is highly professional from the word 'go.' Julie always was—a very boring old word—a good trouper. She plowed on through thick and thin. One thousand performances over three years is three thousand hours—four months and five days of twenty-four hours a day. I had my secretary figure it out one day. That is quite a hell of a long time to have been *vis-à-vis* with somebody, through summers hot, winters cold, that sort of thing. She has an honesty and integrity, an openness, a quality of the English equivalent of the girl next door. She reminds me of some of the English ladies at Metro [Goldwyn-Mayer]: Greer [Garson] and Deborah [Kerr]. She is not quite the same as they, but she has that very same quality that has appealed to movie audiences over the years."

But Julie Andrews was not thinking of movies in the late 1950s, except to attend the occasional special film. (She and Tony accepted, as one of the "perks" of her new stardom, reserved seats to the sold-out *Around the World in Eighty Days*.) In fact, she had no show-business aspirations beyond *My Fair Lady*, she said. "I'd like to work awfully hard for another two years, then marry, then have lots of children. I really wouldn't mind retiring, or working in London on one thing a year. I haven't much desire to go on to bigger and better things—what could be bigger and better than this?"

4

Cinderella Marries Her Prince and Goes to Live in *Camelot*

Charles Tucker's prediction of five years earlier came true in March of 1957: Richard Rodgers and Oscar Hammerstein II wrote a musical for Julie Andrews. She would play the title part in *Cinderella*, a role she had suggested to CBS-TV. For the network the previous year, she had done *High Tor* and two appearances on *The Ed Sullivan Show* to promote *My Fair Lady*. The network commissioned Rodgers and Hammerstein to write what was to be their only full-length original work for television. *Cinderella* was telecast on the evening of Sunday, March 31, 1957, to an astonishing 107 million people, pre-empting both Sullivan's show and *The General Electric Theater. Cinderella* was also the first live Broadway-style musical written for television and virtually the only one. It also had a Broadway-sized budget of $385,000, only $15,000 less than *My Fair Lady.*

Besides writing the lyrics, Hammerstein also adapted the libretto for the ninety-minute musical version from the classic fairy tale. He kept the basic plot but excised some clutter and refashioned the characters to be more well-rounded and realistic. Cinderella was now neither a pitiable drudge nor an impossibly put-upon saint. Her wicked stepmother and stepsisters were now less

61

overtly evil and more comically self-involved. Most revolutionary of all, now Cinderella's godmother (no longer called a fairy godmother) was a pretty, young woman who employed her magic wand and other powers only reluctantly.

By the start of rehearsals for the live telecast, Julie had been established as Eliza Doolittle, a kind of Cinderella character, in *My Fair Lady* for more than a year. Edith (later Edie) Adams, a proven television star, who was also known for her Broadway triumph as Rosalind Russell's sister Eileen in *Wonderful Town* and was still performing her Tony-winning role of Daisy Mae in the musical *L'il Abner*, co-starred as Cinderella's godmother. Full-cast rehearsals could be held only on Sundays, since both Andrews and Adams were doing eight performances a week in Broadway shows.

The stepmother was played by Ilka Chase, a veteran of twenty Broadway shows but by 1957 even better known as a television panelist, the author of seven bestselling books, and a syndicated column. Kaye Ballard and Alice Ghostley, rising young actresses and club entertainers, played the stepsisters. Playwright Howard Lindsay and his wife, actress Dorothy Stickney, portrayed the king and queen. Lindsay, with his partner Russel Crouse, had written the long-running play *Life With Father* (in which Lindsay and Stickney starred for three years) and won a Pulitzer Prize for *State of the Union*. Lindsay and Crouse went on to adapt the libretto for *The Sound of Music* from Maria von Trapp's autobiography. Jon Cypher, the only real newcomer in the cast, played the role of the prince. (In 1996, Cypher starred as the toy company executive in the musical *Big*, just around the corner from Andrews in *Victor/Victoria*.)

Ralph Nelson, one of the finest directors on early live television, directed *Cinderella*. Nelson then made a successful transition to directing movies, with *Requiem for a Heavyweight* and *Lilies of the Field* among his credits. The sets and costumes were by William and Jean Eckart. They created a full-skirted ball gown for Julie that they knew was too full for the narrow, two-story studio in which *Cinderella* was done. The fulsome gown was used only for publicity photographs and a simpler, leaner gown was designed for the highly vertical telecast itself. The Eckart costumes were "the first really glittering ones on a television spectacular [as specials were called in those days]," Adams recalled. "Both my baton and my eyelids sparkled."

The producer Richard Lewine, Nelson, and Rodgers and Hammerstein prepared the show as if it were for Broadway, with one important exception: Julie had no understudy. This was to be her *Cinderella* or nobody's. (When her understudy in *My Fair Lady*, Lola Fischer, went on for her it was front-page news, although the show was such a hit it would still sell out.) Rodgers sat in the small, crowded control room throughout the rehearsals. "They were as intensive as for any TV show up to that time," Adams wrote in her autobiography, *Sing a Pretty Song...*, quite a contrast from working with her costar and husband, the innovative and impromptu Ernie Kovacs.

Because Andrews and Adams were both starring on Broadway, they took to having their evening meal together in Julie's dressing room at 4 P.M., except on matinee days. It was a proper English tea. Julie and Tony also went to Ernie and Edie's apartment on Central Park West for dinner several times.

Cinderella was one of the first network specials to be transmitted live in color, albeit only in the Eastern time zone. Only a tiny percentage of Americans anywhere had access to a color television set in 1957, but Jack Gould, the television critic of *The New York Times* wrote in his review that Andrews in the title role of *Cinderella* was "the best reason yet to buy one."

While the score was far from Rodgers and Hammerstein's best, such charming songs as "Ten Minutes Ago," "In My Own Little Corner," "Lovely Night," and "Do I Love You Because You're Beautiful (Or Are You Beautiful Because I Love You?)" helped to make the television musical *Cinderella* unforgettable. The show-stopper, at the end of the first act, was "Impossible," a duet between Adams and Andrews that detailed the unlikelihood of what was about to happen in act two. The song, which they sang riding off to the ball in the converted pumpkin carriage, reinforced Hammerstein's concept that Cinderella had the ability to effect her destiny, at least partially, rather than rely entirely on outside magic. The song was reprised as "It's Possible."

"Just before we went on the air," Julie recalled, "somebody said, rather foolishly, 'do you realize that more people will see this show this evening than could see *My Fair Lady* in a generation!'"

Any nervouseness this remark or anything else may have induced wasn't noticeable. Once again, Julie seemed born to play the part and received her first Emmy nomination for the show. The rest of the cast also sparkled throughout the ninety-minute show, which as a timeless fairy tale should have become an often-repeated television classic. But the black-and-white kinescope of *Cinderella* that was shown in the rest of the country (and recorded during dress rehearsal) was all that survived of the production.

The show was remade in the winter of 1964–1965 with the same score, one new song by Rodgers, and a somewhat revised book by Joseph Shrank (Hammerstein had died). Lesley Ann Warren played the title part, and a different supporting cast, including Ginger Rogers and Walter Pidgeon as the queen and king, and Jo Van Fleet as the stepmother, was used. Warren, a seventeen-year-old new-comer, would become a critical success on Broadway (*Drat, the Cat*) and in her movie career, courtesy of Walt Disney. In 1982 she co-starred with Julie in the movie version of *Victor/Victoria*. Warren's color version of *Cinderella* was repeated and eventually released on videocassette.

In the fall of 1957, Julie and Stanley Holloway starred as a last-minute joint replacement for Ethel Merman in *Crescendo*, a ninety-minute CBS musical spectacular. Rex Harrison had previously signed to star in the show as a visiting Englishman who is entertained by a sampling of most styles of American music: blues, country and western, folk, jazz, sacred, Latin-American, and, of course, musical comedy. Since they had no time to prepare anything else, Andrews and Holloway performed a medley from *My Fair Lady*.

Julie also recorded her first solo non-cast album as an adult in late 1957. She sang twelve of her favorite songs on the album, *The*

Lass With the Delicate Air, released by RCA. The selections, arranged by Irwin Kostal, included "O the Days of the Kerry Dancing," "Canterbury Fair," "London Pride," and "Where'er You Walk," an English folk song which she had often sung as a child with her stepfather, Ted Andrews.

Early in 1958, Julie sang "Blue Moon" on NBC's color television series, *The Dinah Shore Show.* Julie, Dinah Shore, and Chita Rivera sang a trio, "Life Upon the Wicked Stage" from *Showboat.* Three weeks later, Julie was back at CBS, in black and white, singing a duet with Patti Page on Patti's weekly program, *The Big Record.* Other guests on that eclectic musical telecast included Roberta Sherwood, jazzman Woody Herman and his orchestra, and the country-pop duo the Everly Brothers.

In February, 1958, Julie played Eliza Doolittle on Broadway for the last time. She was replaced by Sally Ann Howes, who was making her Broadway debut. Howes was an English stage and screen star and, like Julie, a former child star and the daughter of a show-business father, actor Bobby Howes. (Anne Rogers was already heading up the North American tour of *My Fair Lady* in Julie's role opposite Brian Aherne.) Edward Mulhare, another English actor, had taken over from Harrison as Henry Higgins on Broadway the previous September.

Tony Walton and Julie went on vacation in March to Paris, Venice, and Klosters, Switzerland. She flew into London on April 6, deliberately cutting it close to her West End opening in *My Fair Lady* on April 30, 1958. (Her New York success had made her comparatively wealthy, and arriving home any sooner would have made her liable for British income tax on her American earnings, a situation that was to keep her away from the United Kingdom for much of the next forty years.)

The eighteen-year-old girl who had flown to New York nearly four years before with two battered, vaudeville-seasoned suitcases arrived in London a twenty-two-year-old star with 260 pounds of excess luggage and her pet canary. The canary, Mr. Pocket, was named for the Alec Guinness character in the David Lean movie version of Charles Dickens's *Great Expectations* and had been a parting gift from the Broadway *My Fair Lady* cast. In addition, Julie's seven steamer trunks were en route from America.

On her trimphant return to British soil Julie wore the Alaska sealskin coat that Charles Tucker had given her, a clinging American-designed white wool dress, a seed-pearl and gold locket (another gift from the *My Fair Lady* cast), and a pearl and gold ring from Tony on her right hand. Her father Ted Wells, her brother John, and her half-sister Celia, as well as a score of friends, met Julie's airplane from Zurich. Tony had stayed behind in Switzerland, but returned to London in time for opening night. Julie went home to Walton-on-Thames for just one night then moved into a suite at the Savoy Hotel for the start of rehearsals.

Rex Harrison, Robert Coote, and Stanley Holloway were also returning home for the West End production of *My Fair Lady* at the Theatre Royal, Drury Lane, in Covent Garden where two of the major scenes in the musical, including the opening, are set. This theater had a larger stage than the Mark Hellinger (although it did have a smaller seating capacity) and eight singers were added to the chorus. Zena Dare made the final appearance of her long and distinguished career as Mrs. Higgins. Cecil Beaton redesigned several costumes for the London staging of the show, including two new gowns for Julie. Her only major problem now was to "brush up on my Cockney and put back the heavy accent that I had had to tone down."

Tickets proved every bit as difficult to obtain for *My Fair Lady* in London as they had in New York, and theater fans and socialites were flying in from Europe and the United States for opening night. There was a general air of high expectation unprecedented for an American musical being imported to the West End. One newspaper ran a countdown box each day that proclaimed: "Seven More Days," "Six More Days," and so on. Of course *My Fair Lady* was an "English" musical in content, never forgetting that Shaw was an Irish playwright. "So many people came to see how the British would respond to this Yankee version of one of their popular classics that there was hardly any room left in the theater for the British" Alan Lerner wrote in *The Street Where I Live*.

Opening night of *My Fair Lady* in its spiritual home proved triumphant. "The streets from Drury Lane to the Strand were lined with people," Lerner said, "and it looked more like a coronation than a premiere."

"The British felt that it was Shaw and Eliza Doolittle coming home," said Kitty Carlisle Hart.

Most of the white-tie premiere audience came out of the show agreeing that the musical was indeed as good as "the Yanks" had promised it would be. There was a four-minute standing ovation at the final curtain and eight curtain calls; there would have been more had the conductor not induced the orchestra to start playing "God Save the Queen." One minute after midnight, the previously banned original Broadway cast album of *My Fair Lady* became legally available to radio, television, and record shops in Great Britain and immediately became a bestselling album.

The next morning the newspaper reviews were generally positive, and the critics who also had seen the show in New York felt that the musical had traveled well. The leading lady who had sung in pigtails in *Starlight Roof* ten years before was hailed as generously as the show. One critic even found Julie's West End Eliza "more mature, commanding, and subtle" than the character she had originated on Broadway.

A Royal Command performance of the show took place on the Monday night after the opening with Queen Elizabeth II and Prince Philip in attendance. "It seemed to me that the Queen never laughed at all," Lerner wrote, "and that Prince Philip was having the time of his life." Julie, Harrison, and Holloway, still in costume, were presented to the royal couple after the performance.

In July 1958, Julie recorded two albums in London in the brand new stereophonic format. With Giorgio Tozzi, a leading Metropolitan Opera baritone and the ghost voice for Rossano Brazzi in the movie version of *South Pacific*, she recorded a studio version of *Rose-Marie*, the operetta by Rudolf Friml and Herbert Stothart with lyrics by Otto Harbach and Oscar Hammerstein II. She also recorded *Julie Andrews Sings*, a solo album of a dozen show tunes such as "It Might as Well Be Spring" and "I'm Old-Fashioned," again with Kostal arranging.

To take advantage of the new stereo technology, the London cast recorded a new *My Fair Lady* album on a rainy Sunday, February 1, 1959, at suburban London's Walthamstow Town Hall. A monaural pressing was made at the same time, since stereo albums required a new record player. The London cast album of *My Fair Lady* preserved the songs in the same order as the New York version but offered more polished performances. The London record became the best of some sixty albums produced of the show's score.

Julie recalled that the recording session provided "the first really angry scene" she had caused in her professional career: "I was recording 'Just You Wait' and I was yelling and screaming my lungs out, as the song required. But in the playbacks I didn't hear what I knew was there. By that time I had done the show for something like two and a half years, and I knew what I was talking about. I got really mad and the sound engineers very sweetly agreed to turn whichever knobs had to be turned, and we redid it. And that was that."

During a three-week vacation from *My Fair Lady*, Julie married Tony Walton, on May 10, 1959. Tony designed her white organza wedding dress. The day before the wedding, Julie, in a cotton housecoat, spent the morning at her flat on Eaton Square (to which she had moved from the Savoy after the opening) accepting delivery of wedding presents. She divided the afternoon between her dressmaker, a theatrical designer in Soho (Tony waited outside; he may have designed the gown but he wasn't going to chance seeing her in it before the ceremony), and her mother's house in Walton-on-Thames, where Julie planned the flowers. She had a late-afternoon sitting for a portrait by Pietro Annigoni and dinner with her business manager. She stayed up late writing thank-you notes.

Two thousand fans turned up to watch the wedding party arriving for the ceremony at St. Mary's village church of Oatlands, Weybridge, Surrey. Tony recalled, "Our wedding was kind of a zoo; I wasn't expecting it." Noel Harrison, who was the then somewhat estranged son of Rex and who had been at school with Tony, served as best man. At one point he used his top hat to push spectators aside so that members of the wedding could get through to the church. The reception was held at The Mitre, a three-hundred-year-old inn opposite Hampton Court Palace on the bank of the Thames.

The honeymoon trip took the couple to California, where the twenty-three-year-old bride would appear on *The Jack Benny Hour.* Benny himself greeted the happy couple at Los Angeles Airport. He mentioned her new marriage on the show and another guest, Phil Silvers, danced with the bride. Julie sang "Summertime" and the inevitable *My Fair Lady* medley. For the finale sketch, "The Defiant Ones Like It Hot," a send-up of two current movies, she dressed as a flapper and sang "Ain't We Got Fun," "I'm Just Wild About Harry," and "Music, Music, Music!"

Julie's engagement to Tony, she recalled, had "just evolved. I don't remember one glorious night on bended knee. We were—here's the cliché—just good friends for a very long time, and then it grew into love. I guess you could say we were childhood sweethearts, and I'm very glad we were. On the day we got married I was glad I had known him so long. It's a big step to take, and it's better to do it with someone you know that well."

On August 8, 1959, Julie Andrews played Eliza Doolittle for the last time. She confessed to being "tired-tired, but not bored-tired." As an important part of a legendary show, "you don't want to go on [forever], she said, "but you don't want to go [away], either. The old firm, the old job becomes very dear."

Thus, when she took her applause for more than the thousandth time on her closing night in *My Fair Lady,* tears rolled in rivers through her stage makeup. The audience joined hands and sang "Auld Lang Syne," then the cast gave Julie an ovation. She ran to her dressing room, where she stayed for more than an hour, crying. She later hosted a party at the theater. The next night Anne Rogers, from whom Julie had inherited the role of Polly in *The Boy Friend* and who had just performed in the United States tour of *My Fair Lady,* took over as Eliza Doolittle in London.

After a total of three and a half years in the show, Julie found that her voice "was in a ragged state from night after night of belting. Then I had my tonsils out—at age twenty-three. I thought I would never sing again. It was an enormous period of anxiety about my voice. The next eighteen months were a miracle to me—I got my voice back."

First she hosted a short series of four programs for the BBC in London, *The Julie Andrews Show*, in November and December of 1959. Tony Walton designed the sets. The series was a nostalgia wallow both for its star and the audience who remembered her childhood performances. Ted and Barbara Andrews were guests, as was Vic Oliver, the comedian from *Starlight Roof.*

Camelot had begun to be conceived in early March of 1956 when it was apparent that *My Fair Lady* would be a hit. Lerner, Loewe, and Hart took an informal pledge to work together on another musical. They began to look around for an idea. They considered and rejected musicals based on Mark Twain's *Huckleberry Finn* and the Spencer Tracy–Elizabeth Taylor movie, *Father of the Bride.* Lerner and Hart were intrigued by *The New York Times* review of the book *The Once and Future King*, T. H. White's witty retelling of the King Arthur, Queen Guinevere and Sir Lancelot legend. In actuality, it was four books published in one volume, the first of which was called *The Sword and the Stone.*

Hart, Lerner, and Loewe bought the stage rights to the book from White, who was then living on Alderney, in the Channel Islands. After *My Fair Lady* and *Gigi*, which had won a record nine Oscars, Lerner and Loewe could write anything they wanted to. Only Loewe had some misgivings about Queen Guinevere and Sir Lancelot's cuckolding of King Arthur as the subject for a musical and what that might do to the second act. Financing would have been no problem, but once again CBS put up the entire $400,000 budget. The composer lyricist, and director were riding so high that they decided to produce the show themselves. Julie, still in London, was the first to be asked to join the company, and the first to give her immediate, enthusiastic, long-distance, "yes."

After twenty-one months of collaborating and commuting (Loewe had had a heart attack and was living in Palm Springs), Lerner and Loewe finished writing the musical in July of 1960. Many of the *My Fair Lady* team were rehired, including Hanya Holm as choreographer, Oliver Smith as set designer, Franz Allers as music director, and Robert Coote to play Pellinore, the king who has lost his kingdom and keeps looking for it in his rusty armor.

Hart suggested Richard Burton, whom he knew, for the part of King Arthur. Lerner had heard Burton and his wife Sybil sing some Welsh folk songs one night at the Ira Gershwins. But even if he had not, Lerner said, he would have hired Burton anyway, calling his speaking voice "one of the rare instruments in the contemporary theater." Besides, he was Welsh, and all Welshmen were presumed to sing with perfect pitch. The unknown Robert Goulet emerged on the last day of a long winter of auditions to play Lancelot. The legendary and long-retired movie costume designer, Adrian, now best remembered for Joan Crawford's shoulder pads, was hired as costume designer.

Rehearsals began in September 1960, under the title of *Jenny Kissed Me*. The company of sixty-one included twenty-four chorus singers. One chorus performer was John Cullum, who understudied Burton, eventually replaced Roddy McDowell as Mordred, and went on to star in Lerner and Burton Lane's *On A Clear Day You Can See Forever*. "We all believed in the book immensely, and thought it would be a very beautiful musical," Julie recalled. Because she and the creative team from *My Fair Lady* were involved and Richard Burton had been signed to make his musical debut as King Arthur, advance ticket sales reached a new Broadway record. Great things were expected of *Jenny Kissed Me*. Hart assured everyone that this time it was going to be easy, that there would be none of the agony of *My Fair Lady*. How wrong he was.

"Julie immediately opened up her old tea stand," Lerner remembered, "and at four o'clock everyone knocked off for the customary bit of old England. Everyone that is, but Richard, who retired to his dressing room for more stimulating refreshment." Strangely, Burton's heavy drinking never adversely affected his performance, nor did it cause offstage problems.

When he was drinking heavily, Burton simply became "the wisest, most world-weary king," Julie remembered. He spoke slowly and deliberately, so as not to forget his lines, and the audience never suspected that he didn't always play Arthur that way. Sometimes even she didn't know when Burton had been drinking. One matinee day, he bet another actor in the company that he could drink one whole fifth of vodka before the afternoon performance and another fifth before the evening show, yet leave his costar completely unaware of it. He proceeded to do just that, then asked Julie after the second performance how she thought he had been that day. "A little bit better," she replied.

But there was trouble in Camelot, though none of it directly involved Julie, who by this time was regarded as an accomplished professional, and the least of anyone's worries. Burton was very sure of his acting but not so of his singing. Robert Goulet could sing very well, but no one was too sure of his acting. Still, the three principals got along extremely well. Goulet developed a crush on Julie, who was still relatively newly wedded. "He got nowhere," said Lerner. "At times the clinches [between Andrews and Goulet as Guinevere and Lancelot] seemed to last a few seconds longer than planned, but it was probably due to muscle more than to reciprocal desire."

Desperate, Goulet turned to Burton for advice. Although Sybil Burton was very much around in this pre-*Cleopatra* period, Richard was still womanizing as much as he was drinking. His own attentions were centered on M'el Dowd, who was playing the minor role of the wicked Morgan Le Fey, a role that was cut in the movie version. This time, however, Burton was no help. After Goulet left the room, he asked Lerner, "Why did he come to me? I couldn't get anywhere [with Julie] either."

Burton later said that Julie Andrews was his only leading lady he'd never slept with. "How dare he say such an awful thing about me?" was her retort. Long after Burton's death, Julie admitted that if he had pursued her earlier in the run, she "might have succumbed like everybody else. But, fortunately, I didn't."

During New York rehearsals Adrian, the costume designer, died. He was replaced by his protégé, Tony Duquette, at the suggestion of Janet Gaynor, Adrian's widow. When the show moved to its first out-of-town tryouts in Toronto, Lerner was hospitalized for exhaustion and a bleeding ulcer. As he was leaving the hospital, Moss Hart was admitted, having suffered a massive coronary attack. Loewe wanted to hire a new director immediately, but Lerner wanted to fill in at least until the Boston opening and, in spite of Loewe's objections, he did so.

On opening night in Toronto, at the brand new 3,200-seat O'Keefe Centre, the retitled musical ran four and a half hours. One critic called it *"Götterdämmerung* without the laughs." Even Lerner said, "Only *Tristan und Isolde* rivaled it as a bladder contest." Since Wagnerian opera was not the goal of *Camelot*, massive cuts were made, and Lerner reconstructed the entire show. Still, as Loewe put it, *Camelot* was more medical than musical. A chorus girl ran a needle into her foot onstage. The chief electrician was hospitalized for a bladder problem. A wardrobe mistress's husband was found dead in their flat. "We will all be replaced tomorrow by hospital orderlies," Loewe quipped.

Just by moving to the more intimate Shubert Theatre in Boston, *Camelot* played better than it had in the barn in Toronto. Now Julie's "Where Are the Simple Joys of Maidenhood?" got the laughs it had been missing. But the show was still too long, running for three hours. And Guinevere needed a new song to replace a long first-act farewell scene between her and Lancelot, as he goes off on his quest. Loewe wrote the melody to "Before I Gaze at You Again," but Lerner did not produce the lyrics until the show was moving from Boston to New York. When he approached Julie and asked if she would incorporate the brand-new song at the first Broadway preview, she said, "Of course darling, but do try to get it to me the night before."

"There is no star in theater today, nor perhaps has there ever been one, who would have agreed to that outrageous request, but Julie Andrews," Lerner said. The author acknowledged that *"Camelot* might never have reached its final destination on 44th Street had it not been for Burton and Julie. Both accepted all cuts and changes, including a new second act, without complaint."

Andrews, Lerner said in 1978, met "any challenge with a smile and an unbatted eyelid...always gracious, always willing, an amazingly quick study both musically and dramatically. I cannot remember one moment in the almost seven years we worked together that was anything but joy. Nevertheless, I cannot say in all honesty that I knew her any better at the end of the seven years than I did at the beginning....I occasionally wondered whether Julie knew Julie any better than I did. Obviously she did and obviously she does. The years have revealed her to be very much her own person, aware of where her happiness lies and not easily affected by the heady wine of the fame she achieved. Somewhere along the line she decided it did not lie in the theatre, and the theatre is poorer for it."

By the time "Costalot," as it was now being called by Broadway wags, arrived in New York, many, though not all, of the problems were resolved. Julie was handed her new song the day before the first Broadway performance. By all accounts her premiere rendition of "Before I Gaze at You Again" was seamless.

When *Camelot* opened at the Majestic Theatre on December 3, 1960, a week later than originally announced, most critics agreed with Howard Taubman of *The New York Times*, who found the show only "partly enchanted." Of Lerner and Loewe, Taubman, wrote, "It would be unjust to tax them with not attaining the heights of *My Fair Lady*, but it cannot be denied that they miss their late collaborator, George Bernard Shaw." Of Guinevere he said, "In the slim, airy person of Julie Andrews, a lovely actress and a true singer, she is regal and girlish, cool and eager."

On the strength of advance bookings and the drawing power of its stars (Goulet was hailed as the most exciting male newcomer in years, and Burton replaced Rex Harrison as the king of talk-singing), *Camelot* eventually achieved a respectable two-year, 873-performance run. But in February 1961, sometimes two or three hundred people would walk out of a performance, creating negative word of mouth, and walk-up ticket sales became nonexistent.

Just as ticket sales began to sag, Julie, Burton, and Goulet appeared on a special *Ed Sullivan Show* tribute to Lerner and Loewe, to honor the fifth anniversary of *My Fair Lady*, on March 19, 1961. Andrews and Goulet sang a duet on "It's Almost Like Being in Love" from *Brigadoon*, and Julie sang "Where Are the Simple

Joys of Maidenhood?" She and Burton finished the broadcast with "Camelot" and "What Do the Simple Folk Do?" from their current Lerner and Loewe show. The *Camelot* box office bounced right back, with lines halfway around the block.

Three months into the New York run, Moss Hart reappeared after recuperating from his heart attack. He convinced Lerner to make more changes, and *Camelot* went back into rehearsal, perhaps the only Broadway musical that has ever done so on such a massive scale so long after opening. Soon Hart's "master hand was molding the show into its final shape," Doris Shapiro, Lerner's secretary at the time, wrote in her 1990 memoir *We Danced All Night*. "Box office receipts kept rising." Hart never fully recovered from his heart attack, however, and died in December 1961, at the age of 57.

The *Camelot* original cast album was released right after the show opened and enchanted millions who would never be exposed to the show's tortured dramaturgy, at least not until the inevitable revivals. The show's many truly lovely songs such as: "I Loved You Once in Silence," "If Ever I Would Leave You," "Follow Me," and "Before I Gaze At You Again," rendered it a better recording than a stage vehicle. The album was number one by late spring of 1961, and stayed at the top of the charts for sixty weeks. The movie rights were sold for one million dollars to Warner Brothers.

President John F. Kennedy's love of the show and its original cast recording made *Camelot* legendary after his death in late 1963. His entire presidency is still frequently called "Camelot."

For Julie, ensconced with Tony and a gray French poodle named Shy on a seventeenth-story East Side apartment overlooking Welfare (later renamed Roosevelt) Island, the whole experience had been "a very pleasant time. *Camelot* was just about my size and weight, a good level for me, and I enjoyed it so much more than *My Fair Lady*." Her eighteen-month run in her third hit musical in a row established Julie Andrews as *the* female musical comedy star of the period, at least the new Mary Martin, if not the new Ethel Merman. She found working with Richard Burton exciting, and he termed her one of his three favorite costars, the others being Peter O'Toole and Elizabeth Taylor.

Richard was one of Julie's few co-stars to see her flare up. "Don't muck about with her," he said. "You'll see nature red in eye and tongue. She has a temper, which I only experienced once. I hid in a cupboard whilst others headed for the distant hills."

He also found her "a natural actress who improves all the time. Her comedy timing is superb. She taught me to time laugh lines better. She treated me as if I were a fairly irresponsible younger brother who frequently needed admonishing. And admonished I was. I enjoyed being admonished."

Burton thought she was "very intelligent, but not, I think, intellectual." She should never play "Lady Macbeth, Hedda Gabler, or Anna Karenina." Her forte, rather, was "radiance, shafts of gold, bars of light, all that stuff." Her assets, according to Burton, included "charm, wit, very hard work, and mischief. She's as wicked as a street Arab. Every man I know who knows her is a little bit in love with her."

When the 1961 Tony Awards came around, *Camelot* was not even nominated for Best Musical against *Bye, Bye, Birdie* (the winner), *Do, Re, Mi* and *Irma La Douce*. However, Richard Burton did win the Tony Award for Best Actor in a Musical, Franz Allers won for Conductor and Musical Director (an award no longer given), Oliver Smith was deemed best scenic designer, and Tony Duquette and the late Adrian shared the Costume Design Award. Julie had been nominated as Best Actress in a Musical, but lost the award to Elizabeth Seal in *Irma La Douce*—as did Nancy Walker from *Do, Re, Mi*, and Carol Channing of *Show Girl*.

During the creation of *Camelot* Julie established an important new friendship with T. H. (Tim) White. He introduced her to the peacefulness of Alderney, where she bought a house named Patmos. In 1962, towards the end of her run in *Camelot*, White pronounced her "the most enchanting creature I have ever seen on stage." He started to write a parody of Cavalier poet Robert Herrick's "Upon Julia's Clothes," the first line of which read "As in silks my Julia goes." The second line of White's version was to have been an unflattering comment on Julie's nose, but he never finished the send-up.

White did, however, write a serious poem entitled simply "Julie Andrews," which appeared in a red leather-bound, privately printed volume of his verse. He gave her number twenty-two of one hundred copies. A companion poem, dedicated to Richard Burton, appeared on the page facing White's tribute to her:

JULIE ANDREWS

Helen, whose face was fatal, must have wept
Many long nights alone
And every night men died, she cried
And happy Paris kept sweet Helen

Julie, the thousand prows aimed at her heart,
The tragic queen, comedian and clown,
Keeps Troy together, not apart
Nor lets one tower fall down.

Occasionally the towers would crumble, of course.

5

Julie and Carol and
Mary Poppins

Julie Andrews and Carol Burnett met in late 1960 or early 1961, when Julie was performing in *Camelot* and Carol was starring in the musical *Once Upon a Mattress*. A mutual friend introduced them and took them out to a Chinese restaurant. The friend felt that the two women, then both in their mid-twenties, would get along well, and that Julie having a girl friend would help to fill the hole left in her life by having started working so young and been forced to grow up so fast. She agreed, despite her natural reluctance to meet anyone new after a performance.

"Those arrangements are usually the kiss of death," Julie recalled. "But our meeting was magical. I describe it as two kids who suddenly discover they live on the same block." Burnett, too, immediately felt the energy and synergy of their initial meeting. Their matchmaker never got a word in once the supper began. "We both started performing as kids," Julie explained to Glenn Plaskin of the *New York Daily News*. "We both came from alcoholic families, and we both had been caretakers, which is a tremendous burden for a kid. Being raised in a chaotic household, we were also both super-neat and super-square."

Julie made a guest appearance on Garry Moore's CBS television variety show on May 2, 1961. She was such a success that Moore signed her for three additional visits the following season. In the first program's finale number, Julie teamed up with Carol, who was a series regular, on "Big D," a song about two people from Dallas from Frank Loesser's 1956 Broadway hit *The Most Happy Fella.* The number, which had been arranged by Ernie Flatt in unforgettable fashion, inspired the new duet act to attempt a TV special of their own.

"Everybody was excited about it," Carol Burnett recalled, "except the networks. At the time, although I was a regular on the Garry Moore show, I wasn't yet under contract to CBS, and nobody had heard of Julie west of New Jersey. We went everywhere trying to sell the idea—to NBC, ABC, and XYZ, but nobody was interested." Mike Nichols, then half of the cabaret comedy team Nichols and May, had agreed to write the show, but even that potential contribution by Elaine May's partner moved no one to action.

In 1961–1962 only NBC offered regular network color broadcasts, and Carol used that fact to tweak the CBS top management into a commitment. At a CBS network luncheon at the Waldorf-Astoria Hotel in New York just after Christmas, Carol found herself the only woman at a table with James Aubrey, who was then president of CBS-TV, Mike Dann, east coast programming vice-president, and Oscar Katz, vice-president for network programs.

"I was putting the three of them on, and they didn't realize it for a long time," she remembered. "I kept saying 'It's a shame you boys passed up your chance at Julie and me, but then we do look so much better in color anyway.' They of course wanted to know what the hell I was talking about, and I told them that Julie and I were going to do a special. Aubrey asked why, and I said, 'Because Julie and I have these magical powers.' By then they had figured out that I might be putting them on."

After lunch, the three executives and Carol found that they had to walk the few blocks from the Waldorf-Astoria back to CBS. "Everyone was returning Christmas presents and you couldn't get a cab," Carol recalled. "When we got to the CBS building the men said, 'We'll wait and get you a cab.' I said, 'Oh, don't worry, with my

magical powers I'll probably get a ride.' At that instant a beer truck
appeared, and a big beefy driver with a tattoo yelled out, 'Hey, Carol,
you want a lift?' The men helped me into the cab of the beer truck,
and I rode off to Central Park West, waving to the three of them
standing there with their mouths open."

The telephone in Carol's apartment rang less than an hour later.
It was Katz, who said, "you're a witch—you've got your special."

"I called Julie at her dressing room at *Camelot*—it was a
Wednesday, a matinee day—and there we were," said Carol.

Between the deal and the taping (a new technology at the time),
Julie was doing her best to get better known west of New Jersey.
Having done an eclectic mix of TV shows, including a stint as the
mystery guest on *What's My Line?* and a colorcast on NBC (hosted
by Pulitzer Prize–winning poet and biographer Carl Sandburg)
during which she sang a medley of Sigmund Romberg tunes, she
appeared as the centerpiece of *The Broadway of Lerner and Loewe*.
The color telecast aired February 11, 1962 and featured her costars
from *Camelot*, Richard Burton and Robert Goulet, as well as
Stanley Holloway from *My Fair Lady* and Maurice Chevalier from
the movie *Gigi*. The four men joined Julie in a finale of "I Could
Have Danced All Night."

During this period, Julie also recorded two more Columbia
albums: *Broadway's Fair Julie*, a collection of show tunes with
Henri René and his orchestra, and *Don't Go Into the Lion's Cage
Tonight*, a dozen music hall novelty songs including "Burlington
Bertie from Bow."

Julie and Carol at Carnegie Hall was taped on March 5, 1962
from the stage of the fabled New York concert hall before an invited
live audience. The hour of songs and sketches was aired on the
evening of June 11, 1962. The opening number was Carol's solo,
setting the scene (There'll Be) "No Mozart Tonight (at Carnegie
Hall)." The duet "You're So London" chronicled the opposite
characteristics of the very American Burnett and the veddy British
Andrews ("You're so 'hi, there, how are ya'/I'm so 'how t'y'do'";
"You're so Kensington Gardens and I'm so San Antone"). The finale
was a reprise of "Big D."

"The Nausiev Ballet" was a Mike Nichols and Ken Welch satire of touring Russian dance troupes who appeared on the *Ed Sullivan Show*, the last bastion of American vaudeville. In the sketch, Julie proved the equal of Carol in physical clowning, which would not have surprised English audiences but was a first for her in the United States. Julie did just one solo, an exquisite rendition of "Johnny's So Long at the Fair."

She and Carol performed a devastating parody of *The Sound of Music*, which was then the biggest hit on Broadway, eclipsing both *Camelot* and the (approximately) seventh company of *My Fair Lady*. In "The Pratt Family of Switzerland," Julie played the Maria von Trapp prototype in her best Mary Martin manner and Carol played Cynthia, the only girl among seventeen Pratt boys. The Nichols-Welch songs were perfect parodies of the Rodgers and Hammerstein score that in three years Julie would have to sing straight.

The Carnegie Hall program was one of those rare exhibitions, in any medium, of topflight talent in top form. It showed a broader American audience Julie's versatility and was a total critical triumph for both stars. The show won an Emmy Award for producer-director Joe Hamilton who was also the producer-director for the *Garry Moore Show* and later married Carol. The show itself won the Rose d'Or from the Montreaux International Television Festival in 1963. "We were booed when we won," Carol remembered, "because everyone thought the show was filmed, and of course it was taped. We convinced the audience we had done it in a single performance, and they quieted down."

The success of the show gave Mike Nichols a big push in his desired transition from performer to writer-director. Both Carol and Mike became close friends of Julie and Tony. The material held up so well on the Columbia cast recording that *Julie and Carol at Carnegie Hall* became television's first and only classic original cast album.

Even in these early years of their marriage, Julie made considerably more money than Tony, although she maintained, "this has never made any difference. I get mine in chunks; he gets his regularly, and I expect he'll work far longer than I will." The two salaries were kept separate and, by mutual agreement, money was seldom discussed by the Waltons. "If Tony minds my being Julie Andrews he certainly doesn't let me know it," she said in 1961.

Tony was beginning to make a reputation as a set and costume designer in the theater with such shows as Sandy Wilson's *Valmouth* in London and the musical *Golden Boy* on Broadway. Her marriage, Julie said, "helped me stand on my own two feet." She became pregnant early in 1962, and soon motherhood would add a new dimension to her life without really interrupting the fast climb of her career.

Walt Disney went to see a Wednesday matinee of *Camelot* in the spring of 1962. He owned the rights to T. H. White's *The Sword in the Stone* and was turning it into an animated feature; he wanted to see what Lerner and Loewe had done to the rest of *The Once and Future King* tetralogy. Disney, who never worried about having stars in his movies because his own name as producer usually guaranteed success at the box office, was also looking for an actress to play Mary Poppins in a combination live-action/animated feature.

Like all Disney movies involving animation, *Mary Poppins* had been brewing for some time until all the elements were just right. Watching Julie in the theater—particularly during "What Do the Simple Folk Do?"—convinced Disney that he had found his Mary Poppins. Julie, he felt, had the right kind of sense of humor and he was impressed with her whistling ability in that sprightly number, whistling being very helpful to nannies. Disney sent word during intermission that he would like to see her, then visited Julie's dressing room after the show. He discussed the Poppins role briefly, and invited her and Tony to visit him at the Disney studios in Burbank, "when you've finished here."

"Since I had never made a movie the idea appealed to me greatly," she said. "I had thought a lot about movies, but never very seriously. I had fantasies that I'd make a movie someday, but I had no serious intentions of making them."

"Julie was always putting herself down about movies," Carol Burnett remembered, "never thinking she would look good enough. When the Poppins part came up she asked me, 'Do you think I ought to? Go to work for Walt Disney? The cartoon person?' I assured her that Disney did other things besides cartoons, but she was a little worried about it. But when she came out to Hollywood she became totally enthusiastic. I don't think she ever came out here to be the great big star of the world, but she was very excited about that one movie."

"I must say I will be forever grateful to that man," Julie said of Disney. "Tony and I flew out after *Camelot* to take a look and liked it enormously. It was so easy to see what he was trying to do with *Mary Poppins* and I loved that very slight flavor of vaudeville to it." While they visited, Disney also personally escorted the couple through Disneyland.

Tony was offered a job as overall design director so that the couple could be together with their new child, who was due to be born in November. They were entertained lavishly, at Disney's watchful insistence. But it was the Robert and Richard Sherman score that really convinced Julie. After hearing the songs, including "Chim Chim Cheree" and "Supercalifragilisticexpialidocious," she was sold. She signed a contract for a $150,000 salary for the film plus a living allowance, since she was technically a resident of London temporarily stationed in New York. Tony got a separate fee for his set and costume design work. Then the couple returned to London to have their first baby.

Emma Kate Walton was born on November 27, 1962 at the London Clinic. Julie had mothered her three younger brothers, particularly Chris, who was eleven years younger than she, and she attributed her notable whistling ability to those three boys. She had long wanted children of her own and she wanted more than one. "I'd like a family of three or five boys," she said, "weather and tide permitting, as we say in England. Tony wants girls. I just want a family of little Tonys." Carol Burnett was named Emma's godmother.

Pamela Travers, then fifty-nine years old, was the author of the

Mary Poppins books on which the Disney movie was to be based. Legally she had nothing to say about who played the leading role. Nevertheless, "she rang me up in the hospital the day after I had Emma," Julie recalled. "She said, 'P. Travers here. Speak to me. I want to hear your voice.'" I was still too weak from giving birth and I told her I wanted to recover first. When we finally got together the first thing she said was, 'Well, you've got the nose for it.' I adored her. She was so honest and direct. Tony and I had several lunches with her before we went to Hollywood to do the movie. Later I wrote her a long letter from the set and tried to give her a sort of idea of what we were doing."

The family of three, Tony, Julie, and Emma Kate, with a nanny and a maid, settled into a rented house in Studio City in the San Fernando Valley of Los Angeles in May 1963. They had six months of rest in Alderney behind them. It was pleasant for both new parents, working at the Disney Studios in nearby Burbank even though *My Fair Lady* was in pre-production, with a new Eliza, at Warner Brothers, less than a mile away.

"It may have been that celebrated ill wind," Julie said, years later. "I had *Mary Poppins* to soften the blow."

My Fair Lady was the one movie she had hoped for most, and not being familiar with the motion picture business, even in Britain, Julie didn't really understand the Hollywood star system that had worked against her. Warner Brothers had invested a record $5.5 million in acquiring the screen rights to the musical and Jack Warner, who was both head of the studio and the producer of *My Fair Lady*, had been convinced to sign Rex Harrison as Henry Higgins. Warner had wanted to use Cary Grant instead, as box office insurance. Grant himself told Warner, "If you don't hire Rex Harrison, I won't even go to see *My Fair Lady*." Harrison was not a potent box office name in America, or anywhere else in movies at that time. But he *was* Henry Higgins.

A string of fair ladies had followed Julie on Broadway and played Eliza rather well, so the feeling at Warner Brothers was that while it might have been difficult to "get" the role on stage, any number of stars who were also good actresses could probably get by on screen, especially under George Cukor's direction—even if the singing had to be dubbed by someone else. At the time, more than half the box office receipts from any Hollywood movie came from outside the United States. Musicals, particularly those with difficult lyrics, were a particularly hard sell in non-English-speaking countries. Warner needed a proven international star as Eliza, and so he hired one.

Julie had stayed in the running for the $17 million production (then a record budget for a movie) simply because she had been brilliant in the part for three and a half years. That just made it all the harder to take when Audrey Hepburn got the part—and a fee of $1 million. Hepburn was not even going to do all her own singing; that job would fall once again to Marni Nixon, the mimic ghost-singer of many movie musicals (without formal acknowledgement or screen credit, as usual). Nixon had sung for Deborah Kerr in *The King and I*, Rosalind Russell in *Gypsy*, and Natalie Wood in *West Side Story*, among others.

The morning she found out about Audrey Hepburn's being cast in the role, Julie was in her agent's office for a conference. He and his associates already knew about the announcement and assumed that Julie did. But she didn't, and asked how *My Fair Lady* was going.

"Haven't you heard?" someone said. "They've signed Audrey Hepburn."

"Oh…I see," was the quiet, composed reply, as Julie struggled to get hold of herself. After a pause, she said, "Well, that's that, isn't it?"

Later that same morning, Julie was riding by the Warner Brothers studios. Out of a protracted, deliberate silence came, in a crystalline, high-pitched voice, "And a good morning to you, Mr. Warner, and the best of luck."

Julie often said that if it had been anyone but Audrey Hepburn, an actress she didn't really know but did admire, she "would have been blazing mad. Of course I wanted to play it. Who wouldn't want to play Eliza? But in a way it's a good thing having to play a different role. People at least will know I can do something else." Some of her other comments at the time smacked of stiff-upper-lipping: "I would other comments at the time smacked of stiff-upper-lipping: "I would have taken the part if Mr. Warner had asked me even though I had had about enough of Eliza," or "I wasn't desperately upset over not getting the role; I didn't hold out much hope in the first place."

Logistically, it would have been possible for Julie to have played both Eliza and Mary Poppins because the principal photography involving Eliza didn't begin until Julie's part in *Mary Poppins* was completed. However she could not have played Eliza and done either *The Americanization of Emily* or *The Sound of Music*. "I was more than compensated by three marvelous roles," she said.

The freeze between Andrews and Warner Bros. would continue through tentative *Camelot* movie negotiations in 1966 and partly thaw only when Jack Warner sold his interest in the studio to Seven Arts in 1967 and became an independent producer. When the new, temporary Warner Brothers Seven Arts paid $3 million for the rights to the Broadway musical *Mame* (an amount at the time second only to the $5.5 million paid for *My Fair Lady*), they considered Julie for the title part—with no resistance from her, even though she was too young for the role.

As for Eliza in *My Fair Lady*, "It's only in later years," Julie said, "that I really wished I had put that role down definitively on film."

During the making of *Mary Poppins* she was surprised by the amount of interest shown in her by the other studios. Disney began showing rough cuts and rushes to other producers, a highly unusual practice. As a result of these informal previews, Julie was signed for both *The Americanization of Emily* and *The Sound of Music* long before *Mary Poppins* had been released.

In the original Mary Poppins book, published in 1934, Pamela ("Don't call me Miss or Mrs., just P. L.") Travers had described Mary as having "shiny black hair, like a wooden Dutch doll, with large hands and feet, pink cheeks, and round blue eyes. She is a plain twenty-seven-year-old who obviously has assumed all the prerogatives of a pretty woman, because everybody falls in love with her." Except for the black hair, Julie proved to be close casting; she was even twenty-seven when she began shooting the movie. Julie said that her characterization of the acid-tongued no-nonsense nanny

"Pop," Julie's tenor stepfather, teaches her lip and tongue control.
1946 PICTORIAL PARADE

At age twelve, with "Mum" and "Pop" after her professional debut in
Starlight Roof, October 1947 RANDALL CARLSEN LTD.

Singing the "Polonaise" from *Mignon* for King George VI, Queen Elizabeth (later the Queen Mother), Princess Elizabeth (later Queen Elizabeth II) and Princess Margaret at a Royal Command Performance, 1948.
THE PRESS ASSOCIATION LTD.

Her ill-fated screen test at MGM, London, aged twelve

As Polly Browne, with the "Perfect Young Ladies" in her Broadway
debut, *The Boy Friend*, 1954 FRIEDMAN-ABELES

As "Poor Little Pierrette,"
The Boy Friend, 1954
THE NEW YORK TIMES

As Eliza Doolittle asking Professor Henry Higgins to give her elocution lessons in *My Fair Lady*, 1956 FRIEDMAN-ABELES

A triumphant dance with Rex Harrison and Robert Coote (Colonel
Pickering) during "The Rain in Spain" number in *My Fair Lady,* 1956
FRIEDMAN-ABELES

With Bing Crosby in the first-ever movie made for television, *High Tor*, 1956 CULVER PICTURES LTD.

Wearing the fancy and full "p.r." dress for Rodgers and Hammerstein's *Cinderella*, a live color telecast, 1957. Costume designers William and Jean Eckhart had to create a simpler, narrower ball gown for the cramped vertical TV studio. CBS TELEVISION

Richard Burton as King Arthur and Julie as Queen Guinevere in *Camelot*,
1961 FRIEDMAN-ABELES

Julie with her husband, set designer Tony Walton, and their newborn daughter, Emma Kate, 1962
UNITED PRESS INTERNATIONAL

Julie with Carol Burnett during rehearsals for the first of their three specials together, *Julie and Carol at Carnegie Hall,* 1962
CBS TELEVISION

was "a little softer, a little rounder" than in the Travers books.

Disney made some other changes as well: The setting was taken from the 1930s back to Edwardian-era London because the latter was more photogenic and sidestepped the problems of the 1930s Depression. The Banks family house where the nanny worked became a sumptuous, velvet-lined Edwardian mansion instead of the "rather dilapidated" house needing a coat of paint called for in the original. The mansion was created on one sound stage while the whole exterior of Cherry Tree Lane was built on another sound stage. But the friendship between Mary Poppins and Bert, the chimney sweep, enacted by Dick Van Dyke, remained platonic, to the great relief of P. L. Travers.

The number of children in the household was reduced from four to two (played by Matthew Garber and Karen Dotrice) while their parents (Glynis Johns and David Tomlinson) were turned into a neglectful suffragette and businessmen, respectively. The writers took these dramatic liberties, they said, to introduce a bit of "harmless" conflict, and to allow Mary to arrive, wind-borne by an umbrella, to save her charges from this supposed parental neglect. As in the book, however, nearly everyone floated in the air at some time or other (most memorably during Ed Wynn's tea party on the ceiling), and Mary Poppins could levitate at will.

"At first I missed the live audience reaction," said Julie of her first movie experience. "But as I grew accustomed to the medium, I found myself enjoying moviemaking more and more. One thing that appealed to me particularly was the permanence. If your performance was good, it was preserved for posterity. Another wonderful thing about movies is that you don't have to be in perfect voice every night."

Although Tony was the designer on *Mary Poppins*, he and Julie rarely saw each other during working hours. Most of his work was, of course, done before the actual shooting began. Since they were brand new parents, both working in movies for the first time, the situation put an obvious strain on the marriage. Though they seldom talked about it, they both understood the underlying fact that Tony would never have been hired as scenic designer for the he had established himself on Broadway by designing the hit *A Funny Thing Happened on the Way to the Forum.*

During filming Julie took great delight in shrieking the highest note she could reach, like a factory whistle, into the microphone hanging over her head. All of her coworkers were amused bar one: the sound technician with his earphones on. "Usually, he'd have to go away for almost half an hour to recover," she said.

It didn't take the shrewd businessmen at Disney Studios even that long to realize what they had on their hands with *Mary Poppins.* In the summer of 1964, while preparing for a late-September release, they set an exploitation budget that was "more than for any other picture" released by the company. They signed contracts for thirty-eight separate Mary Poppins products, including girls' dresses, dolls, houseware, jewelry, a King Features Syndicate cartoon series, and four million books reprinted by various publishers.

The movie opened at Radio City Music Hall in New York, then around the United States, to almost unanimously glowing reviews. A few critics took issue with the interpretation of the Poppins stories, but Bosley Crowther of *The New York Times* was not among them. Instead he wrote:

> In case you are a Mary Poppins zealot who dotes on her just as she is, don't let the intrusion of Mr. Disney and his myrmidons worry you one bit. Be thankful for it and praise heaven that they are still making films. For the visual and aural felicities they have added to this sparkling color film—the enchantments of beautiful production, some deliciously animated sequences, some exciting and nimble dancing, and a spinning musical score—make it the nicest entertainment that has opened at the Music Hall this year....
>
> This is the genuine Mary Poppins that comes sailing in on an east wind...played superbly by Miss Andrews, with her button-shoed feet splayed out to give her an unshakable footing and a look of complete authority, who calmly proceeds to show her changes that wonders will never cease and that there's nothing like a spoonful of sugar to

cease and that there's nothing like a spoonful of sugar to sweeten the medicine.

My Fair Lady opened in mid-October of 1964, just a month after *Mary Poppins,* and to even more lavish praise. Audrey Hepburn's acting and Marni Nixon's singing got good notices, perhaps not so much because they were good as that they weren't as bad as the Andrews partisans had feared they might be. Julie went to see *My Fair Lady* and pronounced it "a wonderful film. It was the first time I had ever seen it from the front. Now I know why people are so crazy about it." Of the dubbed singing, she said neutrally, "I think dubbing is fine as long as you can get away with it."

Audrey Hepburn returned the compliment by slipping into Radio City Music Hall unnoticed, with her then husband Mel Ferrer, while *Mary Poppins* was playing. "We were in such a hurry that we could only stay an hour," Hepburn recounted, "but Julie was simply wonderful, and Mel thought so, too."

So much for the feud between Julie and Audrey that many members of the press, particularly in Europe, had tried to stir up. But Hollywood was still going to have its revenge on Jack Warner, and, indirectly, on Audrey Hepburn. When the Academy Award nominations for 1964 were announced in February of 1965, *My Fair Lady* was nominated in every major category *except* Best Actress, while Julie Andrews was nominated for Best Actress in *Mary Poppins.* With Audrey Hepburn not in the running, Julie was the heavy favorite to win from the moment nominations were out.

Tony Walton was nominated for Best Costume Design for *Mary Poppins,* which was nominated for Best Picture, along with *Dr. Strangelove, Becket, Zorba the Greek,* and *My Fair Lady.*

At the Hollywood Foreign Press Association Golden Globe Awards, which were held between the Oscar nominations and the Awards themselves, Julie won the award for Best Actress in a Musical or Comedy. She thanked, among others, "Jack Warner, for making it all possible." Warner, who received the Golden Globe Best Musical Award for *My Fair Lady* "was sitting right in front of me—it was grand fun," Julie said. Her press agents swore that the whole idea of the acceptance speech had been hers, and she never denied it. When Warner accepted his award he returned the jest by referring to Julie as "what's-her-name."

The high preponderance of overseas, particularly British, nominees prompted Master of Ceremonies Bob Hope to quip, on Academy Awards night (April 5, 1965): "Tonight Hollywood is handing out foreign aid." And for the next three hours the movie industry did just that.

Tony Walton lost to a fellow Briton, Cecil Beaton, who had designed the costumes for both stage and screen versions of *My Fair Lady*. "Oh, no, Tony," Julie said softly to her husband when Beaton's name was announced. Tony applauded dutifully.

"Chim Chim Cheree" from *Mary Poppins* won the Oscar for Best Song for the Sherman brothers, but otherwise it was mostly *My Fair Lady's* night. George Cukor won his first Oscar for directing and Audrey Hepburn (a previous winner for *Roman Holiday* in 1953) presented the Best Actor Oscar to Rex Harrison. A beaming Harrison bounded onto the stage to be hugged and kissed by his not nominated but clearly delighted costar. "I have to thank two fair ladies, I think," said Harrison. "Oh, yes," said Hepburn.

Warner's acceptance of the Best Picture Oscar for *My Fair Lady* proved to be an anti-climax. His speech made no reference to his cast and was delivered in the self-confident tones of a successful businessman being congratulated on a worthwhile $17-million investment. He paid tribute to "the many people who contributed to *My Fair Lady*," without naming names.

The highlight of the evening was the virtual crowning of a new queen of movieland. When Harrison's name had been announced the ABC-TV cameras caught Julie in close-up, licking a very dry, very stiff upper lip. When her own name was announced as Best Actress in her first motion picture, she was suddenly all smiles: the earlier nervousness was gone. En route to posing for pictures with Harrison holding their gold Oscar statuettes (as they surely would have done had she played Eliza again), Julie thanked her audience for the warmest possible welcome to Hollywood: "You Americans are famous for your hospitality," she said, "but this is ridiculous."

6

The Americanization of Julie and The Sound of Money

Julie went straight from filming *Mary Poppins* to *The Americanization of Emily*. She was cast, seemingly against type, as a young English World War II widow who works as a motor pool driver for American Navy officers in England during the day, and who sometimes, out of kindness, sleeps with them at night—especially if she thinks they are doomed to be killed in battle, as her father, brother, and husband all were. Paddy Chayefsky had written the screenplay from a novel by William Bradford Huie and embellished the script with an antiwar message. Among other distinctions, *The Americanization of Emily* was the first antiwar film of the Vietnam era.

It was important to director Arthur Hiller and producer Martin Ransohoff to make this movie in black and white at a time when every kind of movie, even the cheapest B-movie cops-and-robbers story, was being filmed in color, with an eye toward international and television sales. Hiller and Ransohoff wanted to underscore the message of the movie, which also had many comically satirical moments, and better incorporate the crucial black and white newsreel footage of the D-Day invasion. *The Americanization of*

Emily turned out to be the only movie that Julie Andrews made that was not in color.

At age twenty-eight and never having had an acting lesson in her life, Julie admitted that she was "scared to death" at the prospect of making such a serious movie. "I was at a loss without songs," she said. "At least in *Mary Poppins* I would always take comfort in the knowledge that I would be doing a song and would feel secure eventually. But in *Emily* there were no songs to hang on to." Yet that was precisely why she had chosen the straight dramatic role, "because it proposed another huge challenge: I'd *have* to act. It would also give me the chance to prove to myself and the public that I could do something besides musical comedy."

Ransohoff, chairman of the board of Filmways and the most independent of independent producers, had made a fortune on several hit television series (*The Beverly Hillbillies, Green Acres*) and made money on his first six motion pictures. He rented his offices at, and released most of his movies through, Metro Goldwyn Mayer. His associate producer, John Calley, called Ransohoff, who had previously been a small-time businessman in Connecticut, "an L. B. Mayer without overhead." (Calley went on to become executive vice president for production at Warner Brothers, an independent producer and, in 1996, president and chief operating officer of Sony Pictures Corp. which had taken over MGM's old lot.)

"He speaks for himself," Julie said of Ransohoff, "he stands or falls by himself. He didn't depend on anybody to achieve his success. And if you don't like it, he couldn't care less." Ransohoff took chances with some of his movies—*The Loved One* and *Catch-22* among them—"and he certainly took a chance on me. A lot of people told Marty he was out of his mind to pick me. When my agent suggested I read the script I got very excited about it, but I didn't think I had much chance to get the part."

Ironically, one of those who thought she was wrong for the role was Blake Edwards, a writer-director she had met only once, casually, at that point. When the film's first director, William Wyler, walked out in a disagreement over the movie's concept, and before Hiller replaced him, Edwards was asked his opinion on the casting.

About Julie Andrews for Emily, he said, "No, I don't think she's right." Years later he said, "And she wasn't right, in terms of the screenplay. I would have bet you against her doing it well, which is interesting now. But she brought something to it that changed Emily without changing the screenplay, and it worked."

Ransohoff had seen forty minutes of rough-cut footage of *Mary Poppins*. "After three minutes of the stuff I knew Julie was our girl," he said. "I just took that one look and knew she was right for Emily. She did not generate obvious, overt sexuality. She is not a sex symbol, but she has a classic sensuousness. She also had a certain refinement—another classic quality—rather than an overabundance of physical equipment, which gave her a great deal of sex appeal, slightly more refined and highbred than most."

James Garner, the nominal star of the picture by virtue of his previous success with Ransohoff's *Wheeler Dealers*, had costar approval written into his contract and could have vetoed the movie novice. He didn't, though, because he had been playing in *The Caine Mutiny Court Martial* on Broadway at the same time as Julie was appearing, just up the street, in *My Fair Lady*. "I didn't know her, but I had seen her in it," Garner said, "and that was good enough for me." Besides, "She has one of the greatest figures in the business, and I fancy myself something of an expert," Garner added.

Garner himself was another gamble for Ransohoff. A successful television star who had played mostly comedic roles in movies, Garner was not an obvious choice for such a dramatic film. In *Emily* he played Lieutenant Commander Charlie Madison, ostensibly an aide to a Navy real-admiral (played by Melvyn Douglas), but actually a "dog robber," a procurer of everything from perfume to the people who wear it. Madison is also an advocate of open cowardice, a doctrine of self-preservation that was counter to the prevailing wartime philosophy, especially in England: "As long as valor remains a virtue, we shall always have soldiers," he said. Charlie was a difficult, atypical suitor for Emily, but they became equally nervous about his ending up in the first wave on the beach at Normandy on D-Day. As Charlie, James Garner gave the best performance of his career.

In a scene set in Madison's hotel room (which looked more like
a black-market clearing house), Chayefsky's script satirized both
the British and the Americans, a sequence that Andrews and
Garner handled particularly well. Emily makes caustic comments
about the avariciousness and rule-bending of the Americans and
Madison takes down the English for their anti-American ingrati-
tude, unconcealed jealousy, and self-imposed, stiff-upper-lip martyr-
dom. At the same time the two characters begin to fall in love.

During shooting Julie still worried about "the absence of an
audience. The audience gives you a push; it makes you realize
you've got to do it right—there will be no second time. Still, I love
the feeling in movies of doing something fresh every day, instead of
the same thing. I find movie work much more exhausting than I had
expected. I suppose my own nervous tension has a good deal to do
with it. And the only way I can ease the tension is to sing, hum, or
whistle. I wonder sometimes what will happen when I do something in the theater again. Will I feel nervous in front of an
audience?"

Julie's tension-breaking singing and whistling (sometimes just a
high note held as long as possible) were done right on the set, in full
hearing of cast and crew. One day as a camera was being reloaded
Julie broke into a faultless chorus of "Melancholy Baby." Garner
and Hiller were delighted to suspend work in favor of a free Julie
Andrews concert, but she was totally oblivious to their watching
her, nor was she even aware of her own singing.

Julie did remember being unhappy about one scene that was
already "in the can": "Marty and I were watching the rushes
together, and I was not happy about it at all. We had them set up the
scene again the next day so I could do it all over again. I'm not at all
sure that it was any better the second time, but it was my whim and
he indulged it."

"Arthur Hiller and I thought the scene had worked well,"
Ransohoff recalled, "but Julie thought it could be done another way.
So I gave her and the crew a day to restage and reshoot the scene
her way. When we saw the rough cut of the whole movie a few

weeks later, her scene wasn't in it. I had used the original scene. She burst out laughing. She just couldn't understand why I would redo the scene and spend all that money if I was so sure I was right. I told her that it was just the values in the original were the ones we wanted. Instead of having a big ego attitude, she just laughed. She completely respected my position, but the shock of realizing 'Oh, my God, we've thrown a whole day away' sent her into hysterics."

James Garner, who waited eighteen years to work with Julie again in *Victor/Victoria*, recalled, "We did the first love scene she'd ever done in a movie, and her first real love scene anywhere. She knows only one way to do something—and that's right. In reality she's not like what she's like on screen—certainly not in *Mary Poppins*—but nobody does it better than Julie can. Julie's a little bit more natural at anything than anybody else."

Garner figured that he and Andrews had "kissed over five hundred times, counting rehearsals," during the making of *The Americanization of Emily*. "What a pleasure; she's a great kisser." Not only did she return the compliment: "he was a consummate, divine kisser," but she also confessed to her knees buckling when she got up after one particularly intense kissing scene involving the two of them rolling around on a bed.

"Nobody knows the depths of her talent or personality," Garner said. "She's so fresh she opens her mouth and the whole world blooms. The things about Julie on screen and off camera that made people like her are warmth, levity, and sincerity. That's what makes her the star she is. Throughout the history of films, people have succeeded because of their marvelous human qualities. These people had something on the screen that made people want to see them and come to them. She has that.

"You can't be much of a screen personality without being a pretty damn good actor. Julie is a person that the camera does not affect. She does what she does without being affected by all those lights and forty people around her. Some stars can only do it with all that; some can't do it with any of that. She is a personality who became a superstar. An actor working with a young superstar like

Julie might worry about being acted into the draperies. I wouldn't compete with Julie on those terms for two reasons: I might lose, and I wouldn't care.

"I admire Julie in the way I admire Audrey Hepburn. It would be unthinkable, people would hate themselves for being jealous of, or mean to, either Julie or Audrey. They give you no reason to. And yet Julie is a very strong-willed girl. But she manages her life so you are never offended by her strong will." Garner found Andrews and Hepburn (with whom he starred in *The Children's Hour*) "similar in their attraction. They are both professional, warm and friendly, hard-to-know and complex. It is not a facade. They don't give to anybody past a certain line, but they give to everybody up to that line. They don't give people problems and make them feel bad. If something is bothering them they don't show it to everybody else."

Arthur Hiller, who was directing only his fourth feature film, said of Julie, "She's utter perfection. She's got great compassion—on the screen and off." (Hiller went on to a distinguished career, directing movies such as *Love Story*. In 1997 he was president of the Academy of Motion Picture Arts and Sciences.)

Even before *Emily* was released, Marty Ransohoff was convinced that Julie Andrews would be the next movie superstar. "She's the most exciting thing I've seen in ten years," he said in 1966. "There's an open honesty in her face that's like magic—it lights up the screen." He also found her easy to work with, "a dream. She is cooperative and has ideas, and is anxious to help. All conversations with her are on an intellectual level. She brings quality to a project. She's infectious around the set, with a sense of humor that has a great effect on other performers and a great positiveness both behind the scenes and in front of the camera. A film can be damaged by a growler, but Julie lifts up a production. She is totally lacking in the kind of ego that says she knows it all and is always right."

The Americanization of Emily opened in the winter of 1964–1965, right between *Mary Poppins* and *The Sound of Music*. It was overshadowed by both and the reviews were decidedly mixed. Some critics were confused by the intent of the screenplay, the apparent seriousness of the antiwar theme coupled with what they considered a sell-out ending. A few saw Julie's performance as bland and stereotyped, but most critics agreed that, thanks to her comedic and dramatic abilities, she could have a career in movies, even without singing.

"It wasn't that I was so good," Julie said, "it was just such a surprise to see me in it. I don't think of myself as any great shakes as an actress. That's why I consider myself lucky when an *Emily* comes along. I'd love to do more serious roles like that. But films like *Emily* aren't available too readily. The script was so good; it had something to say."

"I wasn't trying to say a damned thing in *The Sound of Music*," director Robert Wise acknowledged. "That's as good a face as I can put on it. People just feel good when they see it; there's a sense of warmth, of well-being, of happiness and joy."

Julie did not greet the prospect of playing Maria in *The Sound of Music* with either great happiness or joy, although her competitive spirit was at work in the effort. At a luncheon Darryl Zanuck and several other Twentieth Century-Fox executives held to discuss the part, Wise pointedly announced that the film versions of *The Sound of Music* and *My Fair Lady* would be showing in New York at the same time on opposite sides of Broadway and then sat back and awaited the reaction. "Julie looked at each of us in turn without speaking," he recalled. "Then she threw back her head and laughed. 'All right then. Let's show them, eh, fellows?' That was the new Julie Andrews talking."

"We were always putting *The Sound of Music* down," said Carol Burnett, "and Julie always made fun of that happy nun. I'm not sure Richard Rodgers was awfully pleased when she was offered the movie. And I think he was concerned about her being Gwendolyn Goodie Two-Shoes. She sent me pictures from Austria of her in her nun's habit, which was a big laugh."

"I thought it might be awfully saccharine," Julie said. "After all, what can you do with nuns, seven children, and Austria? But Bob Wise and Saul Chaplin decided to get rid of the sugar—no filigree, no carved wood, no Swiss chalets, and they stuck to their guns. We all felt the same way. It helped that it was a motion picture because they could do such sweeping things visually."

Wise, who had already won one Academy Award for directing *West Side Story*, had accepted his new assignment only reluctantly, when the original director, William Wyler, quit, but this time in a cloud of indifference. "I didn't jump at it at all," Wise recalled. "The play was very, very saccharine, and obviously we haven't eliminated that for all people. But we tried to tone it down. We didn't go in for too-cute costumes or turreted castles and we were careful not to overdo colors." Wise finally signed on when Fox agreed to hire Saul Chaplin as associate producer and musical director.

Screenwriter Ernest Lehman, who also had written *West Side Story* and *The King and I*, recalled "a sugary curse" on *The Sound of Music*, which was still running on Broadway. "I saw Burt Lancaster, who was doing *The Leopard*, in the cafeteria one day, and he just looked at me and said, 'Jesus, you must need the money.'"

Even the studio, nearly bankrupt from the $31 million debacle that was *Cleopatra*, starring Elizabeth Taylor, Richard Burton, and Rex Harrison, was hesitant. Of the $8.2 million budget for *The Sound of Music*, $1.25 million had been paid for the rights to the musical which, as Fox production chief Richard Zanuck pointed out, "was not the most distinguished show Rodgers and Hammerstein had ever done." Having an unknown cast would make it even more of a gamble, Zanuck recalled.

In retrospect both Lehman and Zanuck took credit for hiring Julie Andrews and for having the good sense not to cast the more obvious movie musical names, Doris Day or Debbie Reynolds, as Maria von Trapp. (Broadway's original Maria, Mary Martin, was then fifty years old and not considered for the movie.) But it was up to Wise to cast the principals, and he picked Julie after seeing two reels of *Mary Poppins* footage. He also insisted on Christopher Plummer, a distinguished Canadian actor not known for musicals and hardly a major movie marquee name, for the role of Captain Georg von Trapp. "I wanted the character to have bite, incisiveness, and real dimension," he said. "I felt we must go on the basis of the story, and not bastardize it with just big names."

Julie was paid a relatively modest $225,000, an unfortunate flat fee, with no participation in the movie's profits. Plummer and the other actors (who included Peggy Wood as the mother superior, Eleanor Parker as the baroness whom von Trapp does not marry, and Richard Haydn as the impresario who helps the family escape to Switzerland) were paid accordingly. Marni Nixon, the busiest ghost singer in movies, was on hand, and on camera for a change. She played one of the nuns and did her own singing on "How Do You Solve a Problem Like Maria?" and dubbed for Peggy Wood and some other nuns.

Filming started in the spring of 1964, and half of the twenty-two-week shooting schedule was spent on location in Salzburg, Austria. Julie, despite her earlier reservations had a "larky time." Wise remembered that she "always enjoyed a good laugh with the kids. She had marvelous fun in her, and in addition to humor, she had warmth and understanding."

The first sequence filmed was of Julie and the seven von Trapp children bundled up in Maria's bed during a bad thunderstorm, with her singing "My Favorite Things." "I was having trouble getting the proper reactions from two of the kids," Wise said. "All of a sudden I heard this shrill laugh in back of me. It was Julie, putting on an act to make the kids laugh. She did it without announcing it to me or anyone else, but she put the kids at ease and made them easier to work with."

In her own attempt to de-sweeten *The Sound of Music* Julie focused on the "My Favorite Things" sequence. "Maria couldn't be sweetness and light with seven kids on her hands all the time. Seven kids would have to get on one's nerves, so I tried once in a while to show that I might be slightly exhausted by them. On the bed, when they ask me to do this or that and say 'What kind of things do you mean?'—just before I go into 'My Favorite Things'—I thought, 'Oh my God! Children always do ask questions like that.' Maria must have had moments when she bordered on being tired and cross."

The movie gave Julie a chance to cut her hair very short,

"something I'd always wanted to do, though having to bleach it blond was a bit of a shocker, especially my first sight of it."

She also experimented with variations on vaudeville bits from her girlhood, such as catching her guitar case crosswise in the door of the bus Maria takes from the abbey to the von Trapp home. Wise disallowed that Buster Keatonism in what was supposed to be a solemn moment, but allowed another: when Maria turns away from the mother superior, who has just told her she must be a governess instead of a nun, the gangly novitiate sees a post just in time to sidestep it, thereby giving the character a tiny added dimension of confusion.

"She must have eight thousand bits," said one crew member. Many of them took place off camera. One day, to clear tension before a complicated camera move, she did a deliberate trip and fell flat on her face. She was versatile enough, on another occasion, to pratfall on her back. To portray Maria, Julie learned to play a little bit of guitar. One day she flung her instrument aside to fly into an impromptu flamenco dance—still wearning her postulant's habit and high-button shoes.

Scheduled to drive to Munich one weekend to see her friend Svetlana Beriosova dance with the Royal Ballet company on tour, Julie instead hired a bus and took thirty members of the cast and crew. Throughout the sixty-mile trip from Salzburg to Munich, she imitated an English sightseeing coach conductor, sometimes lapsing into bits of Cockney. On the return trip to Salzburg, Julie led group singing and soloed on some Cockney songs.

"It rained nearly every day we were in Austria," Julie recalled, "and did terrible things to our nerves." (It also made the picture run one million dollars over budget.) The rain was at its worst during the filming of the unforgettable opening sequence of *The Sound of Music,* during which the helicopter containing the camera swooped down over the Alps to catch Maria dancing bareheaded in forbidden fields while she sings the title song. There were several days when Julie and the crew would have to wait out the rain before she could go tripping over the mountains again.

On these occasions Julie, Saul Chaplin, and cochoreographer

Marc Breaux, would sing songs on the rainy hillside for hours. She considered the trio's harmonies so good, particularly on the "Hawaiian War Chant," that she named the group the Vocalzones. She also sang solos, such as "Air des Clochettes" ("The Bell Song") from Delibes's *Lakme,* in pure operatic style, exquisitely on every note but with the mannerisms and facial expressions of a twelve-year-old child surprised at the power of her own voice. And she sang the "Indian Love Call" slightly off-key.

"These things were all spontaneous, and they related to the situation at the moment," Julie said. "If the situation is getting depressing, or people are getting pesky or touchy, a little fun always helps. I'll do anything I can think of to relieve any kind of tension."

Dorothy Jeakins, the costume designer on the picture and later on *Hawaii,* led the cheering section of Julie's admirers. "She's extremely pure, extremely human," said Jeakins. "Julie has great zeal and spirit. She's ethereal, yet down-to-earth. Everything she does is fresh and impromptu—and gone—like a whistle or a laugh."

When a member of the company was hospitalized, Julie was the first to visit. She went alone, and stayed for an hour. When daughter Emma's nanny had a birthday during filming, Julie gave her a party. She gave the children in the cast a party, too.

Some people on the set of *The Sound of Music* found Julie's chumminess compulsive ("I've never worked with anyone who said 'thank you' so much," said one veteran grip), and others just plain didn't believe it. "She may be a nun," said one crew member, "but she's a nun with a switchblade."

Christopher Plummer called her "terribly nice, but terribly nervous," and told his then wife, Tammy Grimes, that working with Julie was "like being hit over the head every day with a Hallmark card."

Plummer was having problems on the picture, primarily because he had expected to do his own singing on "The Sound of Music" and "Edelweiss," each of which he was to sing twice. But when he heard that he would be dubbed, Plummer said that he would feel castrated, Lehman recalled, and walked off the movie. Leslie Bricusse, the lyricist and a friend of Plummer's, was asked to try to talk him into returning. Plummer did come back and sang for himself during filming, but later his songs were dubbed in by Bill Lee, a singer of comercials for, among other things, chewing gum. Plummer, according to Bricusse, "was so fed up he began calling it *The Sound of Mucus.*"

Richard Rodgers had written both the words and music for two new songs in the movie version of *The Sound of Music* since four of the stage version's songs had been dropped. Both new songs, "I Have Confidence" and "Something Good," were for Julie, and she liked them both. Her singing of each, the former with sunny bravado, the latter with quiet gratitude, summarized both her approach and appropriateness to the venture. Maria on screen was yet another part that Julie Andrews seemed born to play.

"Julie knew how a character should be played," said Wise, "and she would fight to have it played right. We thrashed it out; she gave some and I gave some." Wise was frankly surprised by "the range of her talent, the depth of it, especially in emotional scenes" and called her "the most unaffected player I'd ever worked with. She was so down to earth, pleasant and natural, it was hard to believe she was really Julie Andrews. She had an open, warm response to work, but then she was used to working, to getting on with the job."

Her success in *The Sound of Music,* which for the next several years was the most successful movie ever made while she became the world's biggest star, was attributable, Wise thought, to a "genuiness about her, an unphoniness. What you see on the screen is an extension of Julie herself. She goes right through the camera onto film and out to the audience. Julie seems to have been born with that magic gene that comes through on screen; this magic gene, whatever it is coming through, commands you to react abnormally to her."

Tony Walton, who had moved back to New York after *Mary Poppins* despite another film offer from Julie's agent, escorted her to the New York premiere of *The Sound of Music* at the Rivoli Theater, in March 1965. The premiere, for which Julie had flown in from California with Emma Kate and her nanny, was a star-studded klieg-lighted event in the old Hollywood style, full of the highest expectations. Those attending included Helen Hayes, Beatrice Lillie, Adlai Stevenson, Salvador Dali, Samuel Goldwyn, and, of course, Richard Rodgers. Bette Davis called Julie "one of the loveliest things I've ever seen." And Mrs. Oscar Hammerstein spoke for the majority about the movie: "I'll have to drag out all those old superlatives about Hollywood. It's as close to perfection as any movie musical I've ever seen. The beauty of it is that you really see Austria—the streams, the valleys, and mountains are the real thing. I know Oscar would have loved it."

Thus no one at the opening was prepared for what happened the next day, least of all Robert Wise and Darryl Zanuck: Every major national film critic in America hated *The Sound of Music.* Typical of the reaction was that of the *New York Herald-Tribune* reviewer Judith Crist, who wrote: "One star and much scenery do not a two-hour-and-fifty-minutes-plus-intermission entertainment make, and the issue must be faced—squarely. That is the way to face *The Sound of Music.* This last, most remunerative and lease inspired, let alone sophisticated, of the Rodgers and Hammerstein collaborations is square and solid sugar. Calorie-counters, diabetics, and grown-ups from eight to eighty best beware."

In fact, nobody liked *The Sound of Music* except the public. The critics had never been so powerless to influence opinion concerning a movie. Advance ticket sales at the Rivoli, already substantial in anticipation of Easter, seemed to increase in geometric proportion to the negative notices. And this pattern was repeated throughout the world, where the picture showed at an astonishing 3,200 theaters, almost one-tenth of the then international total of 35,000. The movie broke box office records in twenty-nine countries, including Great Britain, where it doubled the gross receipts of any previous film shown in that country, and in Thailand, where is was called *Charms of the Heaven-Sound.* (At the Bangkok premiere, King Bhumibol, whose ancestor had been the subject of another Rodgers and Hammerstein musical, *The King and I,* played "Do, Re, Mi" on his clarinet.)

Mulitple visits to the film by individual fans helped boost the box-office total of the picture, and it soon surpassed *Gone With the*

Wind as the most popular movie of all time. Many people saw *The Sound of Music* one hundred times or more, but the clear champion viewer was the woman in Wales who went at least once a day for more than a year. The soundtrack became the bestselling album of all time, even beating out the original Broadway cast of *My Fair Lady*. The record had sold fifteen million units by the time the movie played on network television in 1976; half a million more were sold in the weeks immediately following the broadcast.

It was hard to explain the phenomenal success of *The Sound of Music*, even for those involved. "Who knows?" asked the director, to whom most of the credit was given. Wise won almost every award it is possible to win as a producer or director, including the Director's Guild of America Best Director Award for 1966 and two Oscars, one as director and one as producer.

The Academy Awards were highly responsive to the box office record of *The Sound of Music*, which had been in release for more than a year by the time the Oscar nominees were announced in 1966. The movie received ten nominations (one less than the eleven for *Doctor Zhivago*, another box office smash, but one that had achieved some praise from critics). Julie's nomination for Best Actress gave her a chance to become the first actress to win back-to-back Oscars since Luise Rainer had done it in 1936 and 1937 for *The Great Ziegfeld* and *The Good Earth.*

Julie attended the Oscar ceremonies, with Saul Chaplin, in a triple role: as presenter of the Best Actor Award (to Lee Marvin for *Cat Ballou*), as a nominee, and as the substitute acceptor for Robert Wise who was on location with *The Sand Pebbles* in Hong Kong. Her chief competition was another English Julie—Julie Christie—for her work in *Darling*. Both Julies were highly conspicuous that night: Christie wore a pair of gold lamé self-designed pajamas that made her *look* like an Oscar, as the ceremony's costume coordinator Edith Head noted the next day, and Andrews stood out in a Dorothy Jeakins-designed red-orange lightweight wool dress with a discotheque back and a deep-V wrapped front.

In her ninth-row aisle seat at the ceremonies, Julie Andrews kept wringing her hands together as Chaplin smiled and tried to soothe her nerves. When the editing award went to William Reynolds for *The Sound of Music*, Julie shouted, "Oh boy," and clapped so wildly that she knocked her white mink coat to the floor. Reynolds, in accepting the award, complimented her by saying, "When in doubt, cut to Julie Andrews."

After accepting the Best Director Award for Wise, Julie waited backstage to hear the winner of the Best Actress Award, to be announced by the previous year's Best Actor Award–winner: Rex Harrison. Upon opening the envelope, "Julie," he said, with lips pursed. Then he paused for a perverse split second before adding "…Christie, for *Darling.*" Moments later, when *The Sound of Music* won the Oscar for Best Picture of 1965, for a total of five Academy Awards, Julie Andrews said, "Oh boy" again. "We did it. Isn't that great? Now I'm happy."

7

Svengali and Psychoanalysis

With three movies behind her, three more lined up (the last of which put her into the $1 million per picture category), more scripts than she could read, an Oscar, and unbridled acclaim from the press and public, Julie Andrews should have been sublimely happy. Seemingly effortlessly, she had become the superstar she had set out to be. She bought a new house on a hillside in Coldwater Canyon, just north of Beverly Hills, and lived there with Emma Kate, a nanny, and a butler. A secretary came in daily and Julie had agents and a business manager who adored her and whom she trusted. Tony was still in New York, but in touch almost daily by taped letters or the telephone.

Yet, "I was desperately unhappy," she remembered, "and there was no apparent reason for it. I was successful and I should have been happy. I just felt this depression. I was behaving in a way that sacred hell out of me. It's terrible when all those lovely things are happening to you and you aren't enjoying them. I didn't like myself very much, and I was probably getting too big for my boots. I felt I needed some serious answers about myself."

To get those answers Julie went into psychoanalysis five days a week, for the five years which represented the peak of her Hollywood career, 1963 to 1968. She asked the advice of friends but, she said, "it is the only decision that I have ever made totally, one-hundred percent. It was also the wisest."

Julie's greatest anxiety was over the breaking up of her marriage to Tony Walton, her flourishing romance with Blake Edwards, and the effect of both on her daughter Emma. "You have to remember that I came from a broken home," she said. "I wondered if I was somehow subconsciously trying to re-create that thing which I had seen happen in my own childhood. And if my parents' divorce had inspired my breakup, would that in turn influence Emma's life?"

"Her divorce caused Julie a great deal of anguish," her father agreed. "On top of that came the stirrings of unhappiness she had felt when her mother and I parted. It was clear that neither I nor her stepfather had been able to finish off properly the job that a father has to do. One success after another came to Julie, and she never really had time to stop and take a good hard look at herself. Suddenly she needed assurance that the things she believed in were valid. She was also concerned, as any young mother would be, about bringing up Emma on her own. Julie knows how shattering a broken marriage can be to a child."

After *Mary Poppins*, Julie and Tony had made an agreement, to, in Tony's words "never work on the same thing at the same time. There are enough risks without imposing further ones. If I were to decide to go to Hollywood, whatever happened, and be with Julie, it would be a way of being together. But the few times I have been there and not been able to get on with the work that I find satisfying, I've become impossible to be with. And that's as dangerous as not being there at all. Some husbands of stars can fit into the agent-manager role, but I'm not agently inclined and there's pride involved, too."

Edie Adams, who also had moved to the west coast, remembered Tony calling her from New York, saying, "Please take care of Julie. Don't let her 'go Hollywood.'"

When Julie was filming *Hawaii* in Honolulu, Tony was designing the movie version of *A Funny Thing Happened on the Way to the Forum* in Spain. When he was working on the film *The Seagull* in Sweden, she was starring in *Torn Curtain* and *Thoroughly Modern Millie* in Hollywood. Only his work for the movie *Petulia,* which was filmed in San Francisco, put him within "striking distance" of a reconciliation with his wife, but by then it was too late.

"We are apart a lot and it is a problem," she said. "It's not easy at all. If he were to follow me around and be Mr. Julie Andrews, that wouldn't solve anything. We have periods of being enormously lucky, when we can work it out to be together. The rest of the time we have a sort of joint agreement, not to make any demands on the other and a kind of freedom which I find rather marvelous. It isn't easy, especially with Emma. She adores Tony, and one can see why. He is endlessly patient, very kind, a loving father, and rock solid."

Money was still an issue Tony tried to ignore. "It was mostly pride on my part—no, almost entirely pride," he said. "I couldn't conceivably afford the sort of house Julie has in Hollywood, so that sort of expenditure falls entirely on her." (A house in the London suburb of Wimbledon, where Julie and Tony lived together only a few months, was a joint property. The windswept cottage in Alderney was hers alone.)

One obvious, if extreme, solution would have been for Julie to abandon her career. Tony thought that might have been possible only in the first two years of their marriage, "because we were both in the theater, and it was never so hard to be together. And she's never been that passionate about the theater." But as she became a movie star, she felt that "to retire would probably lead to a dreadful resentment in me."

Tony agreed that Hollywood stardom had really involved her for the first time, "because, despite all her years in the business, this was the first time that she had any real self-confidence, a real feeling that she had a firm grip on things. I don't think she'd like to drop that feeling, not yet anyway. This confidence is the most marvelous and valuable thing about her success, and I wouldn't want to be responsible for taking that away from her."

One of the great strengths of their marriage, Tony felt, had been that they were each capable of taking the pressure off the other, particularly when they were both working in the theater. "At times I'd find myself taking on an almost feminine role, trying to calm, soothe, protect, or whatever," he said. "And then as soon as I was deeply involved, the roles would be reversed. I think if I were an overly dominant kind of male, I'd find this situation harder to cope with. But neither of us is overpoweringly masculine or feminine, so this switching of roles was a way of making a difficult situation work, but it was hardly the final answer. It's very hard for many women to feel really happy about it. They're grateful that this is possible so that they can work and be independent, but ultimately they resent a man's easing up on his dominance for a second."

The only time Tony resented being called "Mr. Julie Andrews" was at Alderney in 1964, at a dinner party. "A speech was made by someone which referred in a pleasant enough way to 'Mr. Julie Andrews,'" he recalled. "It got to me like a shot. I don't know why. Maybe because Alderney was such a private, defended place for us."

In her audio tapes from Hollywood in 1965 and 1966, Julie kept "saying how frightened she was of acting, how unreal the whole thing was. But we got too good at the tapes and a bit too tricky," Tony said. "Every once in a while I'd get one from Julie saying, 'It's midnight and I'm just dragging in from rehearsal,' and I could hear the birds singing in the background."

Early in their marriage, Julie had attempted at times to be a traditional wife; not a cook then or ever, she even prepared his breakfast most mornings. She went with him to Oxford for the opening of the English stage version of *A Funny Thing Happened on the Way to the Forum*. Two women in the foyer of the theater dimly recognized her face, and one asked: "Would you mind telling us if you have anything to do with this production?" Julie Andrews smiled and said, "Certainly. I'm Mrs. Walton. My husband designed the scenery."

But by October of 1966 the Waltons had decided to make their physical separation permanent. Early that month in New York she accompanied him to a preview of the Broadway musical *The Apple Tree*, which he had designed (and which she had turned down, even though her friend Mike Nichols was directing). Tony escorted Julie to the New York premiere of *Hawaii* on October 10. The next day she flew back to Hollywood to finish working on *Thoroughly Modern Millie* and to be with Blake Edwards.

Julie's separation from Tony was no longer a "trial" separation—there had already been enough trials in separation for that—but neither was it a legal separation and the Waltons were to remain legally married for another thirteen months. Julie never did like to say goodbye.

"We just decided to try it this way and see what happens," said Julie. "The split was not brought on by any one particular rift. There were many reasons, all of them intensely personal. But we have known each other much too long to fight. We are very good friends, as corny as that sounds. He is the best counsel, friend, advisor I have. I really do value his advice more than anyone's. He is one of the biggest influences in my life. I can't put my finger on it exactly, because it's in so many areas. But he's terribly bright, a very intelligent boy. His general help has been fantastic. And his parents are the best bloody in-laws anyone could ever have. They're a family-family—extremely close."

The Tony Waltons had never been, even at their happiest, the "family-family" that Julie had craved since infancy and both she and Tony regretted it, at least on Emma Kate's behalf. He complained that even before the separation he had seen his daughter only about a third of the time she had been alive. "I've been over-protective about that I know," Julie admitted. "But for her to see him would involve some kind of upheaval, a trip to New York or something like that. She talks to him on the phone two or three times a week, and sees him whenever they can get together."

While Tony held onto the hope of a reconciliation, Julie had postponed their divorce long past the point of any such possibility, thanks to her lifelong ambivalence and to what her friend Elsie Giorgi called Julie's one "major fault: she hates to disappoint anyone. As a result she does things that are over-taxing and not even worthy of her. She has a great sense of duty and great conscience. Who else would take two years to say, 'We are separated'?"

Mike Nichols had come to Hollywood in the mid-1960s to direct two movies, *Who's Afraid of Virginia Woolf?* and *The Graduate*, and he and Julie occasionally saw each other. While she was filming *Torn Curtain*, she served as hostess at a party Nichols gave at The Daisy, then the "in" nightspot in Beverly Hills. Her hairdresser and makeup man from the movie had stayed late in her dressing room that night to prepare her—"like Cinderella, all fixed up for the party, with pants and a big scarf. That's the sort of thing that should happen to you when you're eighteen. I'm thirty." The guests at the party included Richard Burton and Elizabeth Taylor, Rock Hudson, Lana Turner, and Sean Connery, so Julie made news as a hostess, and she and Mike Nichols made news as a couple.

Julie would also go out with other single men, such as Saul Chaplin or Roddy McDowall, "whatever's needed, whenever," she said. Her one serious attachment during this period was to John Calley, who had urged her toward analysis. She often flew to Los Angeles from the *Hawaii* location to spend the weekend with Calley. Then, when her father Ted Wells came to town, "I had a splendid field day with the gossipmongers. I went everywhere, clinging gaily to his arm. I enjoyed thinking what the fan magazines might be making of it."

Blake Edwards and Julie first met at a party given by Peter Sellers at a Beverly Hills hotel in 1963 to celebrate the completion of *A Shot in the Dark*, the second of the five Pink Panther movies that Edwards directed in which Sellers starred as Inspector Clouseau. "It was a cursory meeting with just the usual bullshit," Edwards recalled. "She said, 'I admire your work,' and I said, 'I admire yours, too.'"

Julie and Blake saw each other infrequently and in passing after that, at the Goldwyn Studios in Hollywood when she was filming interior scenes for *Hawaii* and he was directing *What Did You Do in the War, Daddy?* or at parties in the homes of mutual friends. He wanted to cast her in *Darling Lili* even then and went to her house to talk about it. She had relatives visiting, but wished he could stay for dinner.

But it was an offhanded smart remark he made one night at a party that really brought Blake and Julie together. During a discussion of instant stardom Julie's name came up as an Oscar winner of no prior movie experience. Blake said that the secret of her success was that "she has lilacs for pubic hairs." After Julie had bought three lilac bushes for her new garden, she decided she had one too many. She sent the extra lilac bush to Blake for the garden of his new bachelor house in the hills above the Sunset Strip. "I knew nothing about his remark," she insisted. "I just thought he'd like to have it."

But he was sure that she had heard this line, or that someone had put her up to the joke, and decided to come clean. He repeated the story, and she said, "How did you know?" For the next thirty years Julie and Blake gave one another lilacs on anniversaries and other important occasions.

Julie and Blake insisted that their permanent bonding had come about more prosaically (Hollywood style): they kept passing one another at the corner of Sunset Boulevard and Roxbury Drive while going to (his) and from (her) their respective therapy appointments in Beverly Hills. They finally stopped and talked, and discovered more in common than their belief in analysis.

William Blake Crump was born in Tulsa, Oklahoma in 1922, but he became third-generation Hollywood. His real father abandoned the family before he was born. When he was four, his mother moved to Los Angeles, where she married Jack McEdward, a production manager and assistant director. The boy was "left with an aunt and a bunch of female relatives who raised me." He was shuttled back and forth between Beverly Hills and Tulsa, "depending on my mother's whims." He hated his stepfather and California, and described his childhood as both "pretty stinkin'" and "bizarre and complicated."

McEdward, whose own father had directed the vamp Theda Bara in silent movies, adopted Blake. After graduation from Beverly Hills High School and serving in the Coast Guard in World War II, he worked as an actor (playing the local boxing champion who was floored by Cameron Mitchell in Richard Quine's *Leather Gloves*) and sold two scenarios for Westerns. When Dick Powell was looking for a new vehicle, Blake wrote the *Richard Diamond* radio series. From there he moved into writing and directing B movies and television shows, including creating *Peter Gunn*. His most successful movie work came in the early 1960s, when he directed *The Days of Wine and Roses*, and *Breakfast at Tiffany's*, neither of which he wrote, and *The Pink Panther* and *A Shot in the Dark*, which he did write. From then on, Blake Edwards was the writer, or at least a collaborator, on all of his movies.

When he and Julie started seeing one another regularly, his career was in a relative decline, with his $12 million movie *The Great Race* selling very few tickets. His fourteen-year marriage to Patricia Walker, a former actress, was ending badly. Julie was ending her marriage very slowly, while her career was definitely in its ascendancy; she made three major-budget features one after the other, *Hawaii*, *Torn Curtain*, and *Thoroughly Modern Millie*.

Edwards lived alone in a large, old-style movie director's house above Sunset Strip in the hills of West Hollywood, not more than fifteen minutes from Julie's more modest eight-room house off Coldwater Canyon. He was legally separated from his first wife, who lived in London with their children, Jennifer and Geoffrey, and close to a final divorce. His and Julie's first dates were for dinner in public restaurants. They took weekend cruises together and held hands under the table at a dinner party for eighty at the Bel-Air home of the Anthony Newleys (Joan Collins was then Mrs. Newley), prompting one observing guest to sneer: "She even conducts an affair like Mary Poppins."

"I had a Rolls-Royce convertible then," Edwards recalled of their very first date, "and as we were driving down Sunset Boulevard, I turned to Julie and said, 'This is a hell of a way to be anonymous, driving down Sunset Boulevard in an open Rolls-Royce with Mary Poppins!'" (Her car sported a bumper sticker that said MARY POPPINS IS A JUNKIE, a gift from Mike Nichols.)

Edwards's separation and divorce had been long in the works, and he was affronted by any suggestion that Julie was a homewrecker. "It is as wrong as it can be, and unfair to all concerned, particularly to my wife and children, to say that Julie had anything to do with my marriage breaking up," he said. "It was a combination of a lot of things, and my wife and I are trying to organize our separate lives. But that has nothing to do with Julie."

Before they started going together seriously, Julie and Blake had decided to work on a motion picture together—the one that he had written with her in mind and they had talked about. Paramount had agreed to assume the production of *Darling Lili* (or *Where Were You on the Night You Said You Shot Down Baron Von Richtofen?*) with her in the title role and him directing. Blake said, "While Julie and I are not irrevocably bound together in the deal, we can't really turn back. I think it's risky, our working together, or working with friends in general. I'm determined to keep my personal life apart from my business life, and they inevitably get mixed up if you work with friends. But knowing her and myself at this point, if any two people stand a chance of working together and getting away with it, I'd say we do."

Blake, who was thirteen years older than Julie, quickly developed total admiration for her, both personally and professionally. After knowing her for three years, he said, "I feel certain that whatever it is that makes that girl what she is, is profound and unique. I told her very early in our friendship that she was an unusual girl. She said, 'I'm not, and don't be surprised to find out some day that I'm not.' Whatever Julie is does come through on screen. She is an amazingly good actress for my taste. I am startled at times by the honesty of her performance. Now that I know the lady from whence it comes, I know that she has an enormous vista yet to tread. She has some interesting negative qualities, too—her need to be liked, for example. We all have it to some degree; she has it more than most."

Through the making of his hilarious and underrated picture *The Party*, starring Peter Sellers, and her films *Thoroughly Modern Millie* and *Star!*, Blake and Julie's friendship ripened into a full-fledged romance. On November 14, 1967, Julie filed for a California divorce from Tony Walton, on the usual show-business grounds of mental cruelty. The thirty-two-year-old actress, who had been living apart from her husband for three years, said in a terse statement: "The varying demands of our careers have kept Tony and me apart for long periods of time, thus placing obvious strains on our marriage. It has therefore become clear that a divorce would be in the best interest of all concerned."

Julie and "Blackie" (so called because of his moods and black sense of humor rather than as a diminutive of Blake) started spending more and more time together at his new house in Malibu and, with their three children, in both California and Switzerland, where they began to take winter vacations in 1967. Julie, however, did not appear to be any more eager to commit herself to a second marriage than she had been to finish the first.

She felt very strongly that it was nobody's business but her own and Blake's (and possibly Emma's and Tony's) how she conducted her private life. "How dare 'they' judge another human being?" she asked of those members of the press and public who had turned against movie stars such as Ingrid Bergman for what they considered public adultery. "Who knows what goes on anyone else's life?" Julie decided that "this hypocrisy is the last dregs of the big-star era, when the public and the press decided how a star should behave."

Blake agreed with Julie's sentiments about their affair. "You know that you're going to live your lives the way you want to anyway," he said, "but I'm in a better position than she because I'm not a celebrity. The fans and the fan magazines want to know every move she makes, but she is a very bright girl about that. We both feel that they're gonna say what they're gonna say, anyway. You can't avoid that unless you get out of the business."

"I mostly do what I want to do," Julie said, "and don't care what anyone thinks. I do try not to hurt anyone. People will talk and gossip, and there is nothing you can do, so you might just as well go your own sweet way. There is nothing I wish to announce or tell the world. When there is, I will. Until then, I'd rather leave it alone. I don't think anybody goes out of her way to be a scarlet woman, but

then there is very little I can do about it if that's what they want to
make of it."

Because she was so totally committed to her career at this
point in her life, her social and professional lives were hard to
separate. Julie once spent an entire evening at a party exacting
advice from George Burns; she sat riveted by his explanation of
how he and Jack Benny had made their stardoms last a lifetime.
Burns told her to embrace all entertainment media. Most of Julie's
friends and coworkers attributed her superstardom to the very
qualities they found in her as a person.

"I have always felt that this lady was one of the most unusual
ladies I've ever been near," Blake said. "She has an aura about her that
I'm tremendously impressed with. I have a natural ambivalence
toward actresses. I usually withdraw from them instinctively at the
beginning. They're fine in their place, but I can't have any kind of
relationship with them. She's different. She's vitally professional. Her
instincts are so damn good. You'll never see her throwing her weight
around or being competitive past normal competitiveness, and she
seems to be aware of the pitfalls of this business more than most."

Julie had always played a kind of Galatea to a Pygmalion: at first
it was her resented stepfather, Ted Andrews, then came Charles
Tucker, Cy Feuer, Moss Hart, Tony Walton, and Robert Wise. But
Blake Edwards was to become the most influential person in her
life, more like Svengali to her Trilby. (For several years the pair even
considered making a movie called *Trilby*, then eventually abandoned the idea. They did reconsider it in the 1990s, but for the stage
rather than the screen.) In the early stages of their relationship
Blake was still embarking on a search of his own. "The biggest
problem with me," he said, "is that there really is no Blake Edwards.
I've gone in too many directions so far. Success makes you too
aware of the details and apparatus of our business."

Blake was himself in psychoanalysis, five days a week, for seven
years, and he encouraged Julie's sessions with her analyst. She had
also been influenced strongly toward psychotherapy by John Calley
and a London friend, Masud Khan, Svetlana Beriosova's husand,
who was himself a psychiatrist. "One day I just did it," Julie

recalled. "I rang up everybody I knew who had a psychiatrist and asked who would be good."

At first she tried to keep her analysis a secret. Julie told co-workers on *The Sound of Music* and *Hawaii* not to say anything about it for fear her mother would find out. Eventually of course, Barbara Andrews did find out and pronounced the whole psychiatric profession and Julie's alleged need of its services "bloody nonsense. You understand, we still looked on them as quacks in England."

Julie's friend Elsie Giorgi, a medical doctor and dissatisfied subject of analysis, was equally skeptical. "In analysis she has become a student of it, rather than a patient," Dr. Giorgi said. "I sometimes wonder who's treating whom. Julie has great intuition, as well as a great intellectual curiosity about everything, and I think this is just one more thing she's learning about."

But Julie, who had no religious upbringing whatsoever (her only prayers were uttered just before going on stage: "Oh, God, don't let me fall on my face"), proved to be a zealous convert to psychoanalysis. "I'm only beginning to crystallize the bits and pieces of my life," she said, "and analysis helps. I think I'd have been a rotten mother without analysis. I do have phobias, and there's no doubt about it. I have enormous phobias about singing, stemming from the Broadway days when I was trotted out every night and was pretty much mixed up. Some of the neurotic idiosyncrasies of worry about my throat during the Broadway run of *My Fair Lady* really hung me up. I was in an absolute tizzy. I got phobias and complexes and everything else. The same was almost true of *Star!* I was on camera constantly for months and the pressures were enormous. I worried more than I should have."

Another of her concerns was her tendency to get angry and her expressing anger differently from most people. "I do have a temper, an absolutely fearful one," she said. "But I think I am too controlled a human being to let it be said that I have a temper most people would recognize. What usually happens, funnily enough, is that when I'm really blue I get wacky. I'm funniest when things are really down. I do hate scenes of any kind. They upset me desperately, and

I go out of my way to avoid them. I used to hate goodbyes to an extent that was ridiculous. I still hate both scenes and goodbyes, but now I know why."

Both Richard Burton in *Camelot* and Max von Sydow in *Hawaii* had seen flashes of her temper, which surprised her because "I thought I was kidding them the whole time." Other acquaintances, such as Tammy Grimes, wished Julie would show her temper and her other feelings a bit more. "She's sad and boring," said Grimes, "she's lost Eliza. Her accent is too high. She does just what's right. It would be groovier if she'd do just what's Julie once in a while."

Ambivalence, Julie felt, was "another of my failings. Ambivalence can either be a vice or a virtue. But I am able to see both sides of anything to such an extent that it is terribly hard for me to make a decision or do anything involving a drastic change. My kind of temper, when it does come out, is a stewing kind. I grit my teeth at the things that really do get me upset and I simmer for a while. It's the little things that get me mad. I'm terribly good about coping with big problems. One of my ambitions used to be to throw a great screaming temper tantrum. I can't see myself actually doing it, but I have fantasized it. To do it you have to be pretty damn sure that you're right or you look damn foolish. And because I'm totally ambivalent, I'm never that sure."

But her biggest phobia proved to be a fear of success, or at least a failure to understand why it was happening to her so fast. "You have this panic, this weight," Julie said. "You cope with it day by day, and sometimes everything is chaotic on the surface. I need order—desperately—but I can't have it. And there's never any time. Then there is this very great loneliness. It is hard, the pressure; often I get headaches. But one hopes it is not for nothing."

With Dick Van Dyke (as the chimney sweep Bert), Karen Dotrice and
Matthew Garber (as her charges) in her first movie, *Mary Poppins*, 1964
WALT DISNEY PRODUCTIONS

Conferring with director Robert Wise and costar Christopher Plummer
on the set of *The Sound of Music*, 1964

As Maria in *The Sound of Music*, with her seven charges, 1964
TWENTIETH CENTURY–FOX

Director George Roy Hill (*right*) instructs Julie and Max Von Sydow before shooting a scene for *Hawaii*, Sturbridge village, Massachusetts, 1965. She wore her mink over woolen slacks to ward off the damp winter chill.

Julie walks through *Torn Curtain* and director Alfred Hitchcock watches her every step, 1965. She later distanced herself from the movie.
UNITED PRESS INTERNATIONAL

About to take a flyer with Carol Channing (*center*) and Mary Tyler Moore in *Thoroughly Modern Millie*, 1966 UNIVERSAL PICTURES

Briefly single, in the sunny living room of her Hidden Valley, Beverly Hills, home, 1966 CURT GUNTHER

With producer Saul Chaplin, director Robert Wise (*center*), and choreographer Michael Kidd on the first day of filming *Star!*, 1967
TWENTIETH CENTURY FOX

As the glamorous Gertrude Lawrence in *Star!*, 1967
TWENTIETH CENTURY–FOX

8

Hawaii, Hitchcock, and *Millie*

In 1965, with three successful movies in release, *The Sound of Music* secure as the new box office champion of the world, and an Oscar to certify her acting ability, Julie's only professional problem might be, as she so prophetically put it, "that I'll be considered the nanny of all time."

She began the year by performing, along with Carol Burnett, at Lyndon Johnson's inauguration gala—naturally, they sang "Big D" for the Texas-born president. The year ended with her first solo television special and her first Christmas record album (with André Previn). She was named "Star of the Year" by the American Theater Owners in recognition of her number-one movie star status as a box office draw.

When Julie, Carol, and Mike Nichols were summoned to Washington, D.C. to perform at the inaugural gala, it happened to be during a major snowstorm. Julie arrived by train, skipping a party at the home of Perle Mesta (the "hostess with the mostest" and former Ambassador to Luxembourg who was immortalized in Irving Berlin's *Call Me Madam*). Instead, Julie went to the hotel to meet Carol and wait for Mike. When he did arrive, Carol invited him to her room which was on a different floor from his. Julie, in her inevitable slacks and Carol, in Joe Hamilton's bathrobe, went out to the elevator to wait.

"We sat on a settee across from the elevator and tried to think of something to make Michael laugh," Carol recalled. "We tried a lot of pigeon-toed stuff, then with our feet out, but nothing was funny enough. Julie said, 'I know wot—let's be kissing.' I said, 'I like you a whole lot, Julie, but I don't know.' She talked me into it, and we went into a mad embrace the minute the elevator doors started to open. A woman got out. She didn't recognize us, but the look she gave us....

"Next time the doors opened we went into another mad embrace, and this time it was about ten male heads—none of them Mike's—who had stopped at the wrong floor. By now I'm on the floor in hysterics. Back comes the lady. She keeps looking and very solemnly says, 'You're Carol Burnett, aren't you?' I said, 'Yes, and that's my friend Mary Poppins.' I wasn't gonna be the only one recognized. She goes, and the elevator opens again, and we go into our mad embrace. And damn Mike Nichols! He walks right out, and by us, and says, 'Hi, girls,' like we did it all the time."

Although all of her previous important American television work had been on CBS, Julie's first solo special was on NBC. She had a vague oral agreement with NBC that gave them "first refusal on anything I do." By late 1965 nobody was refusing anything that Julie Andrews chose to do. And if, by the night of November 28, there was someone who had never seen her in the movies or on stage and was still somehow unaware of her, *The Julie Andrews Show* remedied that. The virtually flawless full-color hour of singing, dancing, and comedy featured Gene Kelly as her chief guest star.

He and Julie performed a seemingly effortless soft-shoe number together. She sang "I Could Have Danced All Night," "Try to Remember" from *The Fantasticks*, "Auld Lang Syne" with its rarely heard second verse and, of course, "The Sound of Music." *The Sound of Music*'s conductor and arranger, Irwin Kostal, was also the musical director for *The Julie Andrews Show*, which was technically one of the best-sounding specials on television up to that time. The program drew approximately 35 million viewers, more than either the Barbra Streisand or Frank Sinatra specials of that season and won two Emmys and a George Foster Peabody Award.

Once she had her choice, however, television was Julie's least favorite medium. Even her tough-minded and usually influential agent, Arthur Park, couldn't change her mind about that. "She just isn't crazy about TV," Park said. "She feels there are too many compromises in time, that there isn't enough time to do anything right." Julie wouldn't do a television special again for another four years, and then she did one only because her options had narrowed.

At her peak in movie terms, and with her nanny-image problem still only a wisp of a joke rather than a real concern, the next logical thing seemed to be for Julie to marry Jesus in New England and go to Hawaii on a long honeymoon—and to do it for a real movie-star salary of $400,000.

Max von Sydow, the Swedish actor who had played Christ in the 1965 George Stevens picture *The Greatest Story Ever Told*, was cast in the movie *Hawaii* as Abner Hale, a fundamentalist Protestant missionary who hopes to convert the natives in the Hawaiian Islands to Christianity. Julie was cast as Jerusha Bromley Hale, his unwilling wife due to an arranged marriage who is actually in love with a sea captain, Rafer Hoxworth (played by Richard Harris). The *Hawaii* story, based on a third of James Michener's novel of the same name, appealed to Julie, who was anxious to try another straight, nonmusical character (although she would get to sing a lullaby, "My Wishing Doll," which was nominated for the Oscar for Best Song).

"Oh, marvelous publicity—can't you see it?" she chortled just before the start of filming. "Mary Poppins married Jesus. Gorgeous! She must have flown up to him and said, 'Listen, with my magic and your talent, we'd make a great team. I can fly. You can walk on water. What more do we need?' Actually, come to think of it, who else would Mary Poppins have married? It's the classic mother and father image for our children."

There was less to laugh about once *Hawaii* was actually in production. Shooting started in Sturbridge Village, a reconstructed colonial town in southwestern Massachusetts. The stars couldn't get to the location site because the spring snow in New England had stopped all air traffic, so they were driven up from New York in a limousine. Once in Sturbridge, a paid-admission restoration which had been rented, for $10,000 a day, to double for 1820s Walpole, New Hampshire, Julie learned for the first time the real meaning of the word "superstar."

"That little place, that's where she learned what she was," said William Buell, Julie's longtime makeup man whom she called "Daddy Bill." (Lorraine Roberson, Julie's hairdresser during this period, was called "Mom.") Prior to *Hawaii*, there had been a few incidents, mostly in department stores when Julie was shopping, or with mothers poking their children and saying, "Look, dear, there's Mary Poppins!" But in Sturbridge Village, which was not completely closed to the public during the filming of *Hawaii* (the areas where filming was taking place were merely roped off), mob hysteria took over, reaching its zenith on April 19, Patriots' Day, a government holiday unique to Massachusetts and Maine.

"People started to converge as I was walking to my trailer with these rather nice husky policemen," Julie recalled. "These very sizable, nice policemen were around me, and people would be on one side being pushed back by the husky policemen, and then they would circle around and come in from the other side. You could hear them saying, 'Look, it's Mary Poppins,' to their children. They didn't mean any harm, it was a lark for them. But then I got into my trailer and I was alone in eight square feet of space, alone in this island. You could hear them outside giggling and joshing and pushing. And the trailer was swaying. They were scratching at the walls. I pulled down the shades and sat there alone. I thought, 'My God, how alone I am. I can't send for anybody. I can't get out.'"

On another occasion, a zealous fan managed to steal an as-yet unused costume bonnet from Julie's trailer dressing room. The bonnet could not be remade in time, and had to be dropped from the movie. Whenever and wherever she went to eat around Sturbridge, she was mobbed by adoring fans. For a weekend sight-seeing trip with Tony, when he came up from New York, she requested a small, older-model car so that the two of them could go out unrecognized. The ploy worked, and they spent a rare quiet Friday afternoon and evening driving through the Sturbridge area. They spent the rest of the weekend in New York at a modest hotel where a superstar was not expected to stay and consequently were not bothered. They also took in the new Neil Simon hit play, *The Odd Couple*, directed by Mike Nichols.

From Sturbridge Village, the *Hawaii* company returned to Hollywood to shoot some interiors, then traveled to the Kahala section of Honolulu, where Julie, Max, Richard, and director George Roy Hill all had large rented houses. Unusually, this movie was filmed more or less chronologically, from Abner Hale's graduation from divinity school in New Hampshire to his marriage to boarding the ship to Hawaii to their arrival in the islands, and straight through to twenty years later.

"I fell in love with Hawaii," Julie said. "There had been Sturbridge, all cool and New Englandish, and then there was Hawaii—it was quite a change. To watch the dawn in those islands is one of the memorable experiences of a lifetime. Hawaii is gorgeous and fabulous. Where else could you drive up to a road stand and get a paper plate with a hamburger, French fries, mustard, and an orchid?"

Julie became so infatuated with Hawaii that she bought an interest in a macadamia nut orchard and returned to the islands frequently in later years for vacations. Emma Kate stayed with Julie at the Kahala house "every moment of the time," along with her nanny, Kay, and Julie's half-brother Christopher. Julie screened movies at her home, including Jean-Luc Godard's *Breathless*, and she gave parties, including one for all the nannies, tutors, and other household help in the company. When she had time off during the day she often relaxed alone on a secluded beach near the set in a bikini. She flew home on odd weekends to see John Calley.

"Although I loved the islands unashamedly," Julie remembered, "it was ten times harder working there, and six months was too long." In particular, she remembered hot, long, uncomfortable days on the Oahu beaches and three weeks offshore, filming the sea voyage scenes on the 150-ton 1936 Danish schooner *Grethe*, which had been converted to an early nineteenth-century two-masted brigantine. (Alan Villiers, author and seaman, had sailed it with his wife and a crew of nine from Copenhagen to the islands in about three months.)

The storm-at-sea scenes were done for the first two days without Julie. "The actors playing the sailors all got seasick," she recalled. "They all came back to shore and said, 'Dose up, it's going to be hell.' So the morning I was to go out I ate nine pancakes for ballast, took six Dramamines, and belted down a large scotch. I was so drunk I was the only one who wasn't sick."

The $12 million picture was falling badly behind schedule so studio executives flew out from Hollywood. They found director Hill spending most of his time working with the Polynesians, most of whom had no training as actors yet were crucial to the action. Julie felt that she was not getting enough of the director's attention, and he was fired by producer Walter Mirisch, who hired Arthur Hiller to replace him. Julie acquiesced in Hill's firing by staying silent, partly because she had worked so well with Hiller on *The Americanization of Emily*.

The Polynesians included Jocelyne La Garde, a French-speaking Tahitian standing six feet tall and weighing three hundred pounds. La Garde was making her acting debut as Malama, the Polynesian queen (so effectively that she got an Oscar nomination in the supporting actress category). La Garde and Manu Tupou, a Tongan who played her consort Keoki, led the Polynesians out on strike until Hill was reinstated. Julie thought that Le Garde and Tupou "had their nerve," refusing to work, and she would have no part of their strike. But once Hill was back on the picture and had time to devote to her, he and Julie became such good friends that she asked him to direct her next movie, *Thoroughly Modern Millie*.

Another irony of the situation was that Hill had fought to cast Julie as Jerusha in the first place. "Of course I wanted her," Hill explained. "It's awfully hard to get a girl who can play a convincing young lady of breeding of the 1820s in New England. What other names spring to mind? People of the 1820s—particularly in New England—were closer to the lands of their birth than to the Americans of today. There was a great stillness in the people of that time. That is what I tried to get, and that is what Julie has. She is reserved, yet warm and aristocratic."

Julie did not entirely agree with that assessment. "At first I thought I was miscast as the missionary's wife," she countered. "Miscast may not be precisely the right word. I didn't think I was in total sympathy with the lady. I wasn't as subdued as she was. My personality is more bubbly. And I felt I wasn't doing anything, just repressing myself and being her. I had never met anyone like Jerusha. She left her home, turned away from the man she really loved to stay with a husband she didn't love, to suffer the hardships and deprivations of a missionary's wife on an untamed island. I don't think I would have done that. But George was patient with me, Max was a lovely and a marvelous actor to work with, and finally I loved the work and the part."

Shortly after she arrived in Honolulu, Julie went to visit the wax museum, "and I almost dropped in my tracks. There was a wax figure of the first lady missionary in Hawaii, and if that lady isn't the very image of me! I had an eerie feeling that I was destined by fate for this part."

Julie's most important scene in *Hawaii* was the one in which she gave birth to a child. It was shot in the converted Navy warehouse in Honolulu that was serving as a studio and it took seventeen hours over a period of six days. "All I produced was a lump of celluloid," she said. "But I don't think I could have done the scene without having had a baby myself. There was a real doctor counseling on the set, and after every take he would put his hand on my head and ask if I felt all right, just as if I *were* having a baby. Opening night in New York, I noticed that women were fastened on the screen during that scene. The men, I think, rather didn't like it."

The secondary casting of the epic, even apart from the Polynesians, was interesting. Costume designer Dorothy Jeakins also made her film debut as a very touching Mrs. Hale, Abner's mother, in a part that was originally much longer and included a moving farewell scene with Max but was reduced to an almost silent walk-on in the final cut. Von Sydow's two small platinum-haired sons, Henrik and Clas, played his and Julie's sons in the movie. Gene

Hackman, John Cullum, George Rose, and Michael Constantine played small parts, as did a pre-*All in the Family* Carroll O'Connor and Heather Menzies, who had played the second von Trapp daughter, Louisa, in *The Sound of Music*. As for the Polynesians, despite their differences over the director, Julie said, "I adored them and I believe they were rather fond of me."

Before Richard Harris, who had the smallest of the three lead roles, left the islands, he, Max, and Julie threw the cast a dinner party at the Kahala Hilton Hotel. Don Ho was brought in to sing. He and Julie did a duet of his hit "I'll Remember You," with Julie repeating each verse as he sang it because she didn't know the words. Asked to sing a solo, she said, "I'm sorry, but of all the songs I've sung the only one I can remember all the words to is 'I Could Have Danced All Night.'" So she sang that to the aloha-shirted and muumuued crowd, and nothing else.

During *Hawaii*, Julie developed two satisfying professional relationships, one with George Roy Hill, and the second with Max von Sydow. The Swedish star was her favorite leading man she said, "The unqualified front-runner, the most generous man I've ever met, with a light, lovely sense of humor." It would be twenty years before Julie and Max would work together again in *Duet for One*.

Max found that Julie "made fun of herself and her part in a marvelous way, and yet she is so goddamned professional even in the most difficult situations. She doesn't behave like the cliché star. She has a temper, but she is also a disciplined lady, and does not use her temper just because she feels like it. She is nice with people, but she is determined to do things right, and she will stick up for what she thinks is right. She doesn't show off.

"I learned a lot from her about movie discipline. I have a tendency to tenseness all day when I'm on a picture, to stay with my part the whole time—which made me too exhausted too early in the day. She, on the other hand, has a great ability to walk into a part and then out of it again, to do her part one minute and then relax the next—to do other things, write letters, see people, listen to music, sing, and laugh, and then go right back to being Jerusha."

When *Hawaii* opened, it had fourteen black-tie charity premieres in various cities. Julie attended the first of them, in New York on October 10, 1966, with Tony, although they were already estranged. Critics were kinder to Julie than to the film, which was bogged down with its slow pace and epic length. Her father Ted Wells said *Hawaii* convinced him for the first time that his daughter could act as well as sing. Of her own efforts in *Hawaii*, Julie said, "I did have reservations about myself—one always does—but I do like little bits that I did." *Hawaii* was rewarded with eight Academy Awards nominations, basically for its big effort. All the nominations, except for La Garde's as Best Actress in a Supporting Role, were in technical categories and the movie won no Oscars. It turned a slight profit.

With barely a week between the two movies, Julie ended *Hawaii* and began *Torn Curtain*, the spy story that was to become Alfred Hitchcock's fiftieth movie. Julie had hated the Brian Moore script, but her agents had convinced her that working with Hitchcock and costar Paul Newman would be the best (meaning the most lucrative) thing that she could do at the moment. Because she wanted to work with those two men she agreed, and plunged ahead with the picture despite a severe case of fatigue from *Hawaii*. She was paid $750,000 against ten percent of the gross, more than Newman, who was nonetheless billed ahead of her.

Torn Curtain waited for her return from the islands, so when production started in November of 1965 the movie was already behind schedule. The setting of the story was Copenhagen and East Berlin, but all shooting involving the two stars took place entirely on the Universal Studios back lot—and it looked it. Although *Torn Curtain* was not a big budget film, what money was spent (about $5 million) went to salaries and not to production values. Perhaps that was why everybody, including Hitchcock, seemed to walk through *Torn Curtain*.

For the first time in her life on stage or screen, Julie was playing a contemporary woman, Sarah Sherman, the secretary/mistress to an American scientist (played by Paul Newman), who supposedly defected to the Communists. Sarah stubbornly follows him from

Copenhagen to Berlin, although he has told her not to complicate both their lives by doing so. The movie opens with Julie and Paul, who are not married nor are they contemplating it, in bed together, although they were far from nude.

This was a shock to many admirers of Julie's happy nanny/nun persona, and entirely unacceptable to the National Roman Catholic Office for Motion Pictures, the successor to the Legion of Decency, which condemned the picture as "morally objectionable in part for all," for its "gratuitous introduction of premarital sex between its sympathetic protagonists." The Catholic Office also said that the movie's "detailed treatment of a realistically brutal killing [was] questionable on moral grounds," and concluded with a warning: "Parents should be aware that the 'Mary Poppins' image of the female lead (Julie Andrews), shattered in this film, cannot serve as any criterion of the film's acceptability for their children."

Julie, of course, took a different view of the opening love scene. "As it was necessary to the story to establish our close relationship, I saw no harm in it," she said. "Paul Newman was such a nice man; we didn't take it seriously, and had a lot of giggles over it. It didn't last long, so I don't see what all the fuss is about. I prefer to be known as an actress, not an image."

Making *Torn Curtain* did not provide either the fun or the professional satisfaction that Julie's four previous movies had. Costume designer Edith Head helped her with her dress for the Theater Owners of America convention. On the set, Newman was nice enough (he called her "the last of the really great dames"), but a close friendship never developed between them. Even Julie's clowning on the set of *Torn Curtain* was more forced and less funny than before.

When Hitchcock complained at one point of a spotlight "making a hell of a line over her head," she demurely put her hands on her hips and said, "That's my halo." Another day she was lying on the bed in what was supposed to be her Copenhagen hotel room, and suddenly she said to the director, "Won't the camera be looking up my skirt?" Newman squatted down next to the camera and looked. "Yeah, that's the idea," he said. "Oh, you beastly thing," she retorted.

"I say, did you see the cartoon about Mary Poppins? She is sailing through the air with her umbrella, and there are two little boys on the ground looking up. One of them says, 'Coo, you can see right up her skirt.'" Everybody on the set laughed, but dutifully rather than heartily.

Hitchcock said he got his inspiration for *Torn Curtain* from the story of the British diplomats Burgess and MacLean, who had defected to the U.S.S.R. in the 1950s. "I said to myself, 'What did Mrs. MacLean think of the whole thing,'" Hitchcock recalled, "and the first third of the film is more or less from a woman's point of view." That approach did not work, unfortunately, because the audience was way ahead of Julie's character on each aspect of the action. Also, in those days, an amiable top-billed star such as Paul Newman could never be a defector or any type of villain, so there was no suspense.

That three well-known perfectionists such as Alfred Hitchcock, Paul Newman, and Julie Andrews could have made the slipshod bundle of clichés that *Torn Curtain* became is still a minor wonder. That the movie made money on its initial release in the summer of 1966 (although filmed after *Hawaii*, it was released before it) was a major miracle, and a tribute to all three names and their combined potency at the box office, despite the critics' justifiably acidic reviews.

Julie was privately so upset by the final result that she urged her good friends not to see *Torn Curtain*. Even publicly, though she tried to be discreet, some of her resentment over the experience came through. "I did not have to act in *Torn Curtain*," she said. "I merely went along for the ride. I don't feel that the part demanded much of me, other than to look glamorous, which Mr. Hitchcock can always arrange better than anyone. I did have reservations about this film, but I wasn't agonized by it. The kick of it was working for Hitchcock. That's what I did it for, and that's what I got out of it. So that's that."

Her next movie, made for Universal, as was *Torn Curtain*, was an entirely opposite experience, and a musical to boot: *Thoroughly Modern Millie*. For almost two years Julie had been looking forward to making the movie version of *The Public Eye*, Peter Shaffer's one-act play, with Mike Nichols as her director. It was to have been produced by Ross Hunter, who previously had worked with Doris Day, Lana Turner, and Sandra Dee. But Nichols was tied up with his movie debut, *Who's Afraid of Virginia Woolf?*, and was committed to direct *The Apple Tree* on Broadway that summer of 1966. Hunter had also produced the other half of Shaffer's double bill of one-acts, *The Private Ear*, as *The Pad (And How to Use It)*, though it proved to be a large bore and a total critical and box office failure. Thus *The Public Eye* dissipated. However, Julie still had a deal to work with Hunter and Universal, at another $750,000 against ten percent of the gross.

What Hunter really wanted to work on was a movie version of *The Boy Friend* with Julie recreating her role of Polly Browne. But the property was owned by MGM, who would not sell it to either Hunter's production company or Universal. (MGM filmed *The Boy Friend* in 1971, starring Twiggy and Christopher Gable and directed by Ken Russell, in a play-within-a-play manner very different from the original; it was not a success.) Hunter instead decided to make *Thoroughly Modern Millie*, which was first conceived as a comedy about a young career girl in New York in the 1920s, and not as a musical.

"I read the script [by Richard Morris] as a favor to Ross Hunter," Julie said. "I thought it would be the last chance I'd have to do the ingenue. After all, when you're thirty-two, how many more chances can you have? It was my last fling at a part like that."

She was so enthusiastic about the concept of *Thoroughly Modern Millie* that she canceled a much-needed vacation and put off all other movie work, including *Star!*, which actually wasn't ready yet. Julie persuaded Hunter to hire George Roy Hill, who worked with Morris on the conversion of his script into a musical. They used existing songs of the 1920s, such as "Baby Face," "Poor Butterfly," and "Japanese Sandman." Sammy Cahn and Jimmy Van Heusen wrote four new songs, including the title number, "Jimmy," "The Tapioca," and "Trinkt Le Chaim." Mary Tyler Moore, Carol Channing, James Fox, John Gavin, and Beatrice Lillie were signed to play the other major roles. The budget was boosted to $8 million.

Julie found herself "very excited about *Millie;* it had great style, it was wild and wacky, it had a marvelous cast. The way the script was written, the character walked a fine line between a selfish, tough, ambitious girl and a fine lady. The challenge was to be that whole person. I hope one didn't fall one way or t'other. The picture was *very* twenties—high style, but not high camp."

In the title role of Millie, Julie played an essentially sweet girl who tries to be a flapper but is so naive that she is surrounded by a ring of white slavers (led by Lillie) and extremely rich socialites (Fox, Moore, and Channing) but doesn't even realize it. Millie also falls in love with her boss (Gavin). Ross Hunter claimed to have found "a new Julie. She had a lot of sex appeal and a clean look. I've never worked with anyone like her, and I've worked with them all. She is probably one of the greatest stars ever in the business."

Although on screen she was to be once again "Julie Andrews As You Love Her—Singing, Dancing, Delighting," as the studio's ad campaign had stated, making *Millie* was not the romp it might have been. She was going through a difficult personal period: the separation from Tony was in motion, she began appearing with Blake at dinner parties around Hollywood and, having made three more movies in a row without a break, she was tired.

There were professional worries as well: She was contending with the film debuts of both Carol Channing and Mary Tyler Moore, George Roy Hill's debut as a musical director, and a studio that was finding its most financially successful movie ever to be *Torn Curtain*, and was determined to better both its and her record with this picture. Julie responded to all these needs. She did not stint on the help she gave her costars; one day when she was not needed on the set, Julie came in to read her lines off camera for Channing to react to, instead of having Carol's stand-in read the lines. Hunter and Channing were both flabbergasted. "I've never had anyone help me the way Julie did," said Carol. "That would be unheard of for any other star," said Hunter.

Carol told Julie after the incident, "If it had been my stand-in, I wouldn't have spoken the same way to her."

Julie said, "Yes, I knew that, that's what I'm here."

"I always played to Julie," said Carol. "She was the one who was listening. She grabbed the words right out of my mouth."

When Channing lost her Broadway *Hello, Dolly!* role to Barbra Streisand for the movie version (as she had previously lost *Gentlemen Prefer Blondes* to Marilyn Monroe), Julie wired her "Don't worry, Carol, you'll get your *Mary Poppins.*"

"Now wasn't that just the right thing to say?" said Carol.

But Channing was more impressed with Julie's determination than with her sweetness. "With Julie it's not 'Who loves me? How sweet am I? Do you think I'm dear?' and all that sort of stuff. Instead it's work, work, work. She's completely career, and businesslike. She's all for the goal, and it doesn't matter if she's subtle about it—and to me that's the most feminine thing there is. She's dead-on honest. What she wants is ability around her; it makes her better. If you have that ability, or can develop it, she's all with you.

"There was a fly on the set during one close-up," Channing remembered. "Julie jumped up and said, 'Well, we are going to get that fly, damn it, we are going to get it.' The director had a flyswatter, and he was just going to swat it when she grabbed it out of his hand and swatted the fly and killed it. Now, you know you can't do that to a man, and I laughed and said, 'Julie, honey, you are the kind of woman who pushes the elevator button first when you are standing there with a man,' and she said, 'Why not, for heaven's sake?'"

Hill, directing his second movie with Julie and not at all emasculated by the loss of his flyswatter, said of his star: "There was a period when she seemed a little too good to be true, but she has at last gone beyond that. If I had searched the earth for a different movie for Julie after *Hawaii*, I couldn't have come up with a better one than *Millie*. Jerusha was subdued by nature. Millie was so alive that Julie came in every day with a thousand ideas of what to do. She fell completely into the style of the picture and was great fun on the set. We were hysterical and helpless with laughter most of the time."

Hill didn't need her help as much as Julie thought he did.

During one scene between Julie and Mary Tyler Moore, the two women objected to his direction. He said he would walk away and let them direct the scene themselves. They tried for an hour with no success, and pleaded with him to come back.

Universal executives took one look at the rough-cut footage of *Millie* that Ross Hunter showed them and decided that the picture should be shown in 70mm as a reserved-seat attraction for Easter of 1967 in New York and for the summer in London, Los Angeles, and the rest of the world. For this kind of road show, long enough to require an intermission, and to allow higher ticket prices, almost all the footage already shot would have to be left in the movie. Julie and George Roy Hill were distressed by this decision, thinking that they had had a very good, possibly even great, "little" picture on their hands. Andrews made a list of seventy grievances, mostly having to do with length, and pleaded with Universal to cut the film (particularly the Jewish wedding song "Trinkt Le Chaim," which had been nothing more than a cynical sop to the Jewish members of the vast theater party and matinee audience).

Julie's pressing to release *Thoroughly Modern Millie* as a regular movie was based on artistic considerations but Lew Wasserman, president of MCA, which owned Universal, saw a chance to cash in on the current popularity of both road shows and Julie Andrews. The studio made none of her suggested cuts, and that left her eternally cool to Universal. "Their way, it was blown up too far out of proportion from its original conception," she said. But MCA was proven to have been commercially, if not artistically, correct when the picture was released as a longer road show and broke *Torn Curtain's* record as the top grossing movie for Universal to that date.

Millie also established Julie, temporarily, as the only star of that era who could guarantee the success of a movie. George Roy Hill became firmly established as a movie director. Carol Channing got her *"Mary Poppins"* in the form of an Oscar nomination as Best Actress in a Supporting Role, one of seven nominations *Throughly Modern Millie* received. Elmer Bernstein won the Academy Award for his scoring.

Just after *Millie* was made but months before it was released, casting began at Warner Bros. for the screen version of *Camelot.* Jack Warner was personally producing the film, as he had *My Fair Lady,* and he let it be known that he would like Julie to re-create Guinevere in the film—a tacit admission that he had made a mistake the first time around. Her agent said that Julie would be interested in the movie, and Warner Brothers promised to send her a script. But Richard Burton, who had been approached to play King Arthur again, was working in a succession of pictures with his wife Elizabeth Taylor, and was not really interested in *Camelot.* Stories circulated that Julie was asking as much as $1,200,000 just to get even with Jack Warner, but it was doubtful that negotiations ever got that far.

Warner instead signed Richard Harris and Vanessa Redgrave as King Arthur and Queen Guinevere. Director Joshua Logan did not agree with those who felt that Julie Andrews was right for the screen version of any musical that came along. Logan was delighted with Vanessa Redgrave, who herself said at the time, "I'm sure if Julie Andrews wanted to play this part, she'd be playing it."

But Logan, who, with Alan Jay Lerner, had completely over-hauled the conception of *Camelot* in its transition from stage to screen, asked in a sneering tone, "Can you see two men and two armies going to war over Julie Andrews?"

9

Mummy, Home, and Music

Once Emma Kate was born, the role Julie really liked—and played—best was that of mother. "She feels safer with her baby," said Tammy Grimes in 1966. "She becomes all warm and kind of mummy." In 1996, Julie herself said that giving birth to Emma was "the one time in my life I witnessed a miracle."

After she had finished her second three movies in a row, Julie tried to arrange to be at home with her daughter in the late afternoons and evenings and on weekends. In order to spend this time with Emma, Julie preferred to continue working in movies rather than even considering any offers to go back on stage. Julie guarded Emma's privacy obsessively, never giving out the names of the schools Emma attended for fear of kidnapping. From the time her daughter was eighteen months old until she was six, Julie forbade pictures to be taken of herself alone with Emma.

Julie was so covetous of her time with her daughter that even when she dutifully delivered Emma to Tony Walton in New York for a few days' visit, she would reserve the important days, such as Emma's birthday and Christmas, for herself. When Emma was in nursery school Julie drove her there and picked her up five mornings a week in her black 1965 Ford Falcon with simulated wood sides and the "Mary Poppins is a Junkie" bumper sticker. "Julie drove up to the school just like all the other mothers," said her business manager Guy Gadbois, "slightly apologetic about being there."

Emma, a blue-eyed blonde who, in her early years, actually looked more like her father, had short hair like her mother's, shared some of her mannerisms, and many of her interests. Like Julie, Emma would go around the house whistling and singing in a modified British accent. When Julie took up oil painting in the summer of 1966, Emma emulated her, and the four-year-old was likely to be seated right alongside her mother in their pool house with her little box of watercolors. Once, when Julie had an interview at home, Emma, then six, sat quietly in the living room with a sheaf of paper in her lap. Julie asked her what she was doing. "I'm having an interview too, Mummy," was the answer.

During Julie's high-pressure movie period of the mid-1960s, Emma loved to watch her mother on the screen and sometimes would even greet her in real life with "Hi, Julie Andrews!" The three musicals were shown to Emma first; *The Americanization of Emily* and *Torn Curtain* were withheld from her for a few years. Julie let her see *Hawaii* one half at a time, "Not that I think she couldn't take it all, but she might fall asleep, and then I'd be terribly embarrassed," she said.

Emma liked to be sung to sleep by Julie, "but she hated for me to *practice* singing," she said about this heavily musical period stretching from *Thoroughly Modern Millie* to *Star!* that included a Christmas album that Julie recorded with André Previn for a Firestone Tires premium offer in the 1966 season. "She would burst into real tears whenever I practiced, shouting 'Stop it; I don't want you to do it.' She kept trying bravely to conquer it. One day, André and I were practicing at home, and Emma came in. She said, 'Mummy, if I sit very quietly may I watch?,' which she never would have thought to ask before. She sat for a few minutes, looking very uncomfortable, and then asked to leave the room. She had heard all she could stand."

Since Emma was not yet five, she took a nap in the early afternoons, well within range of the pool house where Julie practiced, making it somewhat difficult for Julie to rehearse her songs. "The only time I could do it was driving to the studio early in the morning. There I was, driving down Coldwater Canyon, clinging to the wheel for dear life, completely oblivious to everything around me, singing at the top of my lungs. I'm sure when I pulled up to a light the person in the next car thought to himself, 'Now, who's that crazy woman?'"

If Emma missed her father, she filled the void by clinging to Julie's brother, Chris. Christopher Andrews, Julie's younger half-brother, first lived with Julie and Emma in Hawaii, then in California while he studied photography at the Art Center in Los Angeles. He was twenty when he arrived at the Beverly Hills house in 1966, taking over the bedroom that the butler had once occupied.

Other members of the household at the time included two dogs and a cat. The dog, an almost-white toy poodle named Q-Tip ("Because he looks like a used one," Julie explained) and a black standard poodle named Cobie lived in harmony with the gray and white cat named Bimbo. ("He used to be called Contrapuntal, but Emma thought that was a bit much.") Emma romped regularly with the three animals, but Julie gave them scant attention.

The house was, until late 1969, still in the firm charge of a butler named Covington, called Cov by his mistress, who did most of the cooking and answered the door and the telephone. A laundress came in most days and doubled as a baby-sitter when the nanny was away. Julie had a full-time secretary with whom she worked three days a week at her home or on the movie set and two days a week at the secretary's home. When the kitchen was being remodeled and Covington was away in the Army, Julie, who described herself as "hopeless" in the kitchen, and Emma had many of their suppers at the local hamburger restaurant.

Given her nomadic early existence brought on first by the war, her parents' divorce, and mother's and stepfather's profession, then by her own work in show business, it wasn't surprising that Julie had long sought a place to call home. What was more than a little bit surprising was that this typically English girl found that home in southern California. Julie had first "fallen in love with" the region on her honeymoon with Tony in 1959. When she returned four years

later to work on *Mary Poppins* she told Carol Burnett that "she'd
never been happier anyplace."

"Having bought this house has made me feel truly at home here
in Hollywood," she said. "When I first came I put it down like
everyone else, and said that there was nothing going on here. I
didn't know a soul when I arrived. I hated the fact that I had to drive
everywhere. But now I think that Hollywood is as real as New York
or as real as London or as real as Venice. But to really appreciate it,
you must go away and come back again. Sometimes when I feel
lonely or depressed, it helps me to think that Venice *is* at that
moment, that Rome is teeming. It keeps one from being too
isolated."

The modern white brick, wood, and glass house was plunked
into a private hillside. It was in a cul-de-sac near the top of
Coldwater Canyon known as Hidden Valley and was ideally situated
about fifteen or twenty minutes from all the Hollywood movie
studios and about twenty minutes from downtown Beverly Hills.
Near neighbors included Rock Hudson, Charlton Heston, and Lana
Turner. Producer Aaron Spelling, who Julie didn't know then, lived
right next door. He sent her flowers to welcome her to the
neighborhood.

Despite its central location, Hidden Valley was in semiwild
canyon country and had the feeling of being totally isolated. It was
far from the routes of the sightseeing buses that visited the stars'
homes. Julie preferred it that way. "I like being out of doors, and I
like the country better than the city. My real dad taught me to love
the country. The only salvation for an apartment in London or New
York is if you can see trees, a park, or a river."

The pool and the pool house were across the driveway from the
house and beyond that was an extra lot containing Emma's play-
ground (swings, see-saw, and slide). The property was ringed by
pear, apple, and avocado trees and wild canyon plants. In front of
the house was a flagstone courtyard with a fountain that lit up at
night. At the back of the house, in the best California tradition, was
an eating patio.

Julie had fireplaces in both her living and dining rooms and installed one in her huge bedroom, which comprised the whole upstairs of the house. Because Julie thought she was in her house to stay she remodeled the kitchen and had an adjacent sun porch converted to a family breakfast room. Central air-conditioning was installed and the oak parquet floors were stained dark. Bougain-villea bushes were added to the garden that she had inherited.

The furnishings in the house tended toward elegant things such as Wedgwood white bone china. There was a Grotian Steinmeg grand piano at one end of the living room under a straight open staircase leading down from the bedroom. Behind the staircase was a glass wall facing south that allowed the room to be filled with sunlight for most of the day. In this room was most of Julie's art collection, which she planned to expand. There were two prints by Anna Mahler, daughter of the composer Gustav and a friend of Julie's, a highly unsuccessful head of Julie and a delicate, graceful, three-foot-high statue of an anonymous girl. She also owned a Gyneth Johnstone Italian landscape, an African fertility doll, and five oil paintings by the Oakland California artist Henrietta Berk. Blake Edwards, who also owned several Berks, introduced Julie to the artist's works: semi-abstracts of flowers, children, trees, oceans, and fields in bright warm reds, oranges, blues, and greens.

Julie and André Previn played a favorite game: "If you could buy any five paintings in the world for yourself, what would they be?" According to Previn, "I played it with Julie one afternoon, not limiting her to five, and she chose 'Anything by Turner, but that really is daydreaming—that's just for the game—and any of the strange, wonderful birds and winged creatures by Braque, and anything by Manet, Monet, Pissaro, Sisley—especially *The Canal, The Woodcutter,* and *The Orchard*—Daumier's *The Refugee,* any still life by Redon, like *Bouquet of Wild Flowers,* and any of Nolde's watercolors.'"

"The trouble is one wants so much," Julie said, and she seemed reluctant to buy herself even one major painting for each of her movies. Her business manager Guy Gadbois said she wasn't earning enough to buy what were then $30,000 pictures. While she agreed with Gadbois about her own art collection, she weakened where

Blake was concerned. For Christmas 1967 she gave him Emil
Nolde's *The Singer* and for his birthday in 1968 she gave him a
Persian water jug dating from 1,000 B.C. that she had acquired in
Brussels while filming *Darling Lili.*

Ted Wells had raised his daughter on *The Oxford Book of
English Verse* and *The Golden Treasury* and as a single parent,
Julie found herself reading poetry again. "When I'm very busy, it's
hard to get into a deep novel. But you can pick up a book of poems
and read as much as your heart desires. I go off into another world."
Her favorite poet was Robert Frost, "for his simplicity and sense of
nature."

Recorded classical music was another important part of Julie's
home life. "Whenever I call her or go over there, the record player is
going," said André Previn, "and it is not for my benefit. She really
knows music and loves it." Svetlana Beriosova agreed that Julie had
"great love and understanding of music and dance. I visited her in
California when she was in the midst of *Mary Poppins*, and one
night we just sat listening to Benjamin Britten's *War Requiem* and
ended up hearing it twice."

Julie's stardom made it hard for her to go out in public. "Going
anywhere with her was a little like blockade-running," said André
Previn. But it also gave her access to any studio's current movies to
screen at home instead of going out to a movie with her chums. "I
screen the movies on the smooth wall of the playroom if it's a good
movie," she explained, "on the brick of the living room if it's a bad
movie." That was the sort of "big star" activity that induced
"vehement razzing" from Previn and Nichols who, after all, had
known her when she didn't have to worry about being mobbed at a
movie theater.

When she did go out, it was usually to small dinner parties,
escorted by Blake Edwards. She never drank more than a glass of
wine. "I'm too cautious, too careful a person," Julie explained, "I'd
be terrified of what I'd reveal if I ever really let go." Nonetheless,
her only two "culinary" specialties were two alcoholic drinks. "She
makes the best bullshots in the world," said Carol Burnett. "I always
think, soup and liquor, so good for you."

"And every Christmas," said Julie, to everyone's annoyance and chagrin, I make mulled wine, all icky and sticky. I'm the only one who likes it."

Julie never dieted as such. "My Mum was a great one for balanced meals—fruits and salads, seldom fried things, and all that," she said. "Because she was so strict I now have a passion for things like rice pudding and potatoes." She adopted "the Moss Hart diet" during *My Fair Lady:* eat everything you like, but in half quantity. "I still do that when I need to think about food."

In small groups Julie was at both her wittiest and most enigmatic. "She has a far-out sense of humor," said Previn. "She loves to be the clown, and is much more broadly amusing than one would suspect. She is not above saying things you could not say on a movie screen. I don't know why she is such a reserved lady or seems so, but while she's saying all these things and while she's at her funniest, you're never quite sure what she's thinking."

At home Julie always wore slacks and simple blouses or sweaters and she often wore the same outfit to work. Sometimes she wore the little white anklets that everybody's mother wore in the 1940s and stopped wearing in the 1950s. ("God knows where she gets them," remarked a woman friend.) An admirer of simplicity, Julie had only four pieces of jewelry "that I wear off and on." She wore a plain watch with a plain black strap and, of course, no engagement or wedding ring. For the Hollywood premiere of *Hawaii* she had to borrow a diamond brooch. After *Star!* and the influence of Gertrude Lawrence's ghost, Julie's taste ran to more jewelry on glamorous occasions, but during the day, at home and at work, she wore none.

Her taste in clothes for more public occasions was both old-fashioned and frumpy. She certainly belied the contemporary mid-1960s English "mod" movement, although she flew from New York to Los Angeles after the *Hawaii* premiere in a then-fashionable purple pants suit. At one Hollywood party, she arrived "looking like the chaperone," according to André Previn. "She didn't act it, but she looked it. She was younger than most of the other guests there, but she looked older." Tammy Grimes, who attended the same party, a sit-down dinner with a live rock band and dancing afterward, said, "She wore white gloves. I thought the press was gonna come and give her an award."

"I don't deny that I adore clothes," said Julie. "My greatest pleasure is picking out a new gown. I used to be influenced a lot by Tony. I used to wear a lot of black for some somber reason, until he informed me rather tartly one day that black made my skin look all blotchy."

Tony Walton recalled that Julie had "little interest in the business side of her career and always found it difficult to discuss money." But George Roy Hill and Guy Gadbois disagreed. "She is a fantastic businesswoman," Hill said after making two movies with her. "I'd put a production in her hands before I'd give it to the so-called businessmen in the studios."

"She has a good awareness of her business affairs," Gadbois said. "She is a very conservative person who wants to know what's going on all the time, and she's very inquisitive about where her money's going." Julie's and Gadbois's major disagreement was over a Mercedes she wanted and eventually got. But he urged her to make do with her modest, suburban 1965 Ford Falcon, with a new set of tires, for a while longer, and she did just that.

Her investments, he said, "are of a conservative nature, conservatively diversified." Julie and Gadbois discussed every major expenditure and they met once a week to discuss business. He took care of all household expenses, based on a budget that Julie had approved. She had a small allowance for very personal expenses. "It's her own money, and if she wants something badly enough she'll get it," said Gadbois. "But Julie's sensible enough to know that we're right about the art collection."

Julie's only work during the time off between the finish of filming on *Thoroughly Modern Millie* and the beginning of *Star!* was recording the Christmas album with André Previn, using most of the Los Angeles Philharmonic as a studio orchestra. She was "quite secretly pleased with the Christmas album."

Recording was a medium that Julie had tried to embrace but she was inexplicably unsuccessful at selling albums other than the soundtrack of *The Sound of Music* and the original cast recording of *My Fair Lady,* which were then the two bestselling albums of all time. Her solo collections of songs in the late 1950s and early 1960s had not done well, a factor that prevented her from making more solo albums for a long time. *A Christmas Treasure,* which was released commercially by RCA in 1967, proved to be her last original American album, except for movie soundtracks, until 1983. (Some of her earlier records were re-released in the 1970s however.) It bothered Julie not to succeed in this one medium, especially since she considered herself primarily a singer and had had such fantastic success on stage, and singing in movies and on television. She envied Barbra Streisand's success in all three media as well as records.

One problem may have been that Julie had abhorred recording sessions until the one she did with Previn. "I admire his quiet affirmation that all is right," she said. "In one of the orchestrations on the Christmas album there was a top G at the end, and I hadn't sung a top G since 'I Could Have Danced All Night." He said I could do it, and I did it."

Some of the old Welsh and English Christmas carols they did were in odd keys, but Previn said "I really thing after one hearing she had two-thirds of it down cold. She evidently has instant retention for music. Working with her you find out why she made it so big. Singers are generally a dangerous, unpredictable lot. But Julie comes to any session completely prepared and knowing exactly what to do. She is totally willing to take suggestions, but I don't mean everybody can walk all over her. She is a very good singer who acts rather than a movie star who sings."

She and Previn worked doubly hard on the postproduction dubbing of her musical numbers for *Thoroughly Modern Millie.* Previn served as musical director on the movie, arranging and conducting the twelve musical numbers. Elmer Bernstein scored the instrumental portions of the movie, an unusual but workable bifurcated arrangement necessitated by neither man's complete availability to handle both jobs. Julie and André often worked at night at Twentieth Century–Fox instead of at Universal, because

Julie knew from *The Sound of Music* that the Fox sound facilities were vastly superior to those at Universal. Often Previn's wife, Dory, would be there watching, and Blake Edwards would meet them at the end of the evening, which was often topped off by the four of them going out for ice cream.

"There is, musically, nothing that Julie cannot do," said André Previn, who was then both the permanent conductor of the London Symphony Orchestra and an alumnus of Debbie Reynolds movies. "She is not Leontyne Price, nor should she be that kind of singer. When she was twelve she was on her way to being Gloria Jean, but what was that? She is naturally very musical, with a great love for music. She's an inveterate concert-goer. And the best present anyone can give Julie is a classical record. Her tastes are varied, but she likes the nineteenth century by far the best." Julie's favorite composition then was the *Second Symphony* of Rachmaninoff.

On October 18, 1992, Julie was the guest on the venerable BBC Radio program *Desert Island Discs*, on which celebrities share which items (mostly recordings) they would take with them if they were to be stranded on a desert island. Her choices, and her explanations for those choices, were revealing.

First she chose a recording of "Amberley Wild Brooks" by John Ireland, her first memory of music and a "reminder of my mother." Next she picked "The Lark Ascending" by Ralph Vaughan Williams, because it is "very pastoral" and reminiscent of her father. Her third selection was the Brahms Violin Concerto, which she "[listened to] a lot when I first came to New York for *The Boy Friend.* It helped to take the pressure off when I got lost in the music of it."

Pavarotti's recording of Puccini's opera *Turandot*, especially the aria "Nessun Dorma," with its hopeful message, "Vincero!" (I will conquer!) was her sole vocal choice. Ravel's Piano Concerto in G Major reminded her of when she and Blake were "courting." Aaron Copeland's *Rodeo* evoked her family in general, and she rounded out the list with Prokofiev's Piano Concerto No. 3 in C Major and Elgar's Introduction and Allegro for Strings, Opus 47.

She characterized her selections as "very romantic in nature" and "very British" to "remind me of England." Her favorite book remained T. H. White's *The Once and Future King*. She would take a piano to her desert island with the "hope that it would stay in tune," as her one allowed "luxury." She wished to have "order and safety" on the island, and "to keep out creepy crawlies." If she could bring only one record, it would be the Ravel.

Dory Previn, a lyricist, noticed that whenever Julie began to sing a brand new song, she would ask the lyricist, "What does the song mean?" "We would discuss lyrics, and sometimes she will even lead you into making a change."

Emma Kate increasingly showed creative tendencies, mainly by making up her own clever word-images and painting. "She's a worse romantic that I am," her mother said. "I wouldn't mind her being an actress if that's what she wants some day; I don't think I could stop her if I tried." Julie was determined that if Emma did want a career in entertainment, she would have all the dancing and drama lessons her mother never had and now sorely missed. One of Emma's favorite stuffed toys epitomized her daughter's character, in Julie's opinion. It was a white and purple fabric hippopotamus, about a foot long, around whose neck Emma had placed a dog's collar and leash. "That's my daughter," said Julie, "one day she'll put a leash on a hippopotamus."

Happy as Julie and Emma were in California, there were times when Julie became nostalgic for her old house in Walton-on-Thames. And she regretted that she seldom got to her cottage on Alderney, in the Channel Islands. (Her father looked after it, supervising its use by any members of her family who cared to stay there.) "I never intend to lose the cottage," she said. "It's sweet and small. Alderney is small enough and wild enough and free enough to be totally removed. For the first few days you damn near die and say, "Oh, I'll never stand all this wind through me," but it's such a totally fresh climate that you never want to leave, and when you do you're completely exhilarated."

Christmastime, in particular, made Julie yearn for colder weather than that of southern California. Beginning in 1967, she, Blake, and Emma went to Gstaad, Switzerland, for the holdiays. Blake's children, Jennifer and Geoffrey, joined them from London and Julie's maternal instincts quickly broadened to include them. Jenny and Geoffrey were five and three years older than Emma Kate, respectively, and they called their father's friend "Julie" almost from first meeting. With Blake, Jennifer and Geoffrey moved into Julie's Hidden Valley house in 1969, after the completion of *Darling Lili.*

Jennifer especially responded to Julie as she might to an older sister or youngish aunt. On the *Darling Lili* locations in France and Ireland Jenny and Julie sang a song about their expanded family that they had made up, to the tune of "My Favorite Things"; it began with "Blackie and Julie and Jenny and Geoffrey/Emma and..." and extended on to include half-brothers and sisters. For Julie it was the beginning of the big, happy, family unit that she had so long wished for. The biggest, best-paid movie star in the world, she said, "Emma Kate is my greatest production, and I plan to have lots more."

10

Falling *Star!*

A computer, had it been consulted in 1967, could not have put together a Hollywood movie more certain to become a hit. The star was the most beloved in the world. The director and producer had made the most successful film in history. The budget of $12 million was generous for 1968 and there was expensive location shooting in the south of France, Cape Cod, London, and New York. The songs were by George and Ira Gershwin, Kurt Weill, Noël Coward, and Irving Berlin. As befitted its glamorous subject, the $3 million worth of jewels were from Cartier and the clothes, the most extensive star wardrobe to date, were by Donald Brooks.

Yet *Star!*, about Gertrude Lawrence, starring Julie Andrews, directed by Robert Wise, produced by Saul Chaplin, and financed by Twentieth Century–Fox, who had been solvent again for three years running thanks to *The Sound of Music*, was the most complete disaster in moviemaking history until Michael Cimino's *Heaven's Gate* in 1981. Richard Zanuck, the head of production at Fox, termed *Star!* "my Edsel." "Jesus, but it was embarrassing," said another Fox executive after the highly ballyhooed picture was recut and suffered a disastrous rerelease under the title of *Those Were the Happy Times*.

Ironically, making the movie was a long series of happy times for all concerned and no one involved foresaw even a hint of the total artistic, critical, and commercial failure that *Star!* was to become. Wise had spent most of the three years since *The Sound of Music* preparing the picture, and Julie Andrews looked back on the year of her life spent as Gertrude Lawrence as "the most stimulating thing I've ever done—and the most exhausting—though it put me off rhinestones forever." For Julie, the biggest British musical comedy star since Gertrude Lawrence, the musical film was a fascinating study leading to her generally sympathetic understanding of a woman she never knew nor had even seen perform. The *Star!* experience revealed often eerie parallels in the lives of Andrews and Lawrence—even "one or two rather unpleasant things about myself that I'd rather not think about."

Julie was not yet seventeen when Lawrence died in 1952, shortly after her triumph as Anna opposite Yul Brynner in *The King and I* on Broadway. *Star!* only took Lawrence's life story up to 1941, when Julie was six. "I'd heard some scratchy old records of hers a few times, but that was about it," said Julie. Yet she was the first and only choice to play "Gertie" from her vaudeville debut at sixteen, through 95 percent of all the scenes in the movie. (Several child actresses portrayed the stage star from ages six to fourteen, the first five percent of the film, which was all done in black and white, documentary-style.)

Robert Wise had decided to make another film with Julie Andrews even before they began *The Sound of Music*, and he was smart enough to sign her up for an unnamed second film at the same salary, a comparatively meager $225,000 with no percentage of the profits. Max Lamb, Wise's story editor and a longtime Gertrude Lawrence enthusiast with a large collection of her records, was assigned to find another vehicle for Julie. Lamb convinced Wise that Lawrence's story was just the thing. "I had Max spend six months digging into the Lawrence legend to see what was possible," Wise recalled. "Then I took it to Julie. I wouldn't have made the picture without her; if she hadn't wanted to do it, I'd have been busy on something else. The great drive was not to do the Gertrude Lawrence story, and we were interested in it only as a starring vehicle for Julie. She was always in it."

Wise and Lamb did not assign a screenwriter, although stars almost always saw scripts before they committed to any property. Wise did not want to invest in a writer, buy up the rights to all the books about Gertrude Lawrence (not to mention the rights to all the songs she had sung), "and then have Julie turn it down, leaving me stuck with the Gertie Lawrence story." Instead, Lamb interviewed friends and associates of the late star to see what he could add to the existing written material which was long on quantity but short on depth and insight. As part of his research, Lamb flew to London to see Noël Coward and found him "enormously warm and easy to talk to."

Noël Coward was an important part of the Lawrence story and it would not have been possible to do the film without his cooperation. Wise had already been turned down by Beatrice Lillie who therefore was not portrayed at all in *Star!* despite her importance in her fellow performer's life. Wise recalled his nervous meeting with Coward in London. "If he didn't agree, I knew we'd have to give up the whole idea. But the first thing he said was, 'Who's going to portray me?' Daniel Massey [Coward's godson] was actually his choice, too. We'd been considering him on a list that included Robert Stephens and Peter Cook."

Ian McKellan also auditioned for the role of Noël Coward in *Star!* "I arrived on set, spoke some lines and sang 'Parisian Pierrot,'" he recalled. "When I finished there was spontaneous applause. I thought, and my agent thought, that was that: I had it. I was told it was between me and Dan Massey. Then the tests were sent out to America, to the producer, and word came back—Noël Coward decided his godson must play him."

Although Coward legally went along with the concept, he expressed his deep reservations to his diary after a visit with the English screenwriter, William Fairchild, and his colleague, David Stone. "We argued back and forth," Coward wrote of the "project of which I heartily disapprove." He found the casting of Julie as Gertie, whom he had first met when he was fifteen, "about as suitable as casting the late Princess Royal as Dubarry. However, she's a clever girl and will at least be charming and sing well. *Why* they are doing the film I shall never know. There isn't any real story beyond the fact that she started young in the theater, became an understudy, then a star, lived with Philip Astley, Bert Taylor, etc., married Richard Aldrich, and died. I really do think that the Hollywood mentality is worse than ever."

With Coward's reluctant promise of cooperation, Wise first mentioned the project to Julie at a lunch break during the filming of *The Sound of Music*, made longer by a spell of Alpine rain. As he sketched in the basic details of Lawrence's life, Julie said, "That sounds a lot like me...." Before the rain had stopped, she had agreed to the project as her second picture under her contract with Wise.

"Their lives are somewhat similar," the director explained. "Gertie was a product of music halls, a broken home, and step-parents, too. Physically there's a certain resemblance, although Julie's a far better singer than Gertie ever was. She was the proper age; we were taking Gertie from a young girl into her forties, and Julie can go either way. Both Julie and Gertie had great senses of humor. Gertie was a great clown and had a great love of gagging— Julie does, too."

Julie, who had first been approached to do a stage musical about Gertrude Lawrence when she was appearing in *My Fair Lady*, said that Wise "fired my imagination by saying he didn't want to do the usual, glamorous backstage sort of story," Julie said. "Somehow the way he spoke about the theater, how he wanted the draperies to be green velvet, and how he wanted to use old-fashioned theaters that Gertie used to play in, got me very excited."

Wise then went ahead and bought the rights to the books, including *Gertrude Lawrence as Mrs. A.*, by Richard Aldrich, her last husband, and Lawrence's memoir, *A Star Danced*. He even bought the rights to Lawrence's diaries, which indicated that the books and even some of her friends' and coworkers' memories had been somewhat exaggerated and embroidered.

The production obtained the rights to all the songs Lawrence had sung in public, including "Someone to Watch Over Me," "My Ship," "Someday I'll Find You," "The Physician," and "Jenny."

Fairchild then wrote the screenplay, which was not based on any one particular book, but rather was a composite, suggesting the flavor of Lawrence's on- and off-stage personalities between the two world wars.

In the two months of preproduction on *Star!*, February and March 1967, Julie was fitted for the record ninety-four separate costumes that she would wear in the film. With *The Boy Friend* and *Thoroughly Modern Millie* in her past, Julie was no stranger to the fashions of the 1920s that would predominate in the first half of the film and she was eagerly looking forward to her first fling into the 1930s. Donald Brooks was designing the clothes for his third movie, though he was costume designer for eight Broadway shows and ran a prestigious private design business, but this was the first in which he created costumes for the entire cast.

In designing "between twenty-five hundred and three thousand designs," Brooks said, "I didn't try to make replicas of the clothes of any particular period. Instead, Saul, Bob, and I all immersed ourselves in the various periods and I tried to make the clothes believable. The author establishes the character, and then it must be established visually. Bob looks for character in the face and setting. I look for texture, pattern, and color."

Studio tests led to thirty-six different sets of makeup for Julie's character and twenty different wigs, each of which could be reset significantly at least once. With these aids, during the actual shooting Julie could be forty first thing in the morning, twenty-two at lunch time, and sixteen at sunset, and one day she actually was those three ages in that sequence. To accommodate the wigs, which would also be important to her next movie, *Darling Lili*, Julie cut her short hair even shorter and let it go from lightened blonde back to her natural brown.

In pre-production Julie rehearsed dances with choreographer Michael Kidd since she was to appear in twenty-one of the film's twenty-four musical numbers. Despite her days in vaudeville, Julie was the first to admit, "I don't really dance; if they give me lots of fancy movements, I can make it *look* like I'm dancing." She also prerecorded six of the fifteen songs on which she soloed, including "My Ship," "Jenny," "Someone to Watch Over Me," and "Someday I'll Find You."

When actual filming began in mid-April, Julie began to wear the largest single wardrobe ever fitted onto an actress in one work. Out of a schedule of 149 shooting days, Julie was on camera on all but seventeen which happened to be mostly when Wise and his crew were in London filming childhood scenes with the six juvenile actresses who played Gertie as a girl. Of 1,400 separate camera setups, Julie appeared in 1,372. Wise defended this excessive use of his star by saying, "When a biographical story is being told in film, it is best to have the character be up on the screen nearly all the time rather than having other characters talk about her." Richard Crenna, who played Richard Aldrich, put it another way: "The rest of us are window dressing."

The film set yet another record, for the most sets ever assembled for one movie, 185 in all. There were twenty film sites in London, fourteen locations in New York (which were shot in only eighteen days), and historically important visits to the Cape Cod Playhouse in Dennis, Massachusetts and to the south of France for several scenes at a private, $2-million sea-coast villa called Medi Roc where Lawrence attempted, unsuccessfully, to effect a reconciliation with her daughter (played by Jenny Agutter), whom she had badly neglected in favor of her career.

For one week at the Lyceum Theatre in New York, the cast, abetted by nine hundred extras, simulated the 1926 opening of Gertrude Lawrence in the Gershwins' *Oh, Kay!* Julie sang "Someone to Watch Over Me." It had been six years since she had sung on a Broadway stage, and Julie felt "tingling all over, and suddenly realizing that I'm having the best of both worlds in one movie."

Richard Aldrich, who had been the producer at the Cape Cod Playhouse in 1939 when Gertrude Lawrence worked there, watched Crenna and Andrews recreate scenes of his life at the famous theater that was built in 1790. He saw the scene of his first encounter with Gertie inside the playhouse, she playing the temperamental big star, and he the cool, small-town businessman who was unimpressed. Aldrich also watched the actors run through a rain of rice, after the wedding, to a waiting 1935 Rolls-Royce. While he would make no public comment on Julie's portrayal of Gertie or on Richard Crenna's of himself, as he watched the scene in the playhouse he was heard to whisper, almost to himself, "Remarkable, how much…"

"When I got into the role," said Julie, "I couldn't wait to get my hands on all the things she had done. She was an incredibly multitalented lady. Our voices are different, but I suggested her inflections and cadences here and there. But the routine was unbelievably rigorous; it was like going into training. I got up at 5:45 every day and had to be on the set by 7:00 A.M., and sometimes I didn't get home until 8:00 in the evening. There were only three mornings when I wasn't needed for that first call."

Even on rehearsal days Julie had to go into the studio at 9:00 A.M. and stay until 6:00 P.M., and since she was in virtually every frame of the movie there were three separate shut-downs of filming to rehearse the song and dance numbers. Her lunch hours, usually from 1 to 2:30, were taken up with costume fittings, interviews, out-of-town visitors, and her agents and other business associates. Invariably she would clear out her dressing room for fifteen or twenty minutes of "putting my feet up," which seemed to get her through the rest of the work day. On rare occasions Emma Kate visited the set of *Star!* Every day a doctor arrived to give Julie a vitamin B shot. And at the end of every work day Blake Edwards would arrive to take her home.

Although her father Ted Wells, and her stepmother Win came to Los Angeles for a long visit during the making of *Star!*, Julie's real and almost sole preoccupation was Gertrude Lawrence. "I can't converse on anything outside this movie," she said in the middle of filming. "I just manage to read the morning paper every day and when I go home at night I collapse. The pace of this film is unrelenting and merciless. The whole thing is so fast and furious it's like a gloriously dangerous game which hopefully one will win."

There was, however, the time and the need during the making of *Star!* to think about Gertrude Lawrence: "I found myself reflecting on her a lot, and I realized that in many ways she was a sad and lonely woman. Sometimes I'd get muddled—where did Gertrude leave off and where did I begin?"

To help her sort out the difference, Julie kept a file on her desk labeled "Impressions of Gertrude Lawrence–Confidential." Julie's research showed that Lawrence was "definitely a kook, eccentric, glamorous, and witty. There were the obvious biographical facts we had in common, like separated parents and starting in vaudeville."

Both actresses also had a first marriage ending in divorce, one daughter, and a love affair with a producer. Lawrence made her professional debut at the age of sixteen, in Brixton, singing "Piccadilly" with her father and his woman partner and lover, though not legally Gertie's stepmother. Julie had also played Brixton, when she was fourteen, with her mother and stepfather. (On the same bill then, with Julie, Ted, and Barbara, was Beryl Reid, who played Gertie's "stepmother's" scenes in *Star!*) Julie and Gertie both had played in the Welsh city of Swansea, and both achieved significant later success playing Eliza Doolittle. Moss Hart had directed Gertie in *Lady in the Dark* and directed Julie in *My Fair Lady* fifteen years later.

Julie discovered several other traits that she and Gertrude Lawrence had in common. "We both whistled a lot and we both were always lapsing into bits of Cockney. She had a habit of singing a high note to relieve the tension. I do the same thing, sing as loud and as high as I can. She was extravagant. I am too, even more so after I played her. She would fill her dressing room with flowers; she once bought a large cherry tree because it was in bloom. I'm certainly not as extravagant of gesture, but I think I understand her quite well and I know how she felt. When you're in the theater on matinee day, from noon until midnight, you don't see daylight. You want some living things in your room."

The extravagance parallel had a limit: Lawrence at her peak was earning $3,500 a week on stage while in a good week Julie made $30,000 or more in movies. Also different, Lawrence went $75,000 into debt and drove to bankruptcy court in a Rolls Royce

(Julie was still making do with her little Ford). At the end of making *Star!*, in December 1967, Julie was buying expensive presents. "I'm spending much more now," she said at the time. "I figure, what the hell, since I'm playing her I might as well spend like her. I went berserk for Christmas. Whether it will disappear when the next movie comes along, I don't know."

Another result of playing Gertrude Lawrence was that Julie renewed her interest in expensive clothes and became interested for the first time in jewels ("I wish I could have kept them all"). She found happiness in the designs of Donald Brooks. He went on to create her clothes for *Darling Lili* as well as for her closet. Brooks designed the stunning long, billowy black gown she wore to the 1968 Academy Awards, where she presented the Oscar for Best Picture to Walter Mirisch, her *Hawaii* producer, for *In the Heat of the Night.*

The "hateful things" that Julie found she and Gertie had in common were that they had "an absolute fear of any kind of commitment" and that they were "always putting on an act. She would play at being a mother one minute, a gardener the next, a shopper the next. I'm rather like that."

When she said this, Julie was in her dressing room about to entertain a visitor at lunch. In a perfect, probably unconscious illustration of her last point, she called out to "Mom," her hairdresser and chief fusser (who was in the kitchen), Lorraine Roberson "Is there anything I can do to help?" Julie almost certainly had never helped "Mom" make lunch for company (and had no business in the kitchen at the best of times). But the moment involved an uncomfortably hard truth, calling for a shifting of gears.

Most of all, Julie disliked Lawrence's angry outbursts, being intensely controlled herself. "I'm not as fiery a temperament as she was. She was not a terribly nice person; in fact, she was a real bitch at times."

For that reason perhaps, and because up to that point in her career she had portrayed fictional heroines (with the one exception of the only semi-fictional and highly romanticized Maria von

Trapp), Julie said "this feels like the first *character* I've ever done. But walking the fine line between caricature and tribute, and avoiding impersonations is not easy."

Robert Wise was troubled during the production of *Star!* by Julie's failure to exploit some of the more flamboyant aspects of Lawrence's personality in her portrayal. "If Julie has anything, it is a quality of honesty and truthfulness. That has made her doubtful and given her difficulty with some of the theatricalities of Gertie's behavior. If she has had to work hard on anything, it has been on the volatile and hammy aspects of Gertie. She doesn't quite realize yet how many things she can make her own."

"This is not an attempt at a totally truthful portrait of Gertrude Lawrence," Julie said, "and I didn't feel I was *doing* anything like her. I certainly was not trying to sing like her; I don't think her voice was particularly strong or pretty. When you try to *be* someone, the temptation is to lay it on with mannerisms and speech. But if I did that, I'd only be applying it rather than feeling it myself. So the result was part me, part script, and part her. It was pleasant to play—to be— somebody like that for real for once, but I was not trying to be faithful to the way people remember her—I don't think I could be."

The world premiere of *Star!* at the Dominion Theatre in London had been originally scheduled for July 4, 1968, which would have been Gertrude Lawrence's sixty-seventh birthday. But the opening had been postponed until September 11, then moved up to July 18, in both cases to accommodate the Duke and Duchess of Kent, who were the royal patrons of the premiere for the benefit of the National Advertising Benevolent Society. When the night finally came, Saul Chaplin and Robert Wise and their wives, Darryl and Richard Zanuck, Richard Crenna and his wife, Donald Brooks, William Fairchild, David and Helen Gurley Brown (he was the Fox vice president in charge of story operations), as well as others involved with the picture appeared. So did Noël Coward, Dame Edith Evans, Lord Louis Mountbatten, Cathleen Nesbitt, and Julie's mother, father, stepmother, and two of her brothers.

Noël Coward had a prepremiere cocktail party at his river suite in the Savoy Hotel, for some friends who remembered Gertrude Lawrence. Among them were Cathleen Nesbitt and Anna Massey, whose father, Raymond, had played Higgins in *Pygmalion* opposite Lawrence, and whose brother Daniel was playing Coward in the movie. Although in the end he had contributed heavily to the screenplay, writing his own dialogue for Daniel Massey without screen credit but with a sizable stipend, Coward was skeptical about the final result.

As his group was leaving the Savoy for the Dominion, he said, "It will unquestionably be a marvelous commercial film, and Julie and Danny will be marvelous. So will all those nostalgic, unforgett-able songs. But it won't bear the slightest possible resemblance to the Gertie we knew."

Thus *Star!* arrived though its star didn't. The airplane that had been chartered to stand by at Heathrow Airport to fetch Julie from the Brussels location of *Darling Lili* had never left London. The flower-packed suite booked for her at the Dorchester Hotel would not be used. At the last minute, word came from Brussels that night shooting on *Darling Lili* involving thousands of extras would keep Julie there. The Zanucks were furious and blamed Blake Edwards, Paramount Pictures, and professional jealousy. Crowds, both inside and outside the theater, did not get the word immediately and, disbelievingly and in vain, searched for the star. They were shat-tered when she did not show up. Even the Duchess of Kent asked "where's Julie?"

Without Julie, *Star!* was shown to the public for the first time and the premiere audience came down firmly on two sides: those who remembered Gertrude Lawrence on stage resented the harsh portrait of her as written and played; those who didn't remember her seemed as charmed by *Star!* as they had been by any other Julie Andrews musical.

The London critics divided approximately the same way, al-though they were somewhat harder on the film for taking liberties with a relatively recent life. On the other hand, one critic predicted

that the Dominion Theatre, where *The Sound of Music* had played
for four years, would be given over to Julie Andrews again for the
next four years in *Star!*

After seeing the movie, Noël Coward wrote in his diary that
Julie was "talented, charming, efficient, and very pretty but *not*
very like Gertie. Danny Massey was excellent as me and had the
sense to give an impression rather than try to imitate me. He was
tactless enough to sing better than I do."

When the 174-minute plus intermission musical movie opened
in New York in the fall of 1968, the critics were nothing short of
scathing. Julie also missed that premiere, again pleading pressing
scenes on *Darling Lili*. WCBS-TV's Leonard Harris, speaking for the
majority, said, "*Star!* is a sort of gentile *Funny Girl*, and not nearly
as good. It is a clichéd cataloging of the life and hard times of
Gertrude Lawrence...and it compounds its spurious attitudes
towards show business with its terrible handling of the actual
performance numbers."

Although intermittently entertaining, *Star!* was less than very
good but not the horror most critics made it out to be. Massey's
Oscar-nominated portrayal of Coward alone was worth the price of
admission. And Julie's wistful, solitary rendering of George and Ira
Gershwin's "Someone to Watch Over Me" was a remarkable moment
on film, coming from somewhere deep inside.

Audiences, for whatever reason, stayed away from the road
show release in America, although the film was a modest success in
its first weeks in London. Twentieth Century–Fox withdrew the
picture and rereleased it after some cutting as a regular feature at a
regular price. Still, even the hard core Andrews fans didn't go to see
it, and *Star!* was recalled altogether on July 1, 1969. Further cuts
were made by the studio, taking the film down to two hours,
without consulting Robert Wise. The title was changed first to
Gertie Was a Lady then to *Those Were the Happy Times*. But in
rerelease, the movie lasted only a week.

In those days, however, Hollywood tended to reward expensive
major efforts at Oscar time. *Star!* received eight Academy Award
nominations in 1969, including one in the supporting actor category

for Daniel Massey, one for the costumes of Donald Brooks, and one for the title song by Sammy Cahn and Jimmy Van Heusen. The movie won no Oscars.

Every bit as inexplicably as *The Sound of Music* had become such a phenomenal success and confirmed Julie's position as the box office queen of Hollywood, *Star!* did the opposite. The press and the public, both of whom had adored her for years, suddenly seemed to turn against her. And the turning point, if there was just one, had to be the world premiere of *Star!* in London when Julie failed to appear.

"Of all the premieres," she said, "this was the one I really wanted to go to. This was home, one's family, royalty, and all one's chums. I'd had a dress designed in Dublin, and of all the movies I made, this was the one I cared about most. But they changed the date twice—it was in my contract with Paramount that I would have the night of July 4th off, no matter what—and we were in Belgium, behind schedule and with hundreds of extras involved. Up until three hours before the premiere I thought I was going to make it. Blake had figured out how to use a double for me in a long shot. But as the time got closer, we realized that even with that long shot, which he didn't really want to do, and having the cast and crew wait another hour or so, I could still only fly to London just in time to get to the theater, walk through the front door, and walk right out again. I wouldn't even have got to see my family or friends. So I didn't go."

Both Julie and Blake were embittered by the reaction of the British and American press toward her nonattendance. Blake was even madder because Twentieth Century–Fox executives had called their counterparts at Paramount in Hollywood and begged them to call Blake in Brussels to persuade him to give Julie the night off.

"How could anyone doubt that she wanted to go to the opening and that I wanted her to go?" Blake asked. "It would have been good for Paramount and good for us, too. But it was just impossible."

Both studios were angry with Blake for what they considered his evil influence and final authority over his ladyfriend and star. Paramount was particularly upset since he was spending their money hand over fist and was millions over the budget of *Darling Lili*. (So was she: Julie demanded, and got, eleven dressing rooms at Paramount, for no apparent reason.) What was one night—even with nine hundred extras—more or less? No one in management at either studio doubted that Gertrude Lawrence, faced with the same situation, would have told her producer-director, even if he had been her lover, to go to hell and flown to London for at least two days.

11

The $24 Million Valentine

Despite their stated reservations about, and innate instincts against, working together while romantically involved, Julie and Blake felt committed to *Darling Lili, or Where Were You on the Night You Said You Shot Down Baron von Richtofen?* (The title was shortened on location in Europe when, but not necessarily because, the budget was lengthened.) *Darling Lili* was an original Blake Edwards and William Peter Blatty "play with music," using, as *Star!* had, existing songs of the period—in this case circa 1915, during World War I. Henry Mancini and Johnny Mercer, who had written the Oscar-winning songs "Moon River" for Edwards's *Breakfast at Tiffany's* and "Days of Wine and Roses" for the director's film of the same name, wrote seven new songs for *Darling Lili*, six of them for Julie. These included "Whistling Away the Dark," "I'll Give You Three Guesses," "Smile Away Each Rainy Day," and "A Girl in No Man's Land."

Julie, in her role as British singing idol Lili Smith and German spy Lili Schmidt, would also sing "Keep the Home Fires Burning," "It's a Long Way to Tipperary," "There's a Long, Long Trail A-Winding," and the French national anthem, "La Marseillaise." The chief target of Lili's espionage is a handsome American dawn-patrol air squadron commander who knows all the crucial Allied aerial and troop maneuvers, played by Rock Hudson.

161

In the film, Lili tries to extract secrets from the commander by
seducing him, but falls in love with him instead. Julie, with Blake's
help, was changing her image even further in *Lili* by doing a comic
striptease in a theater where she was only supposed to sing (the
strip is done in a jealous fit to make Hudson's character mad); a
little wrestling match with Rock in bed; and a shower scene in
which she is bare to her cleavage and he is fully clothed.

"I'm trying to be very still in this one," said Julie, during filming.
"Lili isn't a lady who is bouncy. She's somebody who's cool and in
perfect control, and then gets all gibberish."

"We're playing this for realism," said Blake. "The sets, the
action, the people are all as honest as we can make them. Julie
plays an English lady who is loved by England and turns out to be a
German spy. The humor in it arises out of the characters. For
example, Lance Percival is a cowardly Englishman who can only fly
if he drinks, and he likes to drink, so he flies. He crashes and
destroys six planes. There's absolutely nothing inconceivable about
his character."

The flying scenes alone guaranteed a big budget for *Darling
Lili*, as did shooting on location in Ireland, Belgium, and France.
Julie's salary for the picture was $1,100,000 against ten percent of
the gross receipts, a new Hollywood record. Blake, as producer,
director, and coauthor of the screenplay, was also well compensated. Initially the movie was budgeted at $14 million but *Darling
Lili* went over budget in production, and cost its studio millions
more than had been projected. More overage was paid in interest to
investors and taxes because of the delayed release and for the
marketing of the movie, such as it was. This profligacy contributed
to the deaths of movie musicals, the old studio system, and the film
career of Julie Andrews.

Filming began pleasantly enough, on the Paramount lot, in
March 1968. It was a congenial set, partly because Blake had his
handpicked associates around him. His stepfather was serving as
studio production manager and his uncle, Owen Crump, was
executive producer of the movie. Donald Brooks designed Julie's
costumes. Julie was brand new to Paramount and despite the flap

over the *Star!* premiere, there was great excitement at having her on the lot. *Darling Lili* was the object of a great deal of curiosity, but the interior scenes in the early days of shooting posed no particular problems.

The day they shot the shower scene, the director, the star, and her co-star were having a great time, and so was the crew. The scene had been shot three times, and Blake was satisfied with the third take, when Julie, soaking wet, asked "Darling, would you like to do another take?"

"Would you?"

"Not if you're happy."

"You know what you need is to find a fellow, settle down, and marry him."

"'ood 'ave me?" (Lapsing into Eliza-like Cockney.)

"Some damn fool director."

They kissed, and she reached to put her arms around him. "Oh, no, you don't," he said. "You're all wet, and I don't have a change of clothes with me."

Blake said, more seriously, "I'd marry her tomorrow, but she can't marry me right now—her divorce isn't final. We're together, that's the important thing. Of course, if I do marry the leading lady I'll get ten percent of the profits of the picture," he joked.

Up until the *Darling Lili* company moved to its Dublin location, Julie and Blake continued to live in their separate houses. They decided to move in together at Carton, a castle outside the Irish capital that doubled as a movie set in several sequences. It was elegant, private, wooded, and peaceful. Julie said she had never been happier anywhere. Carton was large enough to have four gate houses, several cottages, and unlimited livestock. When Rock Hudson hurt his foot, Julie was able to play Lady Bountiful again, and come down from the big house with a basket of goodies and a solicitous concern for his health. She went for long walks in the summer rain along a secluded path. The whole atmosphere seemed so right that she and Blake planned to rent the castle again the next summer for a vacation though at the last minute they canceled and went on a shorter holiday in Hawaii.

They finally had agreed to live together openly because, in Blake's words, "It seemed dumb not to admit we were in love." Julie, typically less sure of herself in the situation, "kept telling him it wasn't going to work," she recalled.

The Irish weather was extremely uncooperative on the picture. When a gray day was called for in the script, there was endless brilliant sunshine. There were several night scenes, and summer nights in Ireland began at 11:00 P.M. and lasted only until about 3:30 A.M. The Irish crews were not used to big Hollywood productions, especially musicals, and their uncertain work slowed down the schedule considerably. But when the company left Ireland, the crew serenaded Julie with "For She's a Jolly Good Fellow" and "Come Back to Erin."

When *Darling Lili* moved on to Brussels there were more weather problems, more night shooting, and the added obstacle of bureaucratic inefficiency when it came to granting official permission for the use of buildings, a problem that was to be even worse in Paris.

"Everything that could have gone wrong went wrong," Julie remembered. Filming was costing upwards of $70,000 a day and because of the variable weather, scenes weren't matching properly and had to be reshot. One cloudy day when sunshine was needed, they were filming at Diane de Poitiers' sixteenth-century villa, Chateau d'Anet, at Eure-et-Loire, outside Paris. Blake was unsuccessfully trying to match outdoor close-ups of Julie and Rock with footage that had been shot in Ireland. *Darling Lili* was now five weeks behind schedule and an estimated $2 million beyond budget. Although he wanted to reshoot several scenes in Europe, Paramount summoned Edwards and his company back to Hollywood.

Julie enjoyed her European locations and working with Blake. "I was nervous at first," she said, "but this is all kind of fun. Blake very kindly defers to me when it comes to the singing, and if I want to redo something, he lets me redo it. Best of all is that we're together."

Blake, between shots and bouts of bad weather, played Frisbee, and took home movies of Julie and his children, Jennifer, then twelve, and Geoffrey, then nine, who were staying with the couple in a suite at the Bristol Hotel in Paris. (Emma was visiting her father on *The Seagull* location in Stockholm.) During this phase of *Darling Lili*, Julie went shopping in Parisian boutiques and improved her French, a lifelong ambition, by speaking it to the girls who worked in the boutiques and waiters. She mothered Geoffrey and Jennifer, often in a mock–Mary Poppins voice.

Even back at the studio the production was troubled and extravagant. And with each rumor from the set, Julie's press worsened. Suddenly, the Paramount publicity department found itself with more major stars making movies on the lot than at any time in more than a decade. Barbra Streisand and Yves Montand were shooting *On a Clear Day You Can See Forever*, John Wayne was making *True Grit*, Lee Marvin, Jean Seberg, and Clint Eastwood were finishing *Paint Your Wagon*, and Julie and Rock Hudson were filming *Darling Lili*. The studio decided to gather them together one afternoon for a group picture full of stars; a type of publicity photo that hadn't been seen for a long time from any studio.

The actors, uncommonly, were all close to on time, except for Julie who didn't show at all. The other stars, including Hudson, waited, and John Wayne said to Robert Evans, Paramount's head of production, "Are you going to furnish chairs while we wait for the queen?" Evans himself went to the *Darling Lili* set and found her shooting a difficult crying scene that she had to do over and over again. Edwards told Evans he would not interrupt shooting for a publicity photograph, which Evans was forced to tell the other stars, who posed without her. The next morning Julie went to the dressing rooms of Barbra Streisand and some of the others, to apologize for holding them up for nothing.

Blake wanted to return to Europe to reshoot some scenes, but the studio turned him down. The Edwards self-indulgence, or perfectionism depending upon one's viewpoint, had already left Paramount with "$15 million of film and no picture," remarked one top studio production executive. That same executive daily observed Julie's increasing dependence on Blake to make most major decisions. "She's like locked up in a room," he said. "She doesn't make a move without his permission."

Some individual scenes in *Darling Lili* were interesting, conceded the few Paramount officials who had seen the rushes, but they didn't add up to a marketable film of any sort, much less a big Julie Andrews road show, which is exactly what *Darling Lili* would have to be to have any chance of recouping the investment. The opening of the film was postponed for several months, to the spring of 1970, in the hope that it could be salvaged. Edwards spent the extra months of 1969 completely reassembling, recutting and rescoring the movie. In the meantime the interest and taxes on the unreleased film were costing even more money. The total cost of *Darling Lili,* including marketing, ballooned to about $24 million.

Blake's excesses and Julie's seemingly callous superstar behavior quickly caused the press, even in her native England, to attack them with all knives bared. Even the old weekly *Life* magazine, which loved movies and movie stars more than any other mass circulation periodical and had glowingly given Julie the cover in 1965 for *The Sound of Music,* refused to run a second cover story on Julie written by their Hollywood correspondent, John Hallowell, because "it wasn't bitchy enough."

Joyce Haber, a syndicated columnist whose home newspaper was the *Los Angeles Times,* in her heyday ran a series of "blind" items about celebrities, usually involving their alleged sexual exploits. The personalities were always identified by nicknames or initials only. In the case of Julie, Blake, and Rock Hudson, Haber had used the not very subtle appellations of "Miss P and P (Prim and Proper); Mr. X, the director of a major musical, now being filmed, who is conducting an affair with its leading lady, Miss P and P; and Mr. V V (Visually Virile)."

Joyce Haber contended that Julie and Blake had been making fun of Hudson for his allegedly less-than-manly behavior on the set. The columnist reported that Blake had said, "I don't understand people like that," and that Julie had said to Rock, "Remember, *I'm* the leading lady." Haber also claimed that Mr. V V had gone for a weekend to San Francisco and visited one of his favorite leather

With director Blake Edwards on location in Ireland for *Darling Lili*, 1968

Alone with her thoughts during a break from filming *Darling Lili*.

With Omar Sharif in her
"comeback" movie,
The Tamarind Seed, 1974 JEWEL
PRODUCTIONS/PIMLICO FILMS

Julie's only nightclub act,
Caesar's Palace, Las Vegas,
1976 TERRY NELSON

With Rudolph Nureyev in *Julie Andrews' Invitation to the Dance,* 1980
CBS TELEVISION

With Sara Stimson and Walter Matthau in the remake of *Little Miss Marker,* 1979 UNIVERSAL PICTURES

With Dudley Moore
in *10*, 1979
ORION PICTURES
COMPANY

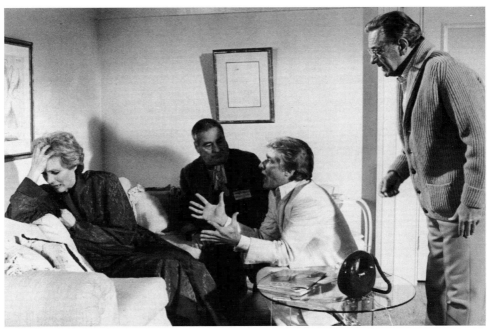

With the other Tinseltown loonies in *S.O.B.*, 1981. Left to right, Robert
Webber, Richard Mulligan and William Holden.
LORIMAR PRODUCTIONS INC.

Julie was literally close to home in *That's Life*, 1986. The movie was filmed on the Malibu property she owned with her husband, writer-director Blake Edwards, and her screen family was played by Jack Lemmon (*center*), his son Chris, Julie's stepdaughter Jennifer Edwards (*left*) and daughter Emma Walton. COLUMBIA PICTURES.

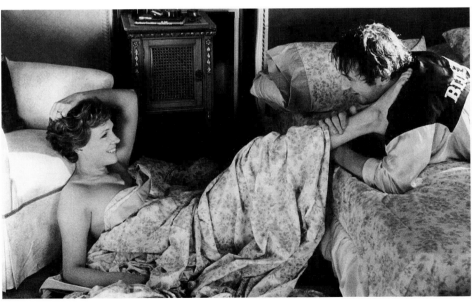

In her finest screen portrayal since *The Americanization of Emily*, Julie has a brief affair with Liam Neeson in *Duet for One*, 1986. CANNON FILMS

Her last movie, until now, opposite Marcello Mastroianni, was *A Fine Romance*, 1992.
ACADEMY ENTERTAINMENT.

In full "drag" for the stage version of *Victor/Victoria*, 1995

A publicity still for her failed sitcom, *Julie,* 1992
ABC TELEVISION

Julie refuses to accept her Tony nomination as Best Actress in a Musical after a matinee, with the press forewarned. She said she preferred to stand with the "egregiously overlooked," who included her husband and everyone else associated with the show; May 8, 1996. AP/ED BAILEY bars, only to walk in the door and find Mr. X leaning against the bar.

Julie and Blake both said that he could not have been in San Francisco at the time that Haber contended he had been, "But suing her would have dignified her," said Julie, who had been the victim of previous attacks by Haber and would be the subject of many more. Julie's only revenge came in her widely quoted remark: "They should give Haber open-heart surgery and go in through the feet." Blake's revenge came twelve years later, in his movie *S.O.B.*, which had been inspired by his and Julie's negative experiences in Hollywood after *Darling Lili*. Loretta Swit played the gossip columnist based on Haber, who by then had long since been fired by the *Los Angeles Times*.

The last straw, even for the few remaining pro-Andrews members of the American press, came in February of 1969. The occasion was Alan Jay Lerner's twenty-fifth anniversary as a librettist and lyricist and a testimonial dinner for the benefit of the American Academy of Dramatic Arts. All the stars who had sung his songs and many who had not were providing the evening's entertainment. Julie was one of four cochairmen, with Rex Harrison, Richard Burton, and Barbra Streisand. Burton was busy filming in Europe and Streisand was excused, with Lerner's permission and urging, because she was needed in Hollywood for *On a Clear Day*. That left Julie and Rex Harrison, performing songs from *My Fair Lady*, as the highlights of the evening.

The affair was held on a Sunday night at New York's Waldorf-Astoria Hotel, and most out-of-town guests flew in the Friday before, just in time for rehearsals. That same Friday evening, Julie called Alan Lerner from California at just about the time she was due to arrive in New York. She said that she was terribly sorry, but she had a spot on her throat and the doctor had told her she shouldn't go to New York; besides, Blake was sick with bronchial pneumonia and she had to stay at home and take care of him. Lerner, of course, was the one person who couldn't plead with her to relent, or tell her to come off it, so he said he understood. His wife, Karen Lerner, however, didn't understand, and she tried everything she could think of to get Julie to honor her long-standing commitment, even resorting to calling André Previn, Lerner's collaborator on *Coco*, in London, to get him to call his old friend Julie.

Despite the worst snowstorm of the season, which had begun to fall at midnight on Saturday, on Sunday evening an estimated two-thirds of the 2,500 ticket-buyers managed to appear at the benefit. Many had walked in high boots down a deserted Park Avenue through deep drifts of snow. Harrison sang "I've Grown Accustomed To Her Face," but the familiar face wasn't there. "I Could Have Danced All Night" was quietly dropped from the program and the only reference to Julie was made by the Master of Ceremonies, cartoonist Al Capp, who read congratulatory telegrams. Capp said, "The one we love the most was from the universally beloved Julie Andrews, which says, "I can't make it." It is signed by her doctor, Sam Shepard, and I believe him and I believe her."

Haber devoted a full syndicated column to Julie's no-show at the Lerner tribute in New York. "Poor Julie will soon run out of excuses," wrote the columnist, "and what will her fans, her public defenders, say then? (I assure you, she has few important defenders in the industry.)"

While Blake tried to salvage *Darling Lili* in the cutting room, Julie returned to television. The commercially and critically successful *The Julie Andrews Show*, originally shown in 1965, had been successfully rebroadcast in 1968. Whatever her falling fortunes in movies, she was still considered a big deal on television.

Despite her feeling that television involved too many compromises in too little time, in November 1969 Julie taped a second special for NBC. *An Evening with Julie Andrews and Harry Belafonte* was directed, at her request, by Gower Champion with Michel Legrand as musical director. She agreed to do the show essentially because Hathaway House, the home for disturbed boys on the old Cecil B. De Mille estate in Hollywood that was her chief charity at the time, was offered the chance to produce the show and earn a percentage of the profits.

The special was staged with just the two performers on camera, singing virtually every song together or to each other, sometimes romantically, as they did for "Scarborough Fair." Champion explained the format by saying, "The really memorable TV specials had been twos: Merman and Martin, Julie and Carol." Belafonte was allowed one calypso number, and Julie had a fast finale medley of *My Fair Lady* and *Mary Poppins*.

The pairing proved to be something of a breakthrough for television in terms of race relations. Belafonte, in an appearance on a Petula Clark special the previous year, had been the focal point of a major scandal when Petula merely touched his arm. This time, he said, "I had no self-consciousness about how we'd relate and I was convinced that Julie had no hangups either. There was no network censorship and Gower never pulled back because of color. We cavort around the stage holding hands, dance and sing cheek to cheek—she's biting and kicking me all through the show. It could have been Frank Sinatra or Robert Goulet instead of me, or Lena Horne instead of her."

Julie, who picked most of the songs for the special after several weeks' close attention to the pop stations on the radio in her—at last—new white Mercedes, succumbed to the finale medley after watching a Lena Horne special and finding herself "never so happy as when she finally settled down to sing 'Stormy Weather.' If I reacted that way to her, I thought maybe some people would feel cheated if I didn't sing something of the past."

She still found working in television "rushed and different, despite a self-imposed ten-week rehearsal schedule, a huge budget, and no distracting audiences for either rehearsals or the final taping." When Julie encountered Carol Burnett in a corridor at NBC, where she was also taping, Julie said, "How do you do it every week? You must have a marvelous nanny."

A friend once described Julie as a lady of standards where men were concerned: "She's either dating or she's married." The situation with Blake didn't fit either category and it began to make her uncomfortable. Then his son Geoffrey came to live with Blake and Julie at her house in Beverly Hills and daughter Jenny soon followed, since she and Julie had developed a particularly strong relationship during the summer spent in Europe filming *Darling Lili*. "We could tell the kids were worried about our living together," Blake recalled. "To them, marriage seemed important."

"So I finally decided what the hell," said Julie. "It was just a piece of paper, and anyway it felt right."

The wedding took place on November 12, 1969 and was held in secret at the Hidden Valley house, at one o'clock in the afternoon, "In the garden by the waterfall," Blake said, "because it's Julie's favorite place." They bought wedding rings and got blood tests from the family doctor the day before the wedding and left the house at eight in the morning on the day of the wedding to get a license outside of Los Angeles County so the press wouldn't find out. Julie informed the staff only that morning, and the children only when they came home from school at noon. "Otherwise they'd have wanted to take the day off from school," Blake explained. Blake and Julie got married, then attended the first screening of *Darling Lili* at Paramount later that afternoon.

A legal family at last, Blake and Julie Edwards bought a bigger house in Beverly Hills and built a beach house at Paradise Cove in Malibu. Under the circumstances, Julie and Blake were pleased with *Darling Lili* and Paramount's decision to release it as a road show in New York and Los Angeles in the spring of 1970. Both Andrews and Edwards seemed to have held on to their professional possibilities and Jennifer had made a creditable acting debut as Heidi in a television version of the classic story.

"From the moment we got married a new quality was added," said Blake, "and we said to each other, 'There's a kind of commitment we've just made that I don't think we made before.' Early on we had certain realities to face. Although Julie's career was important to her, we also had a large family. That's not to say chauvinistically that a woman's place is in the home. But I might survive without the family. I couldn't survive without my profession. I had a bit of trouble in the beginning; it was a kind of childish jealousy. We men endow our women with a bit of mother image, and when our woman turns her attention towards her career and the men in that career, whoever they are—agents, leading men, whoever they are—a little bit of jealousy creeps up. We had a couple of good long talks about it, because Julie won't let me get away with talking rubbish. If she sees me becoming too childish, her favorite phrase is 'Bullshit, Blackie!' In the face of that, what can you do?"

The two-career problem was temporarily solved by the failure of *Darling Lili*. Although many critics liked the movie and it broke box office records in its initial release at Radio City Music Hall in New York, the film didn't do well in the rest of the country or overseas. Suddenly Julie Andrews was box office poison; the two failures in a row finished her movie career, and she was actually paid $1 million *not* to make a filmed version of the Broadway musical *She Loves Me*, a humiliation never suffered by another star before or since. MGM also dropped plans to film Irving Berlin's *Say It With Music*, which Blake and Julie were to have done together.

"I was depressed by the failure of *Star!* and *Darling Lili*," she said, "and I regretted not going into another musical right away to make up for them. But musicals, big or small, just weren't being made then.

"It was really like coming out of a long tunnel—I'd done nothing but work for so long, and I felt great exhaustion. I'm usually very honest with myself, and I think I'd admit it now if I felt I was particularly difficult on the set of *Star!* and *Darling Lili*. I was very tired, and late a number of times, usually because they'd scheduled four or five costume fittings when I should have been eating breakfast or lunch. I decided I was damned well going to get something to eat, and to hell with what people thought. There are times when you have to be rather ruthless if you are trying to survive."

The press, which had already turned against her, played its part in her fast professional demise, a fact which has made Julie timid about interviews ever since. "There's an unwritten law in Hollywood that says once you're on a pedestal let's throw some rocks and knock her off it," she said. Blake termed the attacks on her "vicious" and said they came about because she was "a threat to a lot of ladies and some gentlemen, too, because she appears to be something they have made up."

A changing Hollywood, having created Julie Andrews and used her up, was now ready to throw her out. She wouldn't make another movie until 1974, and that was made at foreign locations for Blake Edwards as part of her English television deal; her next film was made another for five years after *that*—also for Blake—and this time it was only a supporting part. Their fourth film together, *S.O.B.* (1981) would finally tell some of the story of their post-*Darling Lili* frustrations and the decline of both their careers.

In retrospect, it seemed that Hollywood didn't know what to do with Julie Andrews, her wholesome image that she had tried so hard to change, and the director who had helped her to change it. "At the time I didn't think about it," she said. "Trends change, and this year's hit is soon forgotten. How to keep up is the problem. There's a line in *S.O.B.* that says, "Every time I think I know where it's at, it's usually somewhere else." You can only try to do what pleases you. I just tried to pick nice roles."

12

The Vanilla Moments

In 1970 what Julie needed most after her professional debacle and new romance and marriage was time off. "She needs a period of belonging to herself," said her friend Elsie Giorgi. "Anybody who's gone through what she had deserves it. She is thirty-four going on eighteen. But now she is learning to be with herself, and her future happiness depends on how well she learns it. She is strong, though, because she exists through herself and not through the limelight. She writes her own dialogue."

Her friend Svetlana Beriosova agreed: "Julie works just as hard at her life as she does in her profession."

When she herself looked at her life in her early thirties, Julie decided that she had been "sublimely lucky; one should be fairly happy," but added, "it's only later that you gather it all together and see what it means. I was one of those people who was able to learn by doing on the job and get away with it. Half the time I was running to keep up with myself trying to learn what everybody thought I knew."

She worried about her pristine image which the public was apparently then resisting any alteration of, "only to the extent that I would hate to be totally bracketed. There is probably nothing I *couldn't* play, but it is hard enough to find the roles I can do well. I have an enormous inferiority complex when I work with very good actors. I often feel so shallow in my work, and I would love to have a technique to fall back on. On Broadway I never felt quite *enough*. I had to pick myself up by the scruff and give more than I thought I had. I'd be devastated if I had to do Shakespeare. It's very difficult to make an experimental film, and in a way one shouldn't lay oneself open to failure without looking at all the possibilities. Anything I do would have to stack up on my side."

Blake Edwards understood her personal and professional introspection. "All that bad background was bound to have made her insecure and to give her a deep need to find out who or what she is. Having to search has been good for her. Boy, when you explode on the horizon the way she did, you are bound to be insecure and searching. Not that she's neurotic; she isn't at all. She's got quite a cross to bear—I'd hate to be Mary Poppins."

Just as Julie had decided that movies, with their retakes and editing, best suited both her perfectionism and, because of the five-day work weeks, her need to create a stable family life, the movies gave up on her. Musicals were dead, but she might still have had a steady career in straight dramas and comedies and in the little low-budget pictures that were being produced in the wake of *Easy Rider*. But when a tentative offer came to Andrews to take up Vanessa Redgrave's stage role in *The Prime of Miss Jean Brodie* for the film version, Julie put a stop to the discussion. She argued that since Brodie was a teacher of young girls, the role would have been seen as too close to the nanny image she was trying to flee, however unsuccessfully. Maggie Smith went on to win an Oscar for Best Actress as Jean Brodie, a teacher, to be sure, but also a multi-layered, manipulative fascist.

"I've grown relaxed, and less driven," Julie insisted. I have no plans to work to a certain age and then retire. But there's less urgency, suddenly."

In the 1970s, when she couldn't get work, or at least not the kind she preferred (theater, concerts, and television were offered to her constantly), Julie found that her need to pursue success wasn't nearly so great as it had been for most of her life. "When Blake and I first married," she said, "I needed to work less for emotional reasons. I kept very busy with home and family, and was very happy. I found I didn't miss work. My daughter was able to become part of my life. I would never have believed that I'd be able to stop work the way I did. I agreed to do just enough to keep my ego reasonably high. I attended a ballet class for a while, but I found it took up too much time. The days were terribly busy, although I couldn't tell you what I did except get involved with some charities. Finally I got down to essentials: Blake and the children."

In April of 1971, Julie cohosted the Tony Awards, for the first of her three times, with Anthony Quayle. She also made a second special with Carol Burnett, who by now had a regular weekly variety series of her own on CBS. *Julie and Carol at Lincoln Center* was taped on the hot night of July 1, 1971, at the New York cultural complex's Philharmonic (later Avery Fisher) Hall. This second special followed the format of *Julie and Carol at Carnegie Hall*: it was taped in one performance straight through with a live audience of 2,800, to be broadcast on December 7.

"Our Classy Classical Show" replaced "(There'll Be) No Mozart Tonight (at Carnegie Hall)" as a scene-setter. A medley of 1960s pop songs took up where "A History of Musical Comedy" had left off. The "Big D" finale spot was taken over by Julie and Carol, wearing yellow raincoats and galoshes singing "Wait Till the Sun Shines, Nellie." Julie's ballad solo was "He's Gone Away."

While *Julie and Carol at Lincoln Center* was a pleasant professional hour that drew respectably large ratings, it was not the critical smash of the original special nine years earlier. Nor did it need to be. Carol Burnett was an established television star. And while Julie may have been through in the movies, at least temporarily, it became clear that there was always a home for her on the small screen whenever she wanted it.

Finally, in 1972, she did. Sir (later Lord) Lew Grade went to Hollywood to sign what he called the "biggest single deal I have ever completed for ITV." Julie was to star in twenty-four shows for the ATV network in the United Kingdom and ABC-TV in the United States for up to five years plus star in one feature film per year, not necessarily a musical. Her participation in the profits would earn her a minimum of two million pounds (then $5 million) for the first two years, with options to continue, a year at a time, for another three years. Sir Lew said, "I have dreamed of doing a television series with Julie for years. I first met her when I was a theatrical agent and she came into my office, a little girl with a beautiful singing voice. All the American networks have been chasing Julie, but I persevered for three years, and she said she had no excuses left and agreed to sign the contract."

What convinced her to sign, of course, was the movie clause. She had never accepted the verdict of the public and press on *Star!* and *Darling Lili* as the final word on her movie career, and she had had three years to reflect on it. "I pulled through," she said, "largely because I believed in those pictures and disagreed with the critical and popular estimate of them. *Star!* failed because the public wasn't very happy with seeing me in the drunken scenes, but I wanted to show that at times Gertie was almost silly, and they couldn't accept me as a spy in *Lili* and that disappointed me awfully."

Julie had stopped singing for the three years between the end of *Darling Lili* and the beginning of *The Julie Andrews Hour* on television. "There was no incentive to sing," she said, "It's a very lonely business, just you at the piano, practicing, and very hard to do if you have no particular reason. The desire just slipped away. I felt no great anxiety about it. Strange as it may sound, I have never found singing easy or enjoyable. I think I have a fear of finding it so, probably from having a little too much of it when I was young. In the back of my mind and the bottom of my heart I want to lick that."

Getting her voice back into shape for her television show, "There was a terrible moment when I found I was producing sounds, but I thought I'd forgotten how to do it well. It takes about six weeks to put a voice into shape again, and at times I worried that it had really gone for good. But I think it was a sign of maturity to be able to stop singing for so long without worrying too much. When I was a small girl I wanted to be good, but I didn't believe in myself. Maturity took a long time."

Thirty-seven years old when she began *The Julie Andrews*

Hour, Julie said, "Occasionally I feel a bit ridiculous tripping through the daffodils with eighteen young dancers in sneakers. I don't want to grow old, I don't know anybody who does. I'm not as young as I was, and in five more years I won't feel as young as I do now. I may not have the energy to do exhausting jitterbugs or tap dances."

The television series pushed the Mary Poppins image hard, and this time Julie seemed to go along with it. There was one recurring sketch in which Alice Ghostley, a regular on the show, played Julie's roommate; Julie was portrayed as organized, popular, unfailingly cheerful, and Alice as just the opposite. Alice would look into the camera and say, "Isn't she perfect? Don't you hate her?" Julie also played it safe by singing many songs from her past successes, beginning with a medley from *The Boy Friend,* complete with a Charleston, on the first show, and taking few chances with offbeat guest stars.

Robert Goulet, Steve Lawrence, Jack Cassidy, Sid Caesar, Peggy Lee, Joel Grey, the Smothers Brothers, and the real Maria von Trapp all guest-starred on the show. However, Julie could not persuade many other television variety stars of the 1960s to appear on her program. Perry Como, Danny Kaye, and Andy Williams were all announced as guest stars on *The Julie Andrews Hour,* but none of them actually showed up, presumably in retaliation for Julie's failure to be a guest on their weekly shows. (Como did appear on a late 1973 special, *Julie on Sesame Street,* however.)

One unlikely guest appearance by the late pop singer "Mama" Cass Elliott proved a surprise—to Elliott. "I was not prepared to like Julie," she said, "but she surprised me. One night we were working until four in the morning, and the actors were ready to kill each other. Julie was putting out on every take as if it were the last one she'd ever make. I was embarrassed to complain. There's something very special there that you grow to love. If she could just 'free it up' a bit—groovy."

Although the show's writers were using Julie's screen image, they were also concerned about it: the prim and proper nanny persona, so sunny and warm on the big screen, might seem cold and distant in sustained visits to viewers' living rooms. As Linda Hunter, a secretary to both Julie and Blake recounted in her book *The Supersecs*, written with Alice Marchak, Julie sat in on a writers' meeting the first week of the series. The group felt that, in Blake's version, "What we've got to do, Julie, is dirty you up. But it just seems impossible." Smiling sweetly, Julie asked, "Would it help if I balled the band?" "There was this deathly silence," she recalled.

There were a lot of late nights and nothing but early calls while working on the television series although Julie was picked up for work each morning in a helicopter. "A lot of the sacrifices I learned to take for granted," she said, "and didn't notice until I gave up work for a while. When I was doing the show Blake and I swapped roles completely. For the first two months I felt relieved that he was taking care of everything, but then I began feeling left out. He had to cook on the servants' day off. Blackie cooks like a dream—the best I can do is scrambled eggs and a pot of tea—but he uses every pot and opens every cupboard. I clear up the mess so the effort evens up a little."

The Julie Andrews Hour was a critical success and won seven Emmys, including one for Julie as host, and a Silver Rose at the Montreaux International Television Festival. But the show's ratings were abysmal, even after a time slot change, and it was canceled after its first season, having broadcast just twenty-four episodes between September 13, 1972 and March 31, 1973. Some of the show's failure can certainly be ascribed to Julie's inability to transcend her image on television.

"That hurt for a long time," she said. "I found out we'd been canceled at the same time the general public did. There was no personal message, no politeness about it."

Just as Julie was failing in her television series, Blake's career as a Hollywood director seemed to be literally at a bitter end. He fought with MGM over his movie *Wild Rovers*, and quit their *The Carey Treatment* after the completion of principal photography. He was told, in effect, that he would never work in Hollywood again. Since it seemed that Julie wouldn't either, the couple and their combined family headed for Europe. For tax reasons they became residents of Switzerland and settled in Gstaad, where they had gone on vacation so often. Although Blake resisted going at first, they bought a small chalet.

"Instinctively I felt that Julie was right [about going to Switzer-land]," Edwards told *Playboy*. "But I also had to tell her, 'listen, you're fantasizing that little Swiss village. It's not going to work unless we clean up whatever prompts us to live in this mad way. Otherwise we'll just take the madness into Gstaad.' That's exactly what we did for a while."

"It was terrible in the beginning," Andrews said in the same interview. "Blake exploded, my daughter got mononucleosis, Blake's son Geoff resisted the governess like you couldn't believe, and I was utterly miserable, because my idea to stand still and be quiet for a bit just fell to pieces. But when you move away to a quiet spot, people don't come to visit as often, the phone doesn't ring quite so much, things calm down, and you learn to live with yourself. Switzerland was just what we needed, because it provided a kind of sanity for us."

For balance and to maintain a working base in a show business capital, Julie and Blake also bought a house in London's Chester Square.

"My husband gave me a taste of American life," Julie said upon leaving her adopted country after ten years of permanent resi-dence. "Now it is up to me to show him what England has to offer."

England offered them, among other things, several television specials for Sir Lew Grade, all taped in London and shown on both ATV and ABC. These included *Julie on Sesame Street*, with Perry Como, in November 1973; and *Julie's Christmas Special*, with Peter Ustinov and Peggy Lee, in December. In the spring of 1974 she produced *Julie and Dick in Covent Garden*, with Dick Van Dyke, and *Julie and Jackie: "How Sweet It Is,"* for which Jackie Gleason took his first airplane trip in two decades. On the first show, Dick Van Dyke played the Fairy Godmother to Julie's pantomime-style Cinderella; with trick photography she also portrayed the Prince and he, one of the wicked stepsisters. They danced "Won't You Charleston With Me?" from *The Boy Friend*. On the second program, Julie played Ed Norton to Jackie Gleason's Ralph Kramden and as Eliza Doolittle fought with his Joe the Bartender.

Blake Edwards directed many of the specials in London. Once when he was working there and Julie was in Los Angeles, he telephoned her, as he did every night and morning, reaching her at the opposite time of day. As assistant Linda Hunter related in *The Supersecs*, Edwards called from a dinner party, replete with lots of background noise, and told Julie there was someone who wanted to say hello to her. "A moment later a terribly, terribly British accent came over the line: 'hello Julie.' 'Hello,' said Julie. She wondered who it could possibly be, but assuming it must be someone she knew she was too polite to ask the person's identity. Then Blake came back on the line. Curious and just a bit jealous, Julie asked, 'Who was that woman?'

" 'Princess Margaret,' he replied. And then in an attempt to convince her, Blake handed the phone back to his royal companion who put the receiver to her ear just in time to hear Julie's 'Princess Margaret, my ass.'"

Julie also got to make one movie under the original contract with Sir Lew, *The Tamarind Seed*, with Omar Sharif, written and directed by Blake. Julie played a secretary for the British Home Office and Sharif played a military attaché for the Soviet Union. They meet in Barbados, where both are vacationing, causing their respective governments to worry about an exchange of secrets. Their subsequent affair fuels a story of international intrigue. Julie's character's face is disfigured by a bomb in the somewhat downbeat screenplay based on the Evelyn Anthony novel. Earlier in the film, Julie wore a sexy bikini, and there was a love scene between her and Sharif, directed by Blake. "There I was in bed with another man," she said, "and my husband is telling me to do it better!" One critic said that she made love to Sharif "like a competent dietician."

The Tamarind Seed was shot mostly on location in Barbados, Paris, London, and Gstaad, which was supposed to be Canada. Omar, Julie found, was "very disciplined and great fun to work with; he is much loved on the set. He's a most considerate actor, and

I've always adored that aura of quiet romance that he exudes. I didn't discuss bridge with him, though, I would have been out of my depth."

The movie, on its release in the summer of 1974, did well overseas but flopped in the United States, causing a further setback in the careers of both Julie and Blake. He began complaining again about the Hollywood system that had deprived them both of their preferred livelihoods. "I was licking my wounds at that point," Edwards told Charlie Rose in 1996, "it hurt a lot. I said, 'I can't deal with this.' We went to Switzerland, and I said, 'I'm just gonna write—there's not much anybody can do about that. They either buy it or they don't.' I don't have any bosses but myself. But Julie kept saying, 'you know better; you'll get some rest and you'll go back.'"

"She wouldn't let me cop out," he recalled, "she just said, "Bullshit, Blackie, all you have to do is make another hit.'"

He did just that with Peter Sellers and *The Return of the Pink Panther*. Released in 1975, the movie was funded by Lew Grade and costarred Christopher Plummer. Richard Burton and Elizabeth Taylor were in attendance at the premiere in Gstaad. Julie again took a subordinate role. "My life does now depend on what he is doing rather than doing my own things as I used to," she explained. She even accepted a cameo role as a maid in *The Return of the Pink Panther* so they could be together but her two-line part, which she played in a black wig and padding that made her unrecognizable, ended up on the cutting room floor. "I've never been cut out of a picture," she kidded, "and now my own husband does it to me after I worked for free."

Julie wrote two children's books in the early 1970s, *Mandy* and *The Last of the Really Great Whangdoodles*. The first was written for her stepdaughter Jennifer, who extracted the story as a punishment for Julie's swearing; Julie had instituted a systems of "forfeits" for all the family for such misbehavior as not brushing one's teeth. Written under her married name of Julie Edwards, *Mandy* was the story of an orphan girl who longs for a family, while *Whangdoodles* was written, Julie said, "for the child in all of us." The whangdoodle motto was, *"Pax, amor, et lepos in iocando"* ("Peace, love and a great sense of humor"); "our family is rather inclined to embrace it for ourselves," Julie said. "My husband is the real writer in the family," she noted, "his work is the important stuff, but he is my best critic, and my toughest."

Perhaps not. *Time* said that *Mandy* "proves that Julie Andrews has fondly read *The Secret Garden* and deserves every success as a singer and film actress." The trade journal *Publishers Weekly* called *Mandy* "sugar-coated and not very substantial." *The New York Times* said of *The Last of the Really Great Whangdoodles,* "Edwards is more committed to improving her young readers than she is in entertaining them, and her book is sunk by an overload of virtue."

In 1975, Julie returned to television and taped two more specials. *Julie: "My Favorite Things"* was directed by Blake and costarred Peter Sellers. Her daughter Emma appeared in a cameo on a unicycle. Julie sang a Duke Ellington medley and danced with a troupe of Pink Panthers. Sellers played Binky Barclay in a send-up of Busby Berkeley movies, "Flying Down to Brighton." In the second special, *A Salute to Lew Grade—The Master Showman,* Julie sang both "The Sound of Music" and "Wouldn't It Be Loverly?" She and Tom Jones sang the duet "You Will Be My Music."

Charity work still claimed some of Julie's time, and Hathaway House was a concern, even from the distance of London. She returned to Hollywood as Mistress of Ceremonies at the dedication of a new 310-acre, $3,900,000 ranch facility for Hathaway House's disturbed children. California's governor, Ronald Reagan, also attended the dedication. Julie wore white gloves.

After the Vietnam War ended, Julie became involved in the Committee of Responsibility, an organization that brought war-injured Vietnamese children to the United States for medical treatment. This affiliation inspired her and Blake to adopt, in August of 1974 and April of 1975, two orphaned Vietnamese infant girls, whom they renamed Amy Leigh and Joanna Lynn.

"We wanted a child and weren't being successful," Julie recalled. "While we were talking about adoption, André Previn and

Mia Farrow adopted a Vietnamese orphan girl. We took our son and daughter to the Previns' home to see their new daughter before any final decision was made. Emma took some persuading," said Julie, "but finally said, 'All right, Mummy, as long as you don't ask me to baby-sit.' Now she's the biggest mother to the babies of us all."

Both of the infants were flown from Saigon to Europe and taken to Gstaad. They were sickly and fragile upon their arrival but blossomed into healthy toddlers in the Swiss mountain air. They were taken to the United States to become American citizens, but like the rest of the Edwards family in the late 1970s and early 1980's, considered Gstaad their real home. "It's just a village, really," said Julie, "with duckies, piggies, and horses. We have a dream house, with the most beautiful view in the world. The best time is being there. We can close the doors against the world, and hole up and hide. In Gstaad, I have always felt there is nothing that can harm me—ever."

In 1976, Julie organized a concert, which she debuted at her old stomping ground the London Palladium. As was the cabaret fashion of the day, she sang current popular songs made famous by other people. But the act also included most of her traditional favorites, which was appropriate for the venue. "I want to take the audience on a sentimental journey," she said, "for them and for me." She found performing live again both a happy and scary experience. "It isn't the teenaged me in my size-eight Cinderella glass slipper," she explained. "It's me at forty, putting all my accumulated experience on the line."

Caesar's Palace in Las Vegas then made Julie "a tremendous offer I couldn't refuse; Blake talked me into going ahead." The hotel offered Julie $250,000 a week for performing two shows a night. "For what you're paying me I'll sell flowers in the casino," she told the hotel's management. But it turned out to be an unhappy episode for both sides. She sold out two shows a night for a week, but did not draw the gambling crowds that a Las Vegas casino needs to thrive. The remaining seven weeks of her contract were canceled by mutual consent.

"I just about burst a blood vessel every night trying to prove something to myself," she said of the Las Vegas engagement. "I've been afraid since I was a child performing in England; that's why I have to do these things, to get up and work, to prove to myself I can do it. I guess it's because if someone asked me, 'What do you do?' I'd say, 'I sing.'"

Still, the audience response in her hometown of London and the fans' reaction in Las Vegas encouraged Julie to embark on a concert tour in the U.S. and Japan in 1977. For these shows she eliminated the pop songs from her act, and went back to the standard numbers that she did best, such as Jerome Kern's "I'm Old-Fashioned." "I was taught good singing technique early," she explained. "With my perfect enunciation I need a perfect lyric. A lot of the modern things are repetitive. I admire them, but I don't do them justice."

Her staple finale number, whether in London, Las Vegas, or Tokyo, was "I Could Have Danced All Night," and her encore was always "The Sound of Music." These songs, together with "Camelot" she termed, with no trace of sarcasm, "the show's vanilla moments."

In NBC's *America Salutes the Queen*, which aired on November 29, 1977, Julie sang those three songs plus "My Favorite Things." The program, called in Great Britain *The Silver Jubilee Royal Variety Gala*, celebrated Elizabeth II's twenty-five years on the throne. Bob Hope was Master of Ceremonies, and Julie was presented to the Queen backstage. In 1978 Julie guest-starred on *The Muppet Show* where she sang "The Lonely Goatherd" from *The Sound of Music*. That same year, her CBS special *Julie Andrews: One Step Into Spring* featured Miss Piggy, Leslie Uggams, and Leo Sayer.

Although back at work on television and in concerts, Julie continued to refuse the few movie offers she received. She even turned down $500,000 for *International Velvet*. Her chief objection, she said, was, "I don't like what's going on. It's not sour grapes, it's the times. The four-letter words are flying, every other actress bares her bosom in one picture or another, the stories are becoming more and more trashy or totally far out and women have a worse and worse deal of it. I just want to make sure that if I do go back to the screen I don't make a fool of myself. I'm prepared to wait a few years until something right comes along."

She waited only until Blake Edwards cast her in a secondary role in his 1979 R-rated smash hit *10*. This third Andrews-Edwards movie collaboration (her tenth picture, and her first to be rated R) proved to be Blake's biggest commercial success. Coming just after his Pink Panther revival, *10* re-established Blake in Hollywood, just as Julie had predicted a hit picture would. The movie did considerably less for her, however, overshadowed as she was by costars Dudley Moore and Bo Derek. In his first major American movie role, Dudley Moore became a star, even a romantic leading man and almost a sex symbol, "Cuddley Dudley." The beautiful Bo Derek (a ten, on a scale of one to ten, hence the film's title) became an instant movie star, although her fame proved to be shorter-lived than Moore's. Andrews, as the girlfriend Moore leaves to pursue Derek was all but forgotten by the audience too. She and Dudley did sing a duet with him at the piano in this otherwise non-musical movie: Henry Mancini's "It's Easy to Say." (The lyrics were written by Robert Wells.)

"Blake was always thinking of me as Sam," she explained of her first film role in five years, "and although it's not a huge role I did it for him because I was involved with the script for so long and it's such an important step in the development of Blake's work. But it was not a comeback for me, because I never retired."

Dudley said of Julie: "She's a very down-to-earth regular person. I don't think she's ever thought of herself as a huge celebrity, although God knows she is one. She has a huge following even now, but I think she has a need to be liked. We all do, but she's honest about it."

Inexplicably, since Blake wasn't involved, Julie next took on a third remake of *Little Miss Marker*, the movie based on the classic Damon Runyan story that had made Shirley Temple a star back in 1934. In this fourth version, Walter Matthau played Sorrowful Jones, the bookie, and Sara Stimson was cast in the title part. "The character Julie Andrews plays [a penniless heiress who lends her estate to a gambling operation] wasn't even in the original," said

Walter Bernstein, the screenwriter and director of the remake. "I
wanted to take some of the emphasis off the child and put Matthau
in a romantic situation. The role will show the good toughness and
sexuality Julie had in *The Americanization of Emily.*"

It did nothing of the kind, since Julie looked as if she had shot
much of the emotionless film with a migraine headache, and the
movie was a disaster when released, seen only on cable television
in most areas. Yet during the making of *Little Miss Marker,* Julie
charmed yet another leading man. Matthau said, "She's a total
delight, witty, bright, and beautiful. She was exactly what I expected her to be—an excellent person with a great sense of humor.
I can't understand the people who fall into the Mary Poppins trap. I
never expected Julie to be any of the parts she's played, and of
course she isn't."

Julie's next two movies, both for Blake, were calculated to put
her Mary Poppins image to rest forever, if such a thing were
possible. *S.O.B.,* which Blake had been trying to get made for eleven
years (finally making a deal only after the phenomenal success of
10), stood for "Standard Operating Bullshit."

"It's a phrase Blake and I use all the time when something
happens," Julie explained. "The film makes a strong statement
about the way business is done in Hollywood and its standard
operating bullshit. The minute anyone out there thinks you have
something valuable, they are interested. But they couldn't care less
if they don't think your project is going to make lots of money. It's a
crazy business."

In *S.O.B.,* Julie played a parody of herself, in the smallish but
pivitol role of a movie actress best known for family musicals. She
is surrounded by the leeches and loonies of tinseltown, an agent, a
gossip columnist (played by Loretta Swit and based on Joyce
Haber), a quack doctor who dispenses "vitamin" shots, and as-
sorted others. "All the characters are out of real life," she said. "Any
day you can see them out there. It all happened. Although it's done
over the top in terms of comedy, it's mostly a true story."

The character of Julie's husband in *S.O.B.* is a successful
writer-director played by Richard Mulligan, whose current kiddie

musical promises to be a box office disaster. To salvage it, he turns the movie within the movie into a pornographic film. Thus, standing in front of a dozen mirrors, with most of *S.O.B.*'s crazy characters looking on, Julie removes the top half of her red gown and bares her firm "boobies," as her character keeps calling them. The look on her face at that moment says, "Everybody, take your image of me and stuff it."

Julie's defense of the scene was curt: "I'm an actress, and the part called for it. I've always had a rather nice body, but people who had only seen my movies assumed I was either sexless or puritanical."

Unfortunately, nobody much cared one way or the other about Julie's bare breasts and the parody of Hollywood in the late 1960s was almost fifteen years too late. Although Blake had been trying to do the movie for at least eleven of those years, "every studio in Hollywood turned it down. Blake believed in it enough and finally someone took it. I believe the time factor was on our side—by waiting we made a better picture," Julie said. The general public did not involve itself in the problems and frustrations of very wealthy movie-makers, and *S.O.B.* failed at the box office despite a Lear jet whistle-stop publicity campaign by Julie, Robert Preston, Richard Mulligan, and most of the picture's other stars.

Blake had written *Victor/Victoria* with his wife and Peter Sellers in mind. The script was based on the 1933 German movie *Viktor und Viktoria* by Reinhard Schuenzel and Hans Hoenburg. Sellers had died, so Robert Preston replaced him as the gay impresario Toddy. Julie played a starving English opera singer in 1930s Paris who is convinced by Preston's character to pretend to be a man, a Polish count, working as a female impersonator. This allowed Julie to sing in the lower part of her range. Henry Mancini and Leslie Bricusse wrote the songs that Julie and Robert sang in the nightclub sequences, making *Victor/Victoria*, like *Darling Lili*, a movie with music rather than a movie musical. James Garner, Julie's costar in *The Americanization of Emily* eighteen years earlier, played the Chicago gangster who is attracted to "Victor." Lesley Ann Warren played his girlfriend, also a nightclub singer. The movie was made at Pinewood Studios, outside London, on nine soundstages.

When *Victor/Victoria* first arose as a possibility for Blake he was interested, he said, but asked himself, "How can I be more interested, enough so that I will take it on as a project? It wasn't until I thought of the additional element of Toddy being gay and dealing with the homosexual aspects of that world that I suddenly became very intrigued by it. I totally forgot it was a remake, and had something that, for me, was totally original."

Victor/Victoria was a deserved success on its opening in April 1982, and it looked as if Julie could continue in what had become the family business. Jennifer Edwards, twenty-six, was still pursuing an acting career (she played a small part in *S.O.B.*, a hitchhiker); Geoffrey, twenty-two, worked as an assistant editor on *10* and *S.O.B.* for his father; Emma Kate, nineteen, was studying ballet and considering a career in theater. Even the only two children still at home full time, Amy and Joanna, eight and seven, were introduced to their mother's other world. Julie took them to Disneyland, where "we had an exhausting time doing about three days' worth of rides in one," she recalled. (*Mary Poppins* had remained Disney's top-grossing movie; in the world of Disney, at least, Julie was a still superstar.)

Amy and Joanna had never seen their mother's movies, so in late 1981 they were shown the musicals and *Hawaii*. "Joanna fell asleep during *The Sound of Music* and had to be taken off to bed," Julie remembered. The next morning she was in tears. 'I thought you said it was a happy movie.' 'It is in the end,' I told her. 'Well, I saw it,' she said, 'and it was terribly sad.' They are just now starting to understand what it is that Mummy does for a living. Occasionally I take them to the studio with me for haircuts, but otherwise they don't have much contact with the business."

In January of 1983 Julie won a Golden Globe Award for *Victor/Victoria*, her third, followed in February with her third Oscar nomination for Best Actress—eighteen years after her last nomination. "You appreciate it more as you go along in your career,"

Julie told Army Archerd of *Variety*. "At the beginning, if you receive it, you're primarily dazzled." *Victor/Victoria* garnered a total of seven Academy Award nominations, including Robert Preston for Best Supporting Actor, Lesley Ann Warren for Best Supporting Actress, Henry Mancini and Leslie Bricusse for Best Score, and Rodgers Maus for Best Art Director. Only Mancini and Bricusse actually won.

The Writers Guild of America presented Blake Edwards the award for Best Screenplay—Adaptation. *Victor/Victoria* won France's César award for Best Foreign Film. Both Edwards and Andrews were "back" in Hollywood, if they wanted to be, it seemed.

After this first-ever joint success in *Victor/Victoria* (her forgettable supporting role in *10* aside), Julie and Blake began spending more time at their Beverly Hills estate, as well as in Malibu—quite literally back in Hollywood. They even submitted to a lengthy *Playboy* interview by Lawrence Linderman, for the December 1982, issue. The most surprising revelation of this interview was not personal but professional: Despite all the public acclaim she had received, and the wonderful opinions of her friends in the industry, Julie was less happy with *Victor/Victoria* than with any of her other roles to date. "It's the film she's most confused by and least satisfied with," said Blake. "Julie really doesn't have a clear idea of not only what she did but how she did it. At this point it's an enigma to her."

Julie said that was "probably because it was a very difficult, multi-faceted role....There were so many things to be worked out. As someone who likes to be in control, I felt wobbly. There was something else, too: When you get older, you kind of get on to yourself. You know the tricks you play to get by, and you like them less and less if you care about your work. I was trying hard to get away from them and was sometimes falling back....I wish I'd had more time, done fewer tricks and said lines differently."

Yet the accolades and sense of a comeback after *Victor/Victoria* continued. Julie was named Woman of the Year by Harvard University's Hasty Pudding Club. In accepting the award, a trophy in the form of a pot, she asked, "Is it all right if I throw up in it?" The club, appropriately, previewed their latest boys-in-drag show for her. Julie also won the People's Choice Favorite Film Actress Award in 1983.

But when and whether or not she would work again, Julie said, "all depends on whether Blake is involved in the project or approves it, and whether it suits my schedule with the children. My principal occupation is being a wife to my director and a mother to our children. It is the most unlikely marriage, I still think we are a rather odd couple, yet it seems to work. We vowed we would take it a day at a time and never get a great fantasy about the way it was going to be in the future. But he is very good for me, he is straight and tells me when things are rubbish, and frequently pulls me up when I go straying into something that's wrong for me. Life is tremendous fun with him. I always wonder what he is going to come up with next. Just going out to dinner with him is a treat."

After twelve years of her second marriage and her expanded family life, Julie's priorities were clear, at least for the time being. While she would undoubtedly continue to make forays into the show business world that had been with her, quite literally, her entire life, she said, "I certainly wouldn't compare the rewards of watching one's children grow and mature with that of money piling up at the box office. Both are pleasant, but to varying degrees.

"As the old saying goes, you can't take the audience home with you. You can't depend on the loyalty of fans, who, after all is said and done, are just faceless people one seldom sees. And few stars have their fans forever. But a child is forever; that bond and relationship is timeless and doesn't depend on your looks, age, or popularity at the moment."

13

It Never Rains...

The next Andrews-Edwards movie collaboration was disastrous. Blake decided to adapt, together with his psychoanalyst, Milton Wexler, Francois Truffaut's 1977 comedy *The Man Who Loved Women*. As Blake said, it was "a theme with which I've been screwing around forever." Blake's son Geoffrey Edwards was also credited as a cowriter on the screenplay.

Julie worked with her analyst to achieve believability in her role as the psychiatrist whom the womanizing sculptor, played by Burt Reynolds, sees in an attempt to overcome his artistic block. Instead, the patient and the therapist fall in love. The ensuing complications were supposed to add up to a romantic comedy. They didn't and the movie disappeared quickly after its release in late 1983, despite an appearance by the young Kim Basinger as the promiscuous wife of a millionaire and Marilu Henner and Sela Ward as two of the other "loved" women.

Blake's next two movies didn't have roles for Julie, but he influenced her decisions during this crossroads period of her career. He urged her to record an album of middle-of-the-road country music ballads. She even went to Nashville to record *Love Me Tender*. Vinyl and cassette versions of the session were released by Peach River (Runaway) in various configurations, first in the United Kingdom with fourteen tracks, then the United States with

ten tracks, and Japan with sixteen tracks. Johnny Cash sang
backup on the title song. Other cuts included "Crazy," "I Still Miss
Someone," "You Don't Bring Me Flowers," and "Another Somebody
Done Somebody Wrong Song."

"I was bemoaning the fact that I wasn't doing more," Julie told
journalist Henry Fenwick in 1983, "and Blake said, 'why don't you
do something about it?'" She didn't know what to do, she said,
because "my voice is not easy: it's a very identifiable voice but it's a
very white voice. It doesn't have enormous richness or an enormous
gimmick to it. The middle-of-the-road country ballads are not
unlike the ballads I used to sing when I was much younger in
England. There is a direct line."

The producer she found in Nashville, Larry Butler, persuaded
her to "come down to the Mother Lode," which she did. In
Tennessee she ate catfish and found herself singing and recording
in a manner she was unused to: without exact orchestrations and
meticulously rehearsed arrangements—"flying by the seat of one's
pants." She enjoyed the change.

A month before her forty-eighth birthday in 1983, BBC Radio 2
broadcast a retrospective of her career, harking back to her first
program, *Monday Night at Eight* with Kenneth Horne and Peter
Brough, and "Archie Andrews" in *Educating Archie*. "In those days,
all the comedians who later became tremendously famous were
budding talents, and people like Tony Hancock and Eric Sykes, and
Frankie Howerd were very big," Julie recalled. "I watched and
listened to comedians a lot. I wasn't allowed to do very much—
mostly all I did was sing my guest solo and shut up. But I watched a
lot! I could have been a young upstart and everybody took me in as
if I were a member of the family."

The next year marked the thirtieth anniversary of Julie's arrival
in America to star in *The Boy Friend*. In the three decades since she
left England, Julie had become noticeably more mid-Atlantic. For
one thing, she was no longer brewing tea in a silver teapot. She was
still offering it to all visitors, but now she was content to use
teabags, just like any American.

Still ambivalent about many things, a self-described "lady

Libra," Julie was conflicted about being an American and had never changed her citizenship. "My British roots are strong," she said. "I don't know why. I live in America and my work is here. I feel I carry what's British within me wherever I go; I represent my country, though of course I have nothing but affection for America, which has been very generous to me."

Robert Preston, long a Broadway and Tony favorite (he had won Best Actor in a Musical Tony Awards for both the *The Music Man* and *I Do, I Do*) and his *Victor/Victoria* costar cohosted *The Thirty-Eighth Annual Tony Awards* in June of 1984. As part of a tribute to composer-lyricist Stephen Sondheim, Julie sang "Send in the Clowns" from *A Little Night Music*.

During the early- and mid-1980s, Julie's live singing appearances were largely limited to local benefits for her favorite charities. A return to Broadway and concert tours was not yet even considered. "If you're very happy, and I am," she said, "it would be dumb to go off and leave everyone behind." In 1984 in Los Angeles, she and Carol Burnett appeared in (and for) *One Night Only*, to raise money in honor of Operation California's fifth anniversary. The next year, Julie sang at the Beverly Hills Hotel benefit for the John Douglas French Foundation for Alzheimer's Disease.

For Operation California's Mexican Earthquake Relief fund, Julie appeared with Frank Sinatra, Kirk Douglas, John Denver, and the Mexican singing group Paragon in *Placido Domingo and Friends*, a one-night concert at the Universal Amphitheater in August 1986. Jack Elliott conducted the new American Orchestra as Julie and Placido sang, among other things, a duet medley from *West Side Story*. Her solo and duet performances, instead of being electric, were surprisingly bland and, as *Variety* noted, "nothing of her personality made it past the footlights."

That's Life!, Blake Edwards's 1986 "home movie," was filmed under the working title *Crisis* at the Edward's home in Paradise Cove in Malibu, which allowed them to use nonunion crews and make the movie for just $1 million. Milton Wexler (Blake's therapist), who had coadapted *The Man Who Loved Women*, was credited as cowriter with Blake on the film. But actually, the actors, who included Julie, Jack Lemmon, Jennifer Edwards, Emma Walton (Julie's daughter), Chris Lemmon (Jack's son), and Felicia Farr (Jack's wife and Chris's stepmother), improvised most of their own dialogue based on an eighty-page narrative outline provided by the director.

Jack Lemmon and Julie played husband and wife, with Chris Lemmon, Jennifer Edwards, and Emma Walton playing their three children.

In a way, it proved to be Julie's most difficult role: "Blake turned on the camera and said, 'Just be yourself.' I said, 'Whoa! What is that?'"

As in their six prior collaborations, Julie credited Blake with appreciating "other aspects of me that other people didn't see." But she insisted that his work to change her image in movies was "not as calculated as some people would like it to be."

Working with her daughter Emma was "sort of a dream come true," Julie said at the time. "She has been working very seriously toward her acting career. It was Emma's first major role, and for me to share it with her, to watch her enjoy that role, to watch her grow and thrive, was like being handed a wonderful gift that Blake gave to me."

Most of Emma's previous acting experience had been on stage, but she had done some commercial acting and voiceovers prior to *That's Life!* She also had small roles in the movie *Daniel* and three non-Andrews movies by Blake Edwards: *A Fine Mess, Curse of the Pink Panther,* and *Micki & Maude.*

Sometimes, Julie remembered, it was not that easy to distinguish between acting and mothering when she worked with her daughter. "I held Emma in my arms and whispered the thoughts that came into my mind. For a while, I almost forgot we were making a movie. Until after the take I had no idea even what I was saying....All those things you say to your own daughter without thinking. It didn't feel as if we were acting anything. It felt as if we were just continuing on."

Emma told Natalie Gittelson, in an interview for *McCall's*, "She was more of a stage mother than I ever realized—much more concerned about whether my hemline was straight and my makeup on right than she was about herself. And I watched her work in a firsthand way I'd never done before. *That* was an education."

Julie described *That's Life!* as "a drama filled with the comedy one finds in real life. A lot of the situations that occur in the story have happened in our lives, but not only in our family. All the actors were able to fall back on real-life situations for this improvisational film. Each of us had to research our character even more than if it were on the written page."

Duet for One, directed by Andrei Konchalovsky, provided Julie with her finest dramatic role since *The Americanization of Emily* twenty-two years earlier and took her back to England for the filming. The late 1986 release was adapted from a two-character play of the same name by Tom Kempinski. The story, based loosely on the life of cellist Jacqueline du Pré, concerned a famous concert violinist who suffers from multiple sclerosis and gradually deteriorates, physically and emotionally. Max von Sydow, Julie's costar in *Hawaii*, played her psychiatrist, the other original character from the play. Alan Bates played the violinist's estranged husband and Liam Neeson was an itinerant scrap merchant who has a brief affair with Julie's character. Also in the cast were Rupert Everett as the violinist's star pupil and Cathryn Harrison, Rex Harrison's granddaughter.

In *Duet for One*, Julie moved even further beyond her early image. Her character says the "f" word, walks around naked seductively, and goes to bed with her lesbian maid. To research her role, she met with multiple sclerosis patients at a clinic in Bromley, Kent. Julie called the part of the stricken musician "the most desperate and emotionally pained woman I've ever played."

Filming *Duet for One* was "not a joyous experience," said Julie, but it was "a tremendous learning experience—a very harrowing film to make. But I'm awfully glad I did it."

In January of 1987, Andrews received a rare accolade—two simultaneous Golden Globe nominations: one for Best Actress in a Drama for *Duet for One* and the other for Best Actress in a Comedy or Musical for *That's Life!*

In the summer of 1987, Julie and Blake, departing from their usual style of entertaining, hosted a lavish evening for three hundred Operation California supporters, celebrating the organization's eighth anniversary. The party was held under a big white tent at the Edwards's Malibu home. Michael Feinstein and Rich Little entertained, and Phillipine President Corazon Aquino was given, in absentia, the group's Human Achievement Award. An auction raised $108,000 that night. Blake and Julie had been supporters of Operation California, later renamed Operation America, since its founding in 1979 with one flight into famine-ravaged Cambodia. Between 1979 and 1987 Operation California had sent more than $50 million worth of medicine, food, and other emergency aid to the world's disaster areas; most of the money had been raised from entertainment benefits.

Later in the year, she shot a television special, *Julie Andrews: The Sound of Christmas*, in Salzburg, Austria, the first time she had visited the city since making *The Sound of Music* almost twenty-five years before. "It was lovely," she said, "just as if I'd never left." Julie sang "Ave Maria" in the Church of Mondsee. The special also starred Placido Domingo and John Denver and featured the King's Singers, an English choral group. The show won five Emmys, including awards for musical direction, editing, and technical direction, and was nominated for the Roses awards at the Montreaux Television Festival.

In the winter of 1987–1988 Julie released her twenty-fourth album, *Love, Julie*. The nucleus of the record, which included arranger Bob Florence on the synthesizer, had been privately produced as a birthday present for Blake: a group of songs that described the way she felt about her husband, including "Come Rain or Come Shine," "How Deep is the Ocean," and "My Lucky Day." Blake, thrilled with the result, suggested releasing the record commercially, which Julie did on the small USA label, adding additional songs and expanding the sound on others. USA also released a rare single, "The Sound of Christmas" and "O Come All Ye Faithful," with new arrangements and a backup chorus. Ian Fraser, Julie's longtime musical collaborator, produced the sessions.

Beginning on October 29, 1987, just after her fifty-second birthday, Julie embarked on her first solo concert tour in ten years. "A Captivating Evening with Julie Andrews," as the concert was called, took her to the Valley Forge Music Fair in Pennsylvania , the Jackie Gleason Theater for the Performing Arts in Ft. Lauderdale, Florida, the Westbury Music Fair on Long Island, and to other venues in Cleveland, St. Louis, Chicago, Detroit, and Minneapolis. These concerts, which continued into early 1988, were backed by a thirty-nine-piece orchestra and offered a program of material containing, in her words, "all textures, all sounds, all kinds of songs, everything from grand and glorious sweeping ballads to real knockdown drag-out songs."

"I began worrying that I might wake up, five or ten years from now, regretting never having done it one last time," she explained mid-tour. "I was beginning to doubt myself as a singer. I hadn't tested myself really hard for a while, and I needed to shape myself up and get back on my feet. The timing was right. I've been asked to do it for a number of years, but either I was too busy or the children weren't settled."

The hard part, she said, was "getting up and getting on. I was sort of insulated and isolated in the movies. This is more about finding out about me." Her fifteen numbers were calculated to evoke the past, demonstrate her vocal versatility and, just perhaps, tentatively begin to offer some autobiography. Noel Coward's "Don't Put Your Daughter on the Stage, Mrs. Worthington," was a special highlight of the show, with some resonance for her own life. Julie also sang her semi-torchy "Come Rain or Come Shine" from the *Love, Julie* album, and "Le Jazz Hot" from *Victor/Victoria*. Her well-received, extended medley in tribute to the lyrics of Alan Jay Lerner, she said, "was a case of the glove fitting the hand."

The tour demonstrated that Julie's once four-and-a-half octave range had lowered, mellowed, and narrowed, to a still-impressive nearly three octaves. What she characterized as her once "very thin and white" timbre had warmed and thickened.

Now having bared her breasts in two movies, *S.O.B.* and *Duet for One*, Julie also seemed to further her not-so-new raunchy "broad" credentials. "Well, whaddaya know, Mary Poppins sweats," she'd say, drying herself with a towel during the concert. (Her singing diction remained flawless, but many of her hard English "t"'s had become soft California "d"'s in her speech.)

"It's been a revelation to discover that my reasons for performing are entirely different now from what they used to be," Julie told Stephen Holden of *The New York Times*. "In the early days, performing was all I knew. It was my whole identity, and I used it for both gratification and to avoid a lot of soul searching. Now I find I'm doing it just for the sheer joy of doing it."

Those who hoped that the concert tour might presage Julie's returning to Broadway in a "book" musical, were still a few years early, however. "Right now the goal is simply the doing of this show. Who knows where it will lead? A successful Broadway run would mean uprooting the family, asking the kids to change schools and putting up with me being virtually a nun."

In March 1988, she hosted two tributes to co-workers: the American Film Institute Life Achievement Award to Jack Lemmon, which was later aired on CBS, and a tribute to Frederick Loewe at the Shubert Theater in New York.

In 1989 Julie and Carol Burnett reunited for a third special, *Julie & Carol Together Again*, which was to have been taped at Carnegie Hall but ended up being taped at the Pantages Theatre in Hollywood. It represented, by far, the least of the three Andrews-Burnett teamings, reaching its nadir with a ludicrous and instantly dated "Mama Rap" duet. Appropriately, the show opened and closed with a duet of Stephen Sondheim's "Old Friends" from *Merrily We Roll Along*.

Although they might sometimes have gone for long periods without seeing one another, the friendship between Julie and Carol remained solid and impervious to external distractions. "The things I first liked about Carol haven't changed a bit," Julie noted. "She's ingenuous, she's straight, and she's real. What comforts me most in this dizzying world is that I know I can trust Carol completely. She's a sister to me and I love her a lot. I don't think anything could harm that relationship."

Immediately after the taping, Julie left on her 1989 summer concert tour, which included stops in Philadelphia, St. Louis, Miami, Boston, Washington, D.C., and at the Greek Theatre in Hollywood. At the end of the tour she taped her solo concert, with its loosely autobiographical format, for PBS's *Great Performances* series, to be aired in March of 1990.

In this concert, Julie "talked about the really big building blocks of my life: vaudeville, Broadway, and film. I told some personal stories and things. But I didn't let it all hang out. I just told enough, I hope. I think somewhere I'm probably rather shy. I guess I don't want to impose on my family. When you're in the public eye, I think it's very hard for them. I'm always trying to protect them. I just hope that through my music you'll know who I am."

As grueling as touring was for her, and as guaranteed to keep her separated from her family, Julie found it "a tremendous thrill to perform in front of an audience with a forty-piece band. As she told Patti Doten of *The Boston Globe*, "Touring keeps me on my toes and in touch with people, and prevents me from becoming too insulated, spoiled, and closeted. It is both exhausting and very stimulating. But the biggest reason is that I need to air my vocal chords, to open up and really use my voice."

On October 7, 1989, just after her fifty-fourth birthday, Julie became the first actress ever to be awarded a special British Academy of Film and Television Arts (BAFTA) Lifetime Tribute Award for her contribution to film. (Her only other BAFTA award had been given to her twenty-five years earlier, when she was named "Most Promising Newcomer" for *Mary Poppins*.) The award was presented by H.R.H. Anne, the Princess Royal, the long-time president of BAFTA. Princess Anne called Julie "a tremendous ambassador for Britain."

Former costars James Fox (*Thoroughly Modern Millie*), James Coburn (*The Americanization of Emily*), David Tomlinson (*Mary Poppins*), and Millicent Martin (*The Boy Friend*) spoke at the ceremony at the Odeon Leicester Square Cinema. Andrews, in her acceptance speech, said, "I am first and always English, and I carry my country in my heart wherever I go."

Later in the fall, she taped another PBS special, *An Evening with Alan Jay Lerner*. With André Previn, the Royal Philharmonic Orchestra, and the Brighton Festival Choir, Andrews performed her "Magic of Christmas" concert at Royal Albert Hall on December 11, 1989.

In the late 1980s and early 1990s Julie and Blake went through, in his words, "about three years of unadulterated personal hell—with my parents dying, her parents dying, our two adopted kids acting out....It's just total madness, there's no other word for it, like Pandora's Box opened. And the worse it got, the worse it got. I knew while it was going on that it would eventually go away or else it would turn into a comedy. Well, it didn't go away. At one point after a crazy, mad sequence with my parents I was sitting in the car, alternating between laughing and weeping. I remember saying to myself, 'I've got to write this.' I did write it, night and day for three weeks. Black, black humor, and it's all true." Blake's script, with the working title of *It Never Rains...*, may go into production in the summer of 1997.

In 1991, one of their two teenaged adopted daughters was hospitalized for alcohol and cocaine addiction; it turned out that she had been taking drugs since she was eleven years old. A year later, Andrews said to London journalist Jan Moir, "Please God, we're back on track. It wasn't such a surprise when it all unravelled. Since she is an adopted daughter from another country, she has always had a problem as to who she is and where she belongs. I imagine that having Julie Andrews for a mum and Blake Edwards as a dad is hard to deal with, although we took that into consideration. Still, it is her life as much as it was my life. Mine was an odd life and hers is, too. To be thrust into our family must be a very odd existence."

In a PBS interview with Charlie Rose in November of 1996, Blake described a scene in which both of his and Julie's two younger girls were housed in the same drug rehabilitation hospital on opposite sides of a courtyard and "mooning" one another. It certainly sounded like a scene from a Blake Edwards movie.

Julie made her last movie in 1990 (although it was not released until 1992). During filming in France, she got word that her father, Ted Wells, had died at the age of eighty-five, in Yorkshire.

The movie was *A Fine Romance*, based on Francois Billet-doux's successful 1959 play *Tchin-Tchin*, which had starred Anthony Quinn and Margaret Leighton on Broadway. The original title, used for the movie in Europe (albeit sometimes spelled *Chin-Chin*), is from the toast spoken before the clinking of wine or liquor glasses. The plot involves a double adultery in Paris and the South of France. An Englishwoman agrees to meet an Italian man (played by Marcello Mastroianni) to discuss the affair his wife is having with her husband. In trying to resolve the situation, the new acquaintances slip into their own trysting. The movie was released in the United Kingdom as *A Touch of Adultery* and in Japan as *Afternoon Tea in Bed*. Gene Saks directed *A Fine Romance*, which was released for a scant week in New York and sketchily elsewhere. The movie, which was pretty, amiable, talky, short, and unfunny, did make it to video.

In 1991 Julie made her second television movie. *Our Sons* was the story of two mothers and their two gay sons, one of whom is dying of AIDS. In the ABC movie, written by William Hanley and directed by John Erman, Julie played a prosperous businesswoman and widow whose son, played by a then little-known Hugh Grant, is the survivor of the couple. She has come to accept her son's homosexuality. Ann-Margret played the part of the other mother, an uneducated Southern woman who worked as a cocktail waitress and who regards her dying son's sexuality as unforgivable. In the course of the story the two women become somewhat tolerant of one another and more accepting of their sons. Zeljko Ivanek portrayed the dying son.

Julie was attracted to the project, she said, "because it does not get preachy, and it does not take sides. It says that you miss being a grandmother and the heritage that you hoped for when you have a family. It also says that love covers all....A lot of mothers feel guilty for wishing it could be otherwise; there's nothing wrong with that. But having got rid of the guilt, they have to deal with it."

She also noted that her "children have friends who have been affected [by AIDS]. I want this movie to help teach young kids to be more careful, and let parents know that they cannot turn their backs on people they love."

Director Erman found Julie and Ann-Margret as dissimilar as their characters, "like oil and water. There is such an incredible contrast in terms of their personal style. Ann-Margret is like a frightened doe, while Julie is like a proud bird." Ann-Margret agreed that she was nothing like Andrews: "She is very well-organized; I'm not. I'm amazed. She'll be talking business and then go directly into a scene, while I sit alone in my trailer, talking to myself in a Southern drawl, always in character."

Julie told Mary Murphy of *TV Guide* that she had found her character, who represented another major departure for her, in her own raising of her and Blake's five children: "Before I had children, I didn't particularly like kids. I would look at other people's kids and think I didn't want one if they acted like that. But the minute my own child was born, I understood. The umbilical cord opens up such deep emotions. Helping through the teenage years is especially difficult. I can really feel the pain. That's what I identify with most."

Julie also spoke with Michael Szymanski of *The Advocate* in 1991 about the long-standing rumors of her homosexuality. After noting that some of the unfounded gossip stemmed from that long-ago joke she and Carol Burnett had tried to play on Mike Nichols, Julie denied having had any lesbian relationships.

Blake who had another gender-bending movie, *Switch*, in release, also did an interview for *The Advocate* with David Ehrenstein. Blake acknowledged that "gay life has always interested me," partly because, "very early on in my career, before I'd gained any prominence at all, I got the reputation of being gay. I honestly don't know why. At first I found that I deeply resented it and got very angry....I went through years of analysis. The first couple of years I struggled with the idea that maybe I *am* gay, but what am I so afraid of if I am....If I were gay, I'd be the first person to step out and say so. I'd have no problem with that."

That June, 1991, Julie cohosted *The Forty-Fifth Annual Tony*

Awards with Jeremy Irons live on CBS. During the show she sang a medley including "Wouldn't It Be Loverly?" and "I Could Have Danced All Night" from *My Fair Lady* and the title song from *Camelot*. In rehearsal she asked Irons, who had talked-sung the role of Professor Higgins on a studio recording of *My Fair Lady*, to sing with her, but he refused. "No one can beat Rex [Harrison] when it comes to that," he said.

United Nations Secretary General Boutros Boutros-Ghali named Julie UNIFEM Goodwill Ambassador in March of 1992. She made her first visit to UNIFEM beneficiaries in April. In the village of Loboudou, Senegal, she presented a grain grinder to the local women.

The Julie Andrews Rose was introduced at the Chelsea Flower Show in May of 1992. Julie was in London for the launching of the orangey-pink hybrid developed by grower Gareth Fryer and formally named *fryvivacious*. "I'm thrilled and very flattered," she said. "It's an enormous compliment." The rose was not to be for sale in the United States. Experimental seedlings planted in California turned "tall and scraggly," Tom Carruth, a hybrider-horticulturalist, explained to Robert Corbell, the publisher of *Julie Andrews News and Views*, in a 1994 letter. "The flowers fade to a murky color in our sun."

That same month Blake Edwards was honored at the Cannes Film Festival with a retrospective of ten of his movies. With Julie by his side, he debuted his director's cut of the much maligned and underrated *Darling Lili*. The Edwards version was almost half an hour *shorter* than Paramount's 1970 release. Blake was also awarded the French Legion of Honor.

In 1992, Julie and Blake sold the Paradise Cove, Malibu beach house that they had built more than twenty years before, for $8.5 million. The house, with its five bedrooms and a guest cottage on five acres, was completely razed by the new owner, in order to build a faux Tuscan villa. The Edwards sculpture studio, tennis court, swimming pool and thirty steps down to the semiprivate sandy beach were left intact. Having also given up their Beverly Hills estate, Julie and Blake bought one new house halfway in between their two former properties, in Brentwood.

In June, Julie gave a benefit concert at the Whaler's Church in Sag Harbor, on the eastern end of Long Island, raising $50,000 for the three-hundred-year-old shore town's Bay Street Theater. Her daughter Emma Walton and Emma's husband, Stephen Hamilton, year-round residents of Sag Harbor, cofounded the 299-seat theater with Sybil Christopher, who lived in nearby Sagaponack. Sybil Christopher, who had been married to Richard Burton up through *Camelot* and who consequently had known Emma since her babyhood, and Emma were coartistic directors while Stephen was the executive director.

Emma's father, Tony Walton, also a Sag Harbor resident, helped to design the theater, in a building which had been both a torpedo factory and a reggae club. Tony also frequently donated his scenic and costume design expertise to the Bay Street's productions. "Without question, our celebrity opened doors for us initially," Emma admitted to William Harris of *The New York Times*. "But there is a downside: a perception that we are flush...that rich theater in the Hamptons run by Richard Burton's wife and Julie Andrews's daughter. We are constantly cap in hand, and will be forever; that's the nature of the business."

Artistically, Bay Street Theater was a success in its first five seasons. Eight of the theater's first thirteen productions had subsequent runs in Manhattan, including *Three Hotels* by Jon Robin Baitz and *Full Gallop* by Mary Louise Wilson and Mark Hampton. Mercedes Reuhl, Cherry Jones, Dianne Wiest, Ron Rifkin, and Amanda Plummer performed at the theater and Sidney Lumet directed there. Terrence McNally, Lanford Wilson, and Joe Pintauro each wrote a one-act play that was commissioned by Bay Street. The three playlets later ran at the Manhattan Theatre Club under the umbrella title *By the Sea, By the Sea, By the Beautiful Sea*. In 1995, Bay Street had an operating budget of $1.6 million, $500,000 of which came from box office receipts.

"For Steve and me, starting a theater was a way to reconcile what we love to do with living where we wanted to live," Emma said. "It was our great dream to live out here. I've been coming here every summer for twenty years. We were married out here. In order to survive and work in the theater nowadays you have to create your own work. You can't wait for somebody else to employ you."

The London-based *Business Age* decided, in its September 1992 issue and its first survey of the kind, that Julie was the sixty-ninth wealthiest woman in the United Kingdom (despite the fact that she lived in Switzerland and the United States). She was the second-ranking entertainer on the list of 250 women with a fortune that *Business Age* estimated to be $37.4 million, outpaced only by Sheena Easton who ranked thirty-ninth with $67 million. Queen Elizabeth II was tenth on the list with an estimated $170 million. Andrews and Easton were the only performers in the top one hundred names, but Joan Collins, Petula Clark, and Cilla Black were alleged to have personal fortunes in excess of $20 million.

"Blake will be very interested in that," Julie said when told of her wealth ranking. "He'll think I'm hiding something from him. Are you sure it was me?"

Ironically, the magazine noted that Julie had managed to accumulate her wealth despite having steadfastly refused roles in episodic television. Julie's most disastrous foray into television, or into any aspect of show business, occurred in 1992 when she agreed to star in a half-hour situation comedy, *Julie*. The pilot, originally titled *Millie*, had been written by Blake Edwards, who directed his wife in all six episodes that were produced. The show's premise concerned a television variety star who moves to Sioux City, Iowa, to live with her new husband, a veterinarian played by James Farentino. In order to keep their family together, she does her national variety show from a local television studio. The sitcom was bereft of humor and of any chemistry between its costars. The show was so bad that the network, ABC, aired it only after the regular season and the sweeps, placing it among the summer reruns. Even there, *Julie* failed to attract a following and was canceled after just five episodes, leaving one forever in the can.

She made a more uplifting 1992 television appearance on NBC's *Christmas in Washington*, on which she sang "Sunny Bank" and "The Holy Boy" solo, and "The Secret of Christmas" in a duet with Peabo Bryson. She joined President George Bush, Mrs. Bush,

Bryson, Neil Diamond, Midori, the U.S. Naval Academy Glee Club, and the Soul Children of Chicago choir in the finale, "Hark, the Herald Angels Sing."

Before 1992 was over, Julie had redeemed herself totally with a sublime new Philips studio recording of the Rodgers and Hammerstein musical *The King and I*, co-starring Ben Kingsley as the nineteenth-century Siamese monarch and opposite Julie's Anna, the Welsh widow who tutors his children. Operatic mezzo-soprano Marilyn Horne, *Miss Saigon* Tony award–winner Lea Salonga, and Peabo Bryson sang the three other major roles, and John Mauceri conducted the Hollywood Bowl Orchestra. The recording, a Grammy-nominee that employed the glorious Alfred Newman orchestrations, underscoring and bits of dialogue from the 1956 Yul Brynner–Deborah Kerr movie version of *The King and I*, provided a natural match of star and material.

Many of her fans hoped that Julie would undertake a stage revival of the musical in the role of Anna. She did not, preferring to pursue the long-delayed stage musical version of *Victor/Victoria*, leaving the role of Anna in the much-lauded 1996 Broadway revival of *The King and I* to Donna Murphy.

14

Putting It Together

In 1993, thirty-one years after she had left *Camelot* for Hollywood and beyond, Julie Andrews finally came back to the New York theater in *Putting It Together*, a play without much dialogue but including some forty Stephen Sondheim songs. The intimate, five-person piece was devised by Sondheim and Julia McKenzie, who also directed *Putting It Together* in a three-week run at the Old Fire Station Studio Theatre in Oxford, England in 1992, just as Sondheim was finishing a term there as a visiting professor of musical comedy at Oxford University. Producer Cameron Mackintosh, who endowed the fellowship that sponsored Sondheim's professorship, was so taken with *Putting It Together* that he wanted to transfer the program more or less intact to London's West End. Diana Rigg, who also had starred in the London 1988 revision and revival of Sondheim's *Follies*, would play and sing the lead role of the brittle, mouthy, middle-aged, upper-middle-class wife—as she had in the Oxford showcase.

No suitable West End theater was available, so Mackintosh decided to present *Putting It Together* at the off-Broadway Manhattan Theatre Club.

McKenzie, who also had starred in the 1988 version of *Follies* in London, and in the 1977 Broadway production of *Side By Side By Sondheim*, would continue as the director. She, Mackintosh, and musical director Scott McKenzie met with Sondheim at his home in New York City to discuss possible stars of a certain age for the leading role. When the name Julie Andrews came up, Sondheim himself was delegated to approach her and persuade her to agree to sign on. After all, he had known her since 1962, when her then-husband, Tony Walton, had designed the sets for *A Funny Thing Happened on the Way to the Forum*, Sondheim's first Broadway hit as both composer and lyricist. However, Stephen and Julie·never had worked together, nor did he even know if she was available.

She may not have been, before that moment, but when Sondheim's call came, Julie was at least ready to consider a return to the live stage. She had "always said privately, at home, that if Sondheim ever asked me to do a show it might be the one time that I would have to say, simply, yes." Then, too, she and Blake more intently were preparing the adaptation of *Victor/Victoria* for Broadway, which had been more off than on for ten years. Daughters Amy and Joanna, whom she long had given as a reason not to take on any extended job, were now nineteen and eighteen respectively, and ready to leave home for college. Julie could, of course, keep accepting concert dates (her staple repertoire even included two Sondheim songs, "Being Alive" and "Not a Day Goes By"). She found it "depressing" and "irritating," though, to reiterate, in her concert set's autobiographical format, "Then I sang..." or "Then I did...." Rather, "I wanted to wake up my brain, to be contributive, to be of today, rather than thirty years ago."

Also, a limited engagement at the off-Broadway, 299-seat Manhattan Theatre Club could provide a smaller-scale testing of the waters before her big return to Broadway itself in *Victor/Victoria*, to which she now was publicly committed. With four other actor-singers in *Putting It Together*, the show's success or failure would not depend on Julie Andrews. Still, "a part of me said, 'Hold on, now. Let's just think about this a bit.' Sondheim is hardly dabbling in a little pool. It's more like diving into the deep end," she told Patrick Pacheco of *The Los Angeles Times*.

"Stephen's music bares your soul," Andrews continued. "He pierces to the heart of all our lives. That is, if you allow him to get to you, because it can be too painful. The lady I play covers her pain with a lot of wit. Each of our characters starts off by being full of veneer, but very quickly reveal who they are. They're slowly stripped of their illusions."

Putting It Together, as Sondheim himself pointed out, represented the first time Julie would be playing "a contemporary character in a contemporary musical. She hasn't had a chance to do that kind of work." When tickets went on sale for the show, which also starred Stephen Collins, Christopher Durang, Michael Rupert, and Rachel York, fans lined up in freezing February weather and bought up all the seats for its entire four weeks of previews and seven-week run. Scalpers were getting as much as $750 for a pair of $40 tickets.

Julie was paid only scale, $500 a week, for doing the show. She would have to sing one show a night, Tuesday through Friday, and two shows each on Saturdays and Sundays. She also had to share a basement dressing room with Rachel York. There was no star billing, although alphabetically she came first among the five principals. In rehearsals, with almost everyone suffering from voice problems and flu, Julie dispensed tea, sympathy, and cold remedies. Appropriating the perhaps inevitable theme song, "A spoonful of Julie helps the medicine go down," the other four cast members recovered quickly enough to keep the show's opening schedule.

"Rusty" was a word that only began to describe the way Julie felt when she began working on the show with the other four members of the cast. "Does anyone else feel as if they've forgotten everything they ever knew about performing?" she asked one day in rehearsal. "I usually hope to have a lot more time to learn something," Julie told costar Christopher Durang in a *TheaterWeek* interview. "This was actually just three weeks of intense study. That may be okay for a television show, but here I was returning to Broadway for the first time in years and feeling *so* much pressure, and there was no out-of-town tryout....Sondheim's work can be so complicated and I was very nervous. I was singing Sondheim that I had never sung before. And then there were a lot of harmonies to learn, which I love to do but don't sing very often."

Putting It Together opened to unanimous critical acclaim for Andrews, as well it should have; she provided its soul and spine, and showed no trace of nerves. A radiant and striking vision in periwinkle blue evening pajamas, Julie endowed each of her numbers with a heretofore unseen confidence and savvy born of nearly six decades of life lessons. Her first-act finale, the acerbic hymn to a failed marriage, "Could I Leave You?" from *Follies*, was chilling in its hateful ambiguity. And Julie's impeccable diction on the breath-racing nervous-breakdown song (I'm Not) "Getting Married Today" from *Company*, would have made Madame Lilian Stiles-Allen more than proud.

Andrews, without benefit of virtually any spoken lines, gave the most acute and complex performance of her life, singing rather than speaking a gamut of emotions from dark to merely sardonic. "My Husband, the Pig" provided some raunch: "Who can contend with an endless erection that falls on its face when it sees its reflection," she trilled. "Every Day a Little Death" offered some self-analytical angst. Her full-fledged character was, as another lyric had it, "smart, tart, dry as a martini."

William A. Henry III, in *Time,* called *Putting It Together* "the next best thing to a new Sondheim score. The evening glows like a candlelight supper, intimate, tasteful, sophisticated and romantic."

The cast album (a double cassette or compact disc) of *Putting It Together* was recorded over four days during the show's run at the Hit Factory's Studio One in New York, under Stephen Sondheim's personal supervision. The recording captured the most memorable qualities of the 96-performance run, and introduced audiences to a new range (literally and metaphorically) in Andrews's singing and material.

Convinced that all kinds of "good music is coming back," Andrews resumed her solo recording career in 1994. "My own children," she explained, "are coming full circle from heavy metal and grunge to embracing Rodgers and Hammerstein and Duke Ellington." Andrews also liked the privacy and the retake and editing possibilities of the recording process.

Julie Andrews/Broadway: The Music of Richard Rodgers was

recorded in London and Los Angeles with a full orchestra conducted by Ian Fraser, who also had conceived and arranged the album. Fraser had come to America from his native England in the *Camelot* era, 1962, to work with composer/star Anthony Newley and lyricist Leslie Bricusse on the Broadway production of *Stop the World, I Want to Get Off*. Fraser began working with Andrews as a vocal arranger in 1972, on her television series. He became her musical director in 1973, and two of his eleven Emmys came from working with her. He returned with her to Broadway, also after an absence of more than thirty years, to be the musical director and vocal arranger on *Victor/Victoria*.

Jay David Sachs was the producer of these two recordings, *Putting It Together* and *The Music of Richard Rogers*, and of *Here I'll Stay, The Words of Alan Jay Lerner*.

The Rodgers album reflected a more dramatic-narrative style of delivering lyrics than Andrews had demonstrated before, partly the result of her work in *Putting It Together*, partly from the wisdom of experience. Her flawless diction and trademark wistfulness were still intact. The album's highlights included an adventurous "Waltz Carousel" medley, and "Nobody Told Me," with a Rodgers lyric from *No Strings* and "Where or When," with a Hart lyric from *Babes in Arms*. By risking new phrasings, she also made "The Sound of Music" fresh again after thirty years. The Rodgers recording received a deserved Grammy nomination (the first for an Andrews solo album) for Best Traditional Pop Vocal.

Her voice, it was clear, had deepened further, into the mezzo-soprano range, and narrowed further, to two and-a-half octaves, causing her to strain a bit on the waltz medley. "I don't have the instrument I used to," she admitted, "I'm certainly not the coloratura I once was, but I think I know better what to do with what I have."

She also appeared to have learned a lot about running her career by 1994. "I'm not above being smart about what I should do— businesswise," she told David Patrick Stearns of *USA Today*. "I strive to get what I want and people have said that I'm a monster in that department. But that's always said about us ladies who grasp for our own strength."

Sensitive to the sobriquets "The Iron Butterfly" and "the nun with the switchblade" that sometimes were applied to her, Andrews said, "I'm resilient and I'm professional; if that's iron, so be it." She admitted to Patrick Pacheco that "one does build one's defenses so well. There's a certain degree of that very controlled and careful lady and I'm not unaware of it. By nature, I really am a fairly bouncy and sunny individual. There are elements of me in the roles I've played in the past. But people forget that Mary Poppins was just a role, too. I'm more complex than that; it's just a question of allowing those sides to come out."

In 1994 Julie did her first-ever U.S. television commercial and her first magazine advertisement since her Blackglama "What Becomes A Legend Most?" fur ad in several women's magazines in 1982. In the commercial, Andrews pitched Arthritis Foundation pain medicine, which was manufactured by Johnson & Johnson. With a piano playing "I Could Have Danced All Night" in the background, Julie is seen in a theater, wearing a grey knee-length jacket, white blouse, and grey skirt, with her arms crossed. She says, "I love working in the theater, and despite the arthritis that runs in my family, I plan to go right on working." As the visual cuts to her visiting with white-coated personnel in a laboratory, she goes on: "The Arthritis Foundation is working, too, to find a cure. And until they do, they've helped to create new Arthritis Foundation Pain Relievers, for pain relief we can count on...part of the purchase price goes to research into arthritis, so we're helping others as we help ourselves." The print ad offered somewhat the same message. The Center for Science in the Public Interest charged that the medicine in question was nothing more than ordinary aspirin but that it cost $150 more per year than the generic pain reliever. The pharmaceutical company denied the charges, but the ads soon were withdrawn.

In 1995 Julie starred in two PBS *Great Performances* specials, *Some Enchanted Evening: Celebrating Oscar Hammerstein II*, and *Julie Andrews: Back on Broadway*, which chronicled her life leading up to her return to live theater in *Victor/Victoria*. In the tribute to the lyricist, which she hosted, Julie sang "A Cock-Eyed

Optimist" from *South Pacific* as her opening number, and closed with "Edelweiss" from *The Sound of Music*. She also received her sixth personal Emmy nomination, for Outstanding Leading Performance in a Variety or Music Program, on the Japanese (NHK) production *The Sound of Julie Andrews*, which was shown in the United States on the Disney Channel.

Julie and Blake devoted most of 1995 to their oft-postponed stage version of *Victor/ Victoria*. The musical was budgeted at $8.5 million. Julie and Blake put up $2 million of this amount themselves. "I remember asking him if he really thought that was a smart move," she said. "But I couldn't blame him. You put your money where your mouth is."

Originally scheduled to open in April of that year on Broadway, after out-of-town tryouts in Boston, the show was delayed further when a one-million-dollar portion of the show's capitalization dropped out. During this delay, Robert Loggia, who long had been announced for the old Robert Preston role of the gay impresario Toddy, was out and Tony Roberts was in. Loggia, who had been married in Julie's and Blake's living room in Switzerland, also had worked with them in *S.O.B.* The James Garner role of King Marchand, the resolutely heterosexual gangster from Chicago who is attracted to "Victor," went to Michael Nouri, based on his superlative Emile Debeque in *South Pacific* at the Long Beach Civic Light Opera. Rachel York, who had shone along with Julie in *Putting It Together*, was signed for the Lesley Ann Warren part of King's nightclub singer girlfriend.

It was clear why her role was a coup for York, who was in her late twenties and had learned most of her singing technique by listening to Julie Andrews and Ella Fitzgerald and Barbra Streisand records while growing up in Boulder, Colorado. York remained a huge Andrews fan after sharing their dressing room during *Putting It Together* and dancing the tango with her so often in *Victor/Victoria*. "What you see is pretty much what you get," said York. "I can say without hesitation that I've never met a more gracious, classy woman than Julie Andrews."

What was less obvious was why Julie, nearing sixty, and Blake, who was over seventy, would take on such a demanding gamble as a Broadway musical at this stage in their careers. "The stakes are so much higher now," Julie noted. "We're very aware of the chance we're taking."

"For a long time, it was 'over my dead body, I'll never go through that again,'" Blake said about Julie's returning to the stage. "She had five continuous years of Broadway; to this day she has nightmares about it." To Mike Wallace, he acknowledged, "I had to beat her over the head to get her to do this." She agreed to do the recycled role because, she said, "I didn't want to be put out to pasture. When I'm sixty-five I don't want to look back and say 'damn, I wish I'd done that.' This is too good, the kind of role that doesn't often get offered a lady."

Edwards's own "need" to do it was clear-cut, he told Charlie Rose. "I seem to be always re-inventing myself. I'm one of those people that needs to work, needs to do. When I originally did the film I decided almost immediately it was a good stage vehicle. I kept obsessing on that all the time. I needed to do it for me...I needed to do it for Julie, too. She was getting too kind of... 'complacent' is not the word. She needed a challenge. She's one of those people that does her best when she's gotta climb the mountain."

The four best numbers were kept from the movie, with new ones added by Henry Mancini and Leslie Bricusse. After Mancini's death in 1994, Bricusse worked with his collaborator on *Jekyll and Hyde*, Frank Wildhorn. Most prominently missing from the stage version of *Victor/Victoria* was "The Shady Dame from Seville" number, first done by Andrews, then at the end of the movie by Robert Preston, stuffed into her costume and knocking down a line of boy dancers.

"We still have a lot of physicality in the musical numbers," Edwards said, "but it's not clumsy." A nonmusical scene in the movie had established Victoria's extreme poverty by showing her slipping a cockroach from her purse onto her plate after a restaurant meal, so that she could leave without paying. This scene also was cut from the stage show. "You need close-ups for cockroaches," Blake explained.

"We've certainly felt a lot freer," Andrews said. "When we made the movie in 1982, in the back of my head I always felt that it was a bit of a cop-out that King had taken a peek at me and knew I wasn't a boy. In the show, King kisses me not knowing if I'm a woman or a boy."

Working with her husband as her director, Julie said, "can be tough, especially when I don't do something right. But it can be good because we talk a kind of shorthand. Over all, it's more good than bad. We get pretty feisty and heated once in a while. If anything could have torn our marriage apart, this would have. But we don't take theatre arguments home with us. We both know that it's over and done with once it's done."

The show officially opened at the Orpheum Theatre in Minneapolis on June 11, 1995, and proceeded to sell more than $3 million worth of tickets. During its four-week run in Minneapolis (three weeks of which were designated "previews"), *Victor/Victoria* remained a work in progress. Thanks to daily changes, the same show never was performed twice. The net result of new music and lyrics, and different dialogue and direction was more than a half hour cut from the musical before it went on to Chicago for further fine-tuning.

In a *New York Times* Sunday Magazine cover story, "What She'll Do For Love," Philip Weiss wrote of following the show for four months, from early readings through the Minneapolis and Chicago tryouts. He found Edwards "sometimes brittle and impatient" with Julie, even "casually cruel to her." Noting her style of "polite indirectness," Weiss started "keeping count in my notes of all the times she apologizes for herself. 'Can I just say something?' 'So sorry.' 'Sorry. I was late on that.' 'Sorry. I got a cramp half-way through. 'Sorry. So sorry.' 'I'm sorry to be such a pain about this.....' 'I'm terribly sorry but we have to decide which lyrics are being used.'"

Weiss completely detailed the process of putting *Victor/Victoria* together, the cutting and adding of songs, Edwards's appropriating "bits" from the movie and elsewhere, and the mixed midwestern critical and audience reaction to the process. Weiss's piece, which concluded that "she'll do anything for her husband," came out on Julie's birthday and two days before the first New York preview, which helped to give the show a bad advance "buzz," though it didn't hurt the healthy $15-million box-office advance.

Back in New York in time for her sixtieth birthday, October 1, 1995, Julie pronounced herself "scared to death." More than forty-one years after she had made a similar journey to join the cast of *The Boy Friend*, Andrews was riding into Manhattan from the airport to offer up *Victor/Victoria*. "I looked at the city and the skyline," she recalled, "and I thought to myself, we must be crazy aiming for the biggest thing we could imagine, a Broadway hit. It's scary and I would be a fool not to be terrified."

Julie recalled her official *Victor/Victoria* opening night in New York, Wednesday, October 25, 1995, as a bit of a blur. "I was anxious that the show be presented well," she told Bridget LeRoy, Tony Walton's stepdaughter, in an interview featured in the *Peconic Independent* of Long Island. "I was so nervous that I almost didn't hear [the applause that greeted her first entrance]. I know that sounds really dumb, but I was relieved to get through that first night without falling on my face. So many things were riding on that evening: Blake's first appearance on Broadway, my reappearance on Broadway, everything."

The opening night was capped by a glittering party in the grand ballroom of the Marriott Marquis Hotel, which also housed the theater where *Victor/Victoria* was playing. "Paris by Night" was the theme, featuring black satin and white chiffon drapery, and large ice sculptures shaped like Paris landmarks. Veuve Cliquot donated twenty-two cases (4,000 glasses) of its champagne. Julie "spent five minutes there," she recalled. "There were so many people that I couldn't get to see a friend or member of my family, not a single one. Finally the security guy said, 'Listen, it would probably be safer if you just went home.' And I did. I went home and had cornflakes. It wasn't until about a week later that everything simmered down enough for me to enjoy myself."

Among the first-night attendees who partied somewhat longer were Mary Tyler Moore, Robert Goulet, Vanessa Williams, Lauren

Bacall, Pierce Brosnan, Douglas Fairbanks, Jr., Barbara Walters, Robert Loggia, and Frank and Kathie Lee Gifford.

Kathie Lee had been approached before the opening to perform the Wednesday and/or Saturday matinees of *Victor/Victoria*, but she declined for family and professional reasons. (Also Kathie Lee's husband, Frank Gifford had expressed some reservations about the song "Paris Makes Me Horny," even though it was sung by Rachel York.) Julie told Kathie Lee that she understood, saying that she never regretted it when she put the family first, and always regretted it when she didn't. Then she announced that she would be doing all eight performances a week, which she did—for a while.

Once she understood that the *Victor/Victoria* reviews, while mostly favorable to her, were less than stellar overall, "we all sort of figured, well, we just better get on and do the show," Julie told Patrick Pacheco of *Newsday*. "We knew why we were doing the show and, though we were aware of our failings, we thought we'd done pretty well under the circumstances.....I'm not doing the show to get personal kudos. There's a different reason for working these days. That's another reason I wanted to come back to Broadway. I used to be fearful of the theater and aggressive toward an audience as a whole animal. I attributed to them those things that I felt about myself. If I didn't like myself then I was convinced that they didn't like me either. It was stupid, but through the help of friends and a little analysis I'm now able to open my arms to an audience and just say, 'Hi, how wonderful of you to be here. Let's forget the taxman and just have fun.'"

"It's nice not having to be the ingenue anymore," Julie told Joel Siegel on *Good Morning America*, "to be able to say I've been around fairly long and I know what I'm doing—at least I think I know what I'm doing."

Andrews found *Victor/Victoria* "infinitely harder to do" than *My Fair Lady*, and not just because it was forty years later. She had thirteen costume changes, most of them quick and some mechanically cumbersome—and eight songs, five of them in the second act. "We've added a great deal [of music] to the film," she told Chip Deffea of *The New York Post*, "and the singing never comes naturally. I don't have that kind of voice. I *never* have had that kind of voice, although people think I do. I don't just get up and sing like a lark every morning. My voice sounds like a terrible rusty engine most mornings. And then I work it gradually. I have to warm up before going on stage, just as a dancer does."

Julie remembered the great operatic diva Maria Callas coming back stage to see her after a show and saying, "I don't know how you do it eight times a week. I do two performances a week."

One Andrews secret was Dr. Kessler's Drops in a vaporizer as a throat spray. Another was a humidifier whirring in her sixty-degree dressing room. A third was pre-taped high B-flats, which critics had noted her difficulty reaching and which had prompted *Forbidden Broadway*'s Julie parody, "I Couldn't Hit That Note." Rachel York defended the practice, in *Vanity Fair*: "She just pre-recorded them so she doesn't have to hit them eight days a week.....Sarah Brightman pre-recorded her B-flats in *Phantom*. So *come on*."

While she had virtually no social life outside the theater, Julie did see Carol Burnett, who also had returned to New York to do a Broadway show after more than thirty years, starring in the farce *Moon Over Buffalo*. After her initial limited contract, Burnett had agreed to continue with the hit show, but only if she could leave the Tuesday evening performance to her alternate, and thus do only seven performances a week and get two full days in a row off. (Zoe Caldwell made a similar arrangement with her show about Callas, *Master Class*.) It was a strategy for survival that Andrews soon would adopt.

Julie invited Carol for Thanksgiving dinner, 1995, and gave her the name of a good physical therapist—to alleviate the pain from a nightly workout on a raked stage. "When Julie and I first started, we talked about men," Burnett kidded. "Later on we talked about children. Then it was how do we keep in good shape? Now we talk Metamucil."

Andrews and Edwards leased a townhouse on the Upper East Side of Manhattan, which she had loved since first arriving in New York for *The Boy Friend*. She was ensconced on the top floor, where she mostly slept or rested when she wasn't working. He took over the second floor, where he often wrote all night. Since their hours were opposite (and she needed nine hours of sleep more than ever), Julie and Blake saw less of one another than at any other time during their marriage.

They also rented a weekend house in Sag Harbor, Long Island, near Emma, to which Julie was driven, lying down on a futon mattress in the rear of her large sport-utility vehicle, as soon as the last show of the week was over. "I've fallen in love with the Hamptons," she said. "It's a godsend to be able to walk by the sea and breathe the fresh air, and to enjoy the light, which is so extraordinary."

Despite the care she took of herself, Julie became sick three times in 1996, and was out of the show for several weeks in all. In January, she had "a bad flu with bronchitis and God knows what" and missed eleven performances. At the end of February, thinking that she was having a recurrence of the flu, Andrews was rushed to Lenox Hill Hospital for an emergency gallbladder operation. She missed a total of twenty-one performances until she recovered.

The morning after her gallbladder surgery she joked that she might donate her gallstones to Broadway Cares/Equity Fights AIDS to be auctioned off to raise money. (Why not? Michael Nouri's used cigars were fetching $10 and "blown" body mikes from Julie and the rest of the cast went for $5 at the charity's annual sidewalk fair.) She also sat up in her hospital bed, hand writing—in verse—a long note of explanation, in order to comfort her *Victor/Victoria* cast.

During both medical absences, Julie was capably replaced by her understudy, Anne Runolfsson, then thirty years old. But with Andrews out of the show the Marquis Theatre house slipped to about sixty percent of capacity, and the box office gross, which had been averaging $800,000 weekly, went down to around $600,000.

At one point, Twiggy, the 1960s London model who had gone on to play Julie's old role in the movie version of *The Boy Friend* and on Broadway opposite Tommy Tune in *My One And Only*, was approached to take over the *Victor/Victoria* role for three months in 1996 while Julie rested and recovered. Twiggy, who had proven anew that she could sing well enough in the English music hall/

"legit" style on her album *London Pride*, agreed. But the producers withdrew their offer, having decided that a three-month-long absence of Andrews would hurt the box office irreversibly. Twiggy remained a possibility to head up an increasingly unlikely national tour.

In order to preserve Julie's health, Runolfsson also began doing every third Sunday matinee, then every second Sunday, and some Wednesday matinees. Andrews would take occasional evening performances off, such as her sixty-first birthday, October 1, 1996. Sometimes Julie's nights off were unscheduled, and the management office would find out only at 7:20 P.M. that she was not going on at eight o'clock. Then the scramble began to refund ticket holders' money, which was an audience member's right when an above-the-title star would not appear as scheduled. The average eighty-percent-of-capacity audience could dip to as low as twenty-five percent if Andrews canceled a performance.

Julie's previously unannounced days off began when she skipped the Sunday matinee on Tony Awards day, June 2, 1996. She omitted several shows in the last week of June, and the special holiday matinee, July 5—all without any prior notice. This practice prompted Ken Mandelbaum to editorialize in *TheatreWeek*: "There's nothing wrong with skipping some shows; what's wrong here is not warning the public in advance....people are coming into town from all over the place, only to find that (a sometimes perfectly healthy) Andrews is not appearing at a certain performance....Andrews has stated repeatedly that she intends to stay until the show pays back, but it would help matters if she did all shows when she is in good health."

Only when Runolfsson played the lead role did half-price *Victor/Victoria* tickets show up at the TKTS window on Duffy Square. Even when Julie played to sparse houses, as she did for a special Thursday matinee on January 2, 1997 (New Year's Day having been on the usual matinee day, Wednesday), and balcony patrons were reseated in the orchestra, the producers charged full price for tickets, mostly $75 and $55. Then, one Tuesday night in February of 1997, 25-percent-off tickets to *Victor/Victoria* appeared at the TKTS booth, even though Julie was performing that night. The discount continued, as needed, throughout the spring of 1997.

The Drama Desk, an organization of critics, theater editors and press agents, announced its awards nominations in early May, 1996, just prior to the Tony nominees' list. (Unlike the Tonys, the Drama Desk awards were given for outstanding achievement in all of New York City professional theater, whether on Broadway or off-Broadway.) *Victor/Victoria* failed to make the list of six Best Musical nominations, though *Big* did. Julie was nominated as Best Actress in a Musical, Rachel York as Best Featured Actress in a Musical, and Robin Wagner for Best Set Design for a Musical. (He also was nominated in the same category for *Big*.) Otherwise *Victor/Victoria* was ignored by the Drama Desk. The show did win the Best Musical designation from the Outer Critics Circle.

Then came the great Tony flap. When only Julie was nominated from *Victor/Victoria*, she was hurt, stunned, and seething, and determined to protect her "family." Blake said he "wasn't particularly surprised" by the nominating committee's slighting of him and his show, but acknowledged that it had created "a lot of problems" for Julie in her "not knowing how to handle it." He told Charlie Rose that making a stand had been her decision, but that once she had made it, "we discussed how best to do it."

Whether her televised announcement was best or not may never be decided, but her decision to refuse her nomination did drop a bombshell on the awards process. The fourteen-member panel of nominators was criticized for picking four musicals that had originated in nonprofit theater over the two that had been big movies, *Victor/Victoria* and *Big*, which also had a commercial tie-in with F. A. O. Schwartz, the Fifth Avenue toy store depicted in the show. The committee, which included Donald Brooks, Julie's costume designer from *Star!* and *Darling Lili*, choreographer Marge Champion, actor Barnard Hughes, and the doyen of drama critics, Brendan Gill of *The New Yorker*, hardly could be called avant-garde. The youngest committee member, playwright Jon Robin Baitz, said he was "very, very supportive of *Victor/Victoria*." No one else was.

The Tony committee said that Andrews, then arguably the

biggest star on Broadway, couldn't refuse her nomination. Her name stayed on the ballot, but she didn't win. The Tony nominating committee was doubled to twenty-eight for the 1997 awards.

"Believe me, I'm the last person to rock the boat," Julie told Patrick Pacheco. "But it was so hurtful and I personally felt so embarrassed that I was the only one nominated. Even if we had just got three nominations—okay, we take our lumps together. But one?...We deserved many other nominations. It really looked like someone had some kind of an agenda...But, oooh, five minutes before [she made her announcement] I really knew how somebody feels when they are about to be hanged."

HarperCollins repackaged Julie's two children's books in 1996, to capitalize on her new surge in popularity, even to the point of giving the author a new name on the dust jacket. *The Julie Andrews Edwards Treasury: Two Magical Novels* combined the complete texts of her *Mandy* and *The Last of the Really Great Whangdoodles* and sold for $9.98. Since the publisher used the original printing plates, the title pages still proclaimed Julie Edwards as the author of both stories. Her third, much-talked-of children's book, about a ship's cat, was entitled *Babe*—which presumably would have to be changed after the success of the 1995 pig movie of the same name. *Babe* had been "half finished" for about twenty years. "If it weren't for Blake Edwards and being Mrs. Edwards, I wouldn't have the courage to write at all," she said.

At the end of October, 1996, after her sixty-first birthday and the one-year anniversary of *Victor/Victoria* on Broadway, talking to Katie Couric on the *Today* show, Julie pronounced herself, "fine, considering....I do nothing else but the show, and on two-show days it's really rough. But the show gives such joy to audiences, and a lovely message, if there is one."

Although business continued to drop and her voice was getting a bit ragged, she remained committed to starring in the musical until it turned a profit. Originally, that moment had been projected for no later than the one-year anniversary of the New York opening. However, despite a "bump" in box-office after the Tony Awards flap, the summer of 1996 on Broadway was slower in general than usual, a trend to which *Victor/Victoria* was not immune. The spring 1996 opening of the hit revivals of *A Funny Thing Happened on the Way to the Forum* and *The King and I* had given lovers of traditional musicals some alternatives. The new-wave Tony-winners *Rent* and *Bring in Da Noise, Bring in Da Funk* were attracting the new, younger audience. The smash revival of *Chicago* and the promise of *Titanic, Steel Pier, Dream* and *Jekyll and Hyde* took away some of *Victor/Victoria*'s theater-party business, a mainstay of its relative success.

The "break-even" point now was projected to be early summer of 1997. Andrews said, "I can make myself" get through Christmas and New Year's. Liza Minnelli, whom Julie described as "a dear chum," agreed to step into the title role for four weeks beginning on January 7, 1997, which promised to attract a somewhat different audience. Following her vacation, Julie would stay with *Victor/Victoria*, she said.

As it turned out, she did not make it through to the holidays. She was out of *Victor/Victoria* again, for nearly two weeks in November, with pneumonia. When she returned to the show, the first act finale production number "Louis Says" was permanently cut from the show, as it had been temporarily several times already, when Julie was not feeling up to it. Nobody missed it. She relied even more heavily on her pretaped B-flats.

Blake and the creative team reworked the show somewhat for Minnelli, causing some observers to wonder why more changes had not been made all along, to accommodate Andrews and improve the show. Costume designer Willa Kim redesigned some of the costumes for Minnelli, and hair stylist Paul Huntley made a wig that made her "look like Tyrone Power," she said.

Leslie Bricusse, who occasionally wrote both words and music (most notably for the Rex Harrison movie *Dr. Dolittle*), produced a new song for Liza entitled "Who Can I Tell?" It replaced Julie's "Crazy World" in the scene just after Michael Nouri's character, King Marchand, and "Victor" confirm their mutual attraction. Greg Evans wrote, in *Variety*, that "Who Can I Tell?" was "a pop ballad so suitable" to Minnelli's talents that it would "likely take a spot in

[her] concert repertoire for years to come. Her performance of the song here virtually justifies the entire star-replacement gambit."

Another of Julie's first-act songs, "If I Were a Man," was dropped, perhaps because the shorter and bubblier Minnelli's biggest problem with the role was convincing anyone that she could be male. This meant that Liza's first song was the big production number "Le Jazz Hot," which also had been in the movie. Some choreography was added for Minnelli in the restaging of this number. The biggest change of all was in making the character of Victoria American rather than English.

Minnelli, who had won her first Tony for the otherwise forgotten *Flora the Red Menace* in 1964, the same year for which Julie won her *Mary Poppins* Oscar, was invited to meet with Blake and Julie in October 1996 at their Sag Harbor home, ostensibly to talk to Edwards about coproducing an unnamed Broadway show. Liza had been the pioneer, in 1976, of the radical notion of an established Broadway star stepping in for another during a vacation or illness. Minnelli had substituted for Gwen Verdon in the original production of *Chicago* for six weeks during Verdon's illness.

"Julie would do the same for me, I know she would," Minnelli told Harry Haun of *Playbill*. "She really, really needed a rest or she would have injured herself and done some long-range damage if she continued. She had to have four weeks, and that would probably have meant closing the show."

"I want to continue in the show," Julie told the *New York Post*, "but everything in my body was telling me not to."

In October of 1996, the Alan Jay Lerner lyrics album, *Here I'll Stay*, was issued. Andrews had recorded it in London and Hollywood in 1994, again with Ian Fraser, just after the release of the Richard Rodgers album, as the second release of her projected Philips series of recordings of great Broadway music.

While Rodgers and Hammerstein may have written songs *for* her, at times it seemed as if Lerner had written lyrics *through* her, as indeed he had to Fritz Loewe's melodies in *Camelot*, especially. But the entire Andrews–Lerner album was sublime, an even better case of "the glove fitting the hand" as she put it. Making the album had taken her all the way back: "Just listening to the overture to *My Fair Lady* with the huge symphony orchestra play, my legs buckled and I practically sank to my knees." And she recalled Lerner as "a mercurial and wonderful human being, and especially wonderful to me."

Apart from the more expected pleasures of the Lerner album—renditions of songs that she had introduced, Julie offered up some genuine treasures from more obscure shows. Chief among them was "One More Walk Around the Garden," which Lerner had written with Burton Lane for the forgotten *Carmelina*. Julie's haunting version of the song provided a fitting valedictory to Lane, who died at eighty-four just three months after the album's release, the last of his generation of great Broadway composers. Andrews had picked the song as appropriate to "going back to Broadway, this far along in my career."

The same week the Lerner album was released, Emma Walton gave birth to a baby boy named Samuel David Hamilton, Julie's fifth grandchild.

On November 12, 1996 Julie and Blake celebrated their twenty-seventh wedding anniversary. "I *would* be Mary Poppins if I pretended that everything was rosy," she said. "And it ain't. Marriage is the hardest work you're ever going to do. When Blake is dressed up in a tux and has just had a hit movie, or he's directing, he's bright and shiny in my eyes. When he's got a cold and he's in his pajamas and he's unshaven, it's a bad day. I love him more deeply because of the foibles and the fights.

"We vowed when we married that this we would take one day at a time," she told Earl L. Conn, "and not have any fantasies that precluded the realities. I think it's been a very good idea. You don't try to see the long term as much when you deal with the everyday. It probably bears fruit because you concentrate on the moment. I guess the other side of it is that two people have to *want* to do it....It's quite a surprise for both of us. We made that one vow and suddenly it's twenty-five years later!"

For his part, Edwards, "At the risk of sounding like just another fan," as he told Charlie Rose in an interview aired on November 21,

1996, just after their anniversary, Julie "is a remarkable human being; she really, truly is. Her failings are fun. There's nothing really disastrous about them. As long as we've been married, I've never really found anything I truly didn't like about her. There are things that anger the hell out of me because they're so diametrically opposed to my m.o. But I always find myself smiling inside about them."

Blake remembered a time in Switzerland when "I was ·really campaigning to get her to stand up for her rights and speak out more—and not be a victim so much. She took off on me, really gave it to me. And I started to laugh. I said, 'What have I created here? What is this?' Then she really got mad, and said 'You've been after me for years to stand up for what I believe in, and now you're laughing at me for doing it.'"

In a perverse kind of irony, when the Grammy Award nominations were announced in early 1997, *Victor/Victoria* was nominated as best Original Cast Album (along with *Rent, Bring in Da Noise, Bring in Da Funk* and *A Funny Thing Happened on the Way to the Forum*), and the cast album of *The King and I* revival was not cited.

When Minnelli opened in *Victor/Victoria,* Vincent Canby of *The New York Times* found her "alarmingly miscast.... She dominates neither the show nor its only good number, 'Le Jazz Hot' [in which she participates] as little more than a member of the chorus....The show itself chugs along on automatic pilot....Without Ms. Andrews, *Victor/Victoria* is a joke without a punch line."

Costar Tony Roberts was so annoyed at Minnelli's forgetting lines that he called in sick and said he would do so until Julie returned. Cooler heads prevailed, and Roberts returned to work while Minnelli still was in the musical. Then Liza was felled with a throat infection and missed the last four performances of her commitment. She reportedly hinted she might be available, after all, to replace Julie in the show when the time came, but only if Roberts was gone.

After her four-week vacation, with three of the weeks at her "hideaway home" in Switzerland, Julie returned to New York in time to be inducted into the Theater Hall of Fame on February 3,

1997. The honor was voted upon by some 350 members of the American Theater Critics Association and the Theater Hall of Fame. To be eligible for the Hall of Fame, a theater person had to have begun his or her New York (not necessarily Broadway) career at least twenty-five years before nomination and have at least five major credits. *Victor/Victoria* was only Julie's fifth New York show, so she entered the Hall of Fame in her first season of eligibility. Seven others were enshrined with Andrews in the twenty-sixth annual induction, joining more than three hundred members of the Theater Hall of Fame: actors Eileen Atkins, Brian Bedford, and Earl Hyman, and costume designer Florence Klotz; posthumously, *Washington Post* drama critic Richard Coe, costume designer Irene Sharaff, and legendary comedienne Nancy Walker.

Julie returned to her show the next night. She told Rosie O'Donnell that she was "grateful for the rest. I ate too much, slept too much, took walks, and watched my grandchild." She also read, watched videos and the Swiss winter vistas, woke in the middle of the night to make herself bacon-and-egg sandwiches, and ate her first restaurant meal out since she had undertaken *Victor/Victoria* two years earlier. Julie now talked of leaving the show at the end of May, even though the investment would not have been earned back.

On David Letterman's show on February 20, 1997, she sidestepped the controversial goings-on during her absence, genuinely not involved in them, but she said she was pleased for the investors, herself among them, that Minnelli had played to nearly ninety-seven percent of capacity.

"Liza's been an absolute trouper, but the company is happy that 'Mum' is back," said Tony Adams, one of the show's producers and the longtime Edwards associate who was "like Blake's number one son," in Julie's words. "From the beginning," Adams said, "she has been the emotional and spiritual leader, and this company has been through so much that they're like children who automatically look to Julie for that calming influence."

Anne Runolfsson performed virtually all of the Sunday matinees in February, March, and April 1997, giving Julie two days in a row off each week. Despite this lightened workload, Julie got sick again and missed several more performances. At the end of March she used her "weekend" to fly to Hollywood to present a special Oscar to Michael Kidd on the ABC Academy Awards telecast. Appearing radiant and sincere in her tribute to her old friend and colleague, she evoked the Julie Andrews of thirty years before, when she had reigned supreme in the movie capital.

She returned to New York and front-page controversy, in publications as disparate as the *Wall Street Journal* and the *New York Post*. After months of rumors that the insurance underwriters for *Victor/Victoria* were refusing to pay claims owing to her various absences for illness, the show's producers filed a lawsuit against the nine insurance companies that shared the risk, saying that they had rescinded the policy, which the producers had thought would pay up to $2 million for missed Andrews performances due to illness. The insurance companies, led by Lexington Insurance Company of the American Insurance Group Inc. (AIG), claimed that Julie had lied on her application for the coverage about previous respiratory and bone, joint, muscle, back, spine, or neck conditions.

Leslie Scism's front-page *Wall Street Journal* story of April 4, 1997, which detailed the lawsuit, prompted the next day's *Post* full front-page headline "Mary Poppins/Liar, Liar" framing, top and bottom, a photograph of Julie as Maria von Trapp in *The Sound of Music*.

The insurance policy had been bought in March, 1995, for a premium of $157,985. It would have paid the full $8.5 million cost of mounting the musical had Julie not been able to do the musical at all, due to illness or injury. The policy carried a standard two-consecutive-performances deductible, meaning that it would never pay for just one missed show.

The producers claimed losses of $442,435 from her ten missed performances in January, 1996, and another $980,850 in lost revenue during her twenty-one day absence for gallbladder surgery and recovery. Her late 1996 larynx problems represented about another $183,000 in losses, according to the producers' lawsuit, which also said that the insurers refused to pay any of those claims.

The only direct statement about Julie's health in the lawsuit was that she "occasionally experiences mild bronchial symptoms solely in response to specific external factors such as infection, smog, or other environmental factors, and occasionally has mild osteoarthritic symptoms in her hands."

She herself was not available to comment on the charges and countercharges. Peter Cromarty, the press agent for *Victor/Victoria*, said she was in "vocal rest."

On Sunday, June 1, 1997, Julie gave her last performance in the show. On Tuesday, June 3, she was replaced by Raquel Welch, who had signed to do the role for six months.

Personally, after half a lifetime of psychotherapy, she was still groping and growing: "If the therapy is successful you learn to live with what you find, which is a form of liking. I keep telling everybody—I arrived at liking myself and saying 'It's O. K.' at a very late age."

Julie's regrets included not having more children and that she didn't work more on Broadway. This was ironic, as she always had said that being a wife and mother is what most precluded a return to the stage. "If the family is great then I can embark on anything," she told Jonathan Van Meter. "But if they're not great, then I can't concentrate on anything but trying to put it right."

Carol Burnett, for one, thought she had made the right choice: "One of Julie's greatest acts of courage as a woman was to adopt those orphan infants with Blake. She was so devoted to them you completely forgot she wasn't their natural mother....and she gave up years of her professional life to care for them."

Professionally, Julie found it "very hard to get perspective on yourself," but offered a line from *Camelot* as a possible summing-up of her life: King Arthur, when asked to describe his kingdom, says, "It's one of what we all are, which is just a drop in the great blue motion of the shining sea. But it seems some of the drops sparkle, some of them really do sparkle." Julie said, "Perhaps if I've sparkled a little, that would be just fine."

She ruled out no aspect of show business for her future, even working on the stage again, "or anywhere else—weather and tide permitting." She explained to Christopher Durang the origin of that expression: it came from "the early concert party days when my parents performed by the sea, on the actual sand. They used to announce the times of the performances on big placards: 2:30, 4:30, and 6:30 and so on, and then underneath would be written 'weather and tide permitting.' It became a family phrase; I use it all the time."

Julie and Blake seriously were considering leaving the West Coast and buying homes in the Hamptons and Manhattan. "We're exploring our options," she said. After three months off for "sheer, utter silliness" with her family, Andrews was going to be ready for a new challenge: "I'm dying to explore and experiment." At the top of her wish list might be creating "an original role in a Sondheim musical." She also thought it would be "delicious" to play Angela Lansbury's old role, Mrs. Lovett, in the movie version of Sondheim's *Sweeney Todd,* and acknowledged that there had been "discussion" of her doing it.

In March 1997, as she was winding down in *Victor/Victoria,* Julie was surrounded by colleagues from her past: Christopher Plummer as [John] *Barrymore* opened at the theater behind hers. Down 45th Street, the musical *Jekyll and Hyde* by Frank Wildhorn and Leslie Bricusse was in previews. And on the same street, at the Royale Theatre, where Julie had played in *The Boy Friend* forty-three years before, Lesley Ann Warren was about to open in the Johnny Mercer musical *Dream.*

Beginning "to face my own mortality," Julie's "ongoing question" was: "What do I want to do with the rest of my life? I don't know whether it's because of my rocky beginnings, but it seems awfully important to be able to say, at the end of your life—or the end of the day—that you don't regret much, that you've seized the time and shaken it a bit.

"I still would like to contribute a great deal," she said. "There's a lot of life in the old girl yet."

APPENDIX 1

Julie Andrews on the
New York Stage

The Boy Friend: 1954–55; produced by Cy Feuer and Ernest Martin; directed by Vida Hope (and Cy Feuer, uncredited); book, music, and lyrics by Sandy Wilson; choreography by John Heawood; setting and costumes by Reginald Woolley; with John Hewer, Dilys Lay, Ruth Altman, Eric Berry, Ann Wakefield, Bob Scheerer, Geoffrey Hibbert, and Moyna MacGill.

My Fair Lady: 1956–58; produced by Herman Levin; directed by Moss Hart; book and lyrics by Alan Jay Lerner; music by Frederick Loewe; choreography by Hanya Holm; production design by Oliver Smith; costumes by Cecil Beaton; with Rex Harrison, Stanley Holloway, Robert Coote, Cathleen Nesbitt, John Michael King, and Phillipa Bevans.

Camelot: 1960–62; produced by Moss Hart, Alan Jay Lerner, and Frederick Loewe; directed by Moss Hart; book and lyrics by Alan Jay Lerner; music by Frederick Loewe; choreography by Hanya Holm; production design by Oliver Smith; costumes by Adrian and Tony Duquette; with Richard Burton, Roddy McDowall, Robert Goulet, Robert Coote, and M'el Dowd.

Putting It Together: 1993; music and lyrics by Stephen Sondheim;

directed by Julia McKenzie; devised by Stephen Sondheim and Julia McKenzie; musical staging by Bob Avian; Scott McKenzie, musical director; sets by Robin Wagner; costumes by Theoni V. Aldredge; with Stephen Collins, Christopher Durang, Michael Rupert, and Rachel York.

Victor/Victoria: 1995–97; written and directed by Blake Edwards; music by Henry Mancini and Frank Wildhorn; lyrics by Leslie Bricusse; choreography by Rob Marshall; production design by Robin Wagner; with Michael Nouri, Tony Roberts, Rachel York, Gregory Jbara, Richard B. Shull, Adam Heller, and Michael Cripe.

The Films of Julie Andrews

Mary Poppins: 1964; Buena Vista; produced by Walt Disney; directed by Robert Stevenson; music by Robert B. and Richard M. Sherman; with Dick Van Dyke, Glynis Johns, David Tomlinson, Hermione Baddeley, Ed Wynn, Matthew Garber, Karen Dotrice, Elsa Lanchester, Jane Darwell, Arthur Treacher, and Reginald Owen. Oscars went to Julie Andrews for Best Actress; the Shermans for Best Original Score and Best Song ("Chim, Chim, Cheree"), Cotton Warburton for Best Editing, and Peter Ellenshaw for Best Visual Effects. Eight other nominations. Available on videocassette and laserdisc (Disney).

The Americanization of Emily: 1964; Metro–Goldwyn–Mayer (Filmways); produced by Martin Ransohoff; directed by Arthur Hiller; screenplay by Paddy Chayefsky; music by Johnny Mandel; with James Garner, Melvyn Douglas, Joyce Grenfell, James Coburn, and Keenan Wynn. Available on video and laserdisc (MGM/UA).

The Sound of Music: 1965; Twentieth Century–Fox; produced and directed by Robert Wise; screenplay by Ernest Lehman, based on the stage play by Howard Lindsay and Russel Crouse, suggested by the book *Maria Trapp's Story*; music by Richard Rodgers, lyrics by Oscar Hammerstein II (with additional words and music by Richard Rodgers); production design by Boris Leven; with Christopher Plummer, Eleanor Parker, Peggy Wood, Richard Haydn, Charmian Carr, Dan Truhitte, Portia Nelson, Anna Lee, Marni Nixon, Norma Varden, Heather Menzies, Nicholas Hammond, Duane Chase, Angela Cartwright, Debbie Turner, and Kim Karath. Oscars to Wise for Best Picture and Best Director; also Best Editing, Best Sound and Best Music Score: Adaptation. Available on video and laserdisc (CBS/Fox).

Hawaii: 1966; United Artists (the Mirisch Company); produced by Walter Mirisch; directed by George Roy Hill; screenplay by Dalton Trumbo and Daniel Taradash; music by Elmer Bernstein; costumes by Dorothy Jeakins; with Max von Sydow, Richard Harris, Jocelyne La Garde, Manu Topou, Gene Hackman, Carroll O'Connor, and John Cullum. Eight Oscar nominations, no awards. Available on video and laserdisc (CBS/Fox).

Torn Curtain: 1966; Universal; produced and directed by Alfred Hitchcock; screenplay by Brian Moore; music by John Addison; costumes by Edith Head; with Paul Newman, Lila Kedrova, David Opatashu, and Ludwig Donath. Video and laserdisc (MCA)

Thoroughly Modern Millie: 1967; Universal; produced by Ross Hunter, directed by George Roy Hill; screenplay by Richard Morris; music score by Elmer Bernstein; musical numbers scored by André Previn; with Mary Tyler Moore, Carol Channing, James Fox, John Gavin, Beatrice Lillie, Jack Soo, Pat Morita, and Philip Ahn. An Oscar went to Elmer Bernstein for Best Music Score. Five other nominations. Available on video and laserdisc (MCA).

Star!: 1968; Twentieth Century–Fox; produced by Saul Chaplin; directed by Robert Wise; screenplay by William Fairchild; music arranged and conducted by Lennie Hayton; choreography by Michael Kidd; production design by Boris Leven; set decoration by Walter M. Scott; costumes by Donald Brooks; with Daniel Massey, Richard Crenna, Michael Craig, Bruce Forsyth, Beryl Reid, Jenny Agutter, Robert Reed, Tony Lo Bianco, and Garrett Lewis. Six Oscar nominations. Available on video and laserdisc (Fox Video).

Darling Lili: 1970; Paramount; produced and directed by Blake Edwards; screenplay by Blake Edwards and William Peter Blatty; music score by Henry Mancini; new songs by Johnny Mercer and Henry Mancini; costumes by Donald Brooks and Jack Bear; with Rock Hudson, Jeremy Kemp, Lance Percival, Michael Witney, Jacques Marin, Doreen Keough, and Gloria Paul. Three Oscar nominations. Not available on video or laserdisc.

The Tamarind Seed: 1974; Avco–Embassy (ITC); produced by Ken Wales; directed and screenplay by Blake Edwards, based on the novel by Evelyn Anthony; music by John Barry; with Omar Sharif, Anthony Quayle, Daniel O'Herlihy, Sylvia Syms, and Oscar Homolka. Available on video (Embassy).

10: 1979; Warner Brothers (Orion); produced by Blake Edwards and Tony Adams; directed and screenplay by Blake Edwards; music by Henry Mancini; with Dudley Moore, Bo Derek, Robert Webber, Dee Wallace, Sam Jones, Brian Dennehey, Max Showalter. Two Oscar nominations: Henry Mancini for the score, Mancini and Robert Wells for the song "It's Easy to Say." Available on video (Warner) and laserdisc (Coliseum).

Little Miss Marker: 1980; Universal; Jennings Lang, producer; directed and screenplay by Walter Bernstein; music by Henry Mancini; with Walter Matthau, Tony Curtis, Sara Stimson, Bob Newhart, Brian Dennehy, and Lee Grant. Available on video (MCA).

S.O.B.: 1981; Paramount (Lorimar); produced by Blake Edwards and Tony Adams; directed and screenplay by Blake Edwards; music by Henry Mancini; with William Holden, Robert Preston, Richard Mulligan, Shelley Winters, Marisa Berenson, Larry Hagman, Robert Loggia, Stuart Margolin, Craig Stevens, Loretta Swit, Robert Vaughn, Robert Webber, Larry Storch, Rosanna Arquette, Corbin Bernsen, Benson Fong, and Jennifer Edwards. Available on video and laserdisc (CBS/Fox).

Victor/Victoria: Metro–Goldwyn–Mayer; 1982; produced and directed by Blake Edwards; screenplay by Blake Edwards; music by Henry Mancini; lyrics by Leslie Bricusse; with James Garner,

Robert Preston, Lesley Ann Warren, Alex Karras, John Rhys–Davies, Graham Stark, and Peter Arne. Mancini and Bricusse won an Oscar for their score. Six other nominations, including Andrews, Preston, and Warren in acting categories. Available on video and laserdisc (MGM/UA).

The Man Who Loved Women: 1983; produced and directed by Blake Edwards; screenplay by Blake Edwards and Milton Wexler, based on François Truffaut's 1977 movie; with Burt Reynolds, Kim Basinger, Marilu Henner, Barry Corbin, Cynthia Sikes, Tracy Vaccaro, Jennifer Edwards, and Sela Ward. Available on video (Columbia–TriStar).

That's Life!: 1986; Columbia; produced and directed by Blake Edwards; screenplay by Blake Edwards and Milton Wexler (and improvised); music by Henry Mancini; with Jack Lemmon, Sally Kellerman, Chris Lemmon, Jennifer Edwards, Emma Walton, Felicia Farr, Robert Loggia, Cynthia Sikes, Rob Knepper, Dana Sparks, and Matt Lattanzi. Oscar nomination for Best Song. Available on video.

Duet for One: 1986; Cannon; directed by Andrei Konchalovsky; screenplay by Tom Kempinski, and Jeremy Lipp and Andrei Konchalousky; based on the play by Tom Kempinski; with Max von Sydow, Alan Bates, Liam Neeson, Cathryn Harrison, Margaret Courtenay, Macha Meril, and Rupert Everett. Available on video and laserdisc (MGM/UA).

A Fine Romance: 1992; Castle Hill; directed by Gene Saks; screenplay by Ronald Harwood, based on the play *Tchin–Tchin* by Francois Billetdoux; with Marcello Mastroianni, Ian Fitzgibbon, Jean–Pierre Castaldi, Jean–Jacque Dulon, Maria Machado, Denise Grey, Jean–Michel Cannone, and Catherine Jarret. Available on video (Academy Entertainment 1625).

APPENDIX 3

Julie Andrews Discography

The Boy Friend: 1955; original Broadway cast recording, with John Hewer, Dilys Lay, Ruth Altman, Geoffrey Hibbert, Eric Berry, Ann Wakefield and Bob Scheerer; music and lyrics by Sandy Wilson. RCA LOC-1018. Also issued as an album of three 45-rpm extended-play records (RCA EOC-1018). Available on compact disc (RCA 60056).

My Fair Lady: 1956; original Broadway cast recording, with Rex Harrison, Stanley Holloway, and Robert Coote; music by Frederick Loewe, lyrics by Alan Jay Lerner. Columbia OL-5090 (United Kingdom, Phillips RBL-1000; 1957). Also issued as a four-disc extended-play album, Columbia A-5090. On regular compact disc, and on a 1994 Gold Recording, Collector's Edition, Master Sound, with a bonus track featuring chat with the stars; Columbia SK66128.

High Tor: 1956; original television soundtrack, with Bing Crosby and Everett Sloane; music by Arthur Schwartz, lyrics by Maxwell Anderson; music scored and conducted by Joseph J. Lilley (Decca DL 8272). Available on vinyl only.

Cinderella: 1957; original television cast album, with Edith (later Edie) Adams, Alice Ghostley, Kaye Ballard, Ilka Chase, and Jon

237

Cypher; music by Richard Rodgers, lyrics by Oscar Hammerstein II; orchestrations by Robert Russell Bennett; musical director Alfred Antonioni. Columbia OL-5190 (OS-2005 Stereo). Available on compact disc (Columbia).

The Lass with the Delicate Air: 1957; music arranged and conducted by Irwin Kostal; RCA LPM-1403 (LSP-1403 Stereo). Not available on compact disc.

Julie Andrews Sings: 1958; arranged and conducted by Irwin Kostal; RCA LPM-1681 (LSP-1681 Stereo). Not available on compact disc.

Tell It Again: Songs of Sense and Nonsense: 1958; with Martyn Green; Angel 65041 (monaural only). Not available on compact disc.

Rose–Marie: 1958; with Giorgio Tozzi, Meier Tzelniker, Frances Day, Tudor Evans, Frederick Harvey, John Hauxvell, and Marion Keene; music by Rudolf Friml and Herbert Stothart, lyrics by Otto Harbach and Oscar Hammerstein II; conducted by Lehman Engel; RCA LOP 1001 (RE-27143 in United Kingdom). Not available on compact disc.

My Fair Lady: 1959; original London cast recording, with Rex Harrison and Stanley Holloway; composed by Frederick Loewe, lyrics by Alan Jay Lerner; Columbia. Available on compact disc (Columbia).

Camelot: 1961; original Broadway cast recording, with Richard Burton, Robert Goulet, and Roddy McDowall; composed by Frederick Loewe, lyrics by Alan Jay Lerner; Columbia OS-8521 Stereo (CBS-7009 in United Kingdom). Also KOS-2031 (different cover). Available on compact disc (Columbia CK 32602-2).

Broadway's Fair Julie: 1962; with Henri René and his orchestra; Columbia CL 1712, monaural, CS-8512 Stereo. NOT available on compact disc.

Julie and Carol at Carnegie Hall: 1962; original television cast recording, with Carol Burnett; composed and with lyrics by Mike Nichols, Ken Welch, and others; Columbia OL 5840 monaural, OS-2240 Stereo. Issued on compact disc, but no longer available.

Don't Go Into the Lion's Cage Tonight: 1962; arranged and conducted by Robert Mersey; Columbia CS-8686, Stereo. NOT available on compact disc.

Mary Poppins: 1964; original motion picture soundtrack, with Dick Van Dyke; composed and with lyrics by Richard M. and Robert B. Sherman; Buena Vista STER-5005; Stereo. Available on compact disc (Disney).

The Sound of Music: 1965; original motion picture soundtrack; with Christopher Plummer, Peggy Wood, Marni Nixon, Charmian Carr, Dan Truhitte, Heather Menzies, Anna Lee, Portia Nelson, Nicholas Hammond, Duane Chase, Angela Cartwright, Debbie Turner, and Kym Karath; composed by Richard Rodgers, lyrics by Oscar Hammerstein II; arranged and conducted by Irwin Kostal; RCA LSOD-2005 Stereo. Available on compact disc (RCA 66587).

A Christmas Treasure: 1967; with André Previn conducting. Firestone MLP(mono), SLP-7012; 1966; RCA LSP-3029. Available on compact disc (RCA 3829).

Thoroughly Modern Millie: 1969; original motion picture soundtrack, with James Fox and Carol Channing; title song by Sammy Cahn and James Van Heusen; arranged and conducted by André Previn; score by Elmer Bernstein and others. Decca DL1500 (Monaural), DL-71500 (Stereo). (Brunswick STA-8685 in U. K.) Available on compact disc (MCA 10662).

Star!: 1968; original motion picture soundtrack, with Daniel Massey, Bruce Forsyth, and Beryl Reid; songs by Noel Coward, George and Ira Gershwin, and others. Twentieth Century–Fox Records; DTCS 5102 Stereo. (EMI SSL 10233 in Great Britain; 1968.) Available on compact disc, with added material (20th Century–Fox Film Scores 11009-2; 1993).

Darling Lili: 1970; original motion picture soundtrack, with Henry Mancini and his orchestra, Gloria Paul and Le Lycée Francais de Los Angeles Children's Choir; new songs composed by Henri Mancini, lyrics by Johnny Mercer; RCA LSPX-1000 Stereo. RCA SF-8138. NOT available on compact disc, except in Japan as part of Disc Two of a five-disc retrospective, *The Anthology of Henry Mancini*; BVCP7310.

A Little Bit in Love: 1970; Harmony H-30021 (or CHM-687) Stereo. (A reissue from *Broadway's Fair Julie* and *Don't Go Into the Lion's Cage Tonight.*) NOT available on compact disc.

Julie and Carol at Lincoln Center: 1971; original television soundtrack with Carol Burnett; special material by Mitzi Welch and Ken Welch; conducted and arranged by Peter Matz; Columbia S-31153 Stereo. Issued on compact disc (Columbia Special Products 31153), but no longer manufactured.

The World of Julie Andrews: 1972; (In United Kingdom: *The Best of Julie Andrews*); Columbia KG-31970 Stereo. (CBS-68234 in United Kingdom) (A reissue from *Broadway's Fair Julie, Don't Go into the Lion's Cage Tonight* and the *My Fair Lady* London cast album.) Available on compact disc, 1994, United Kingdom (Sony CD 983403 2).

TV's Fair Julie (a reissue of *Broadway's Fair Julie*): 1972; Harmony KH-31958 Stereo. Not available on compact disc.

The Secret of Christmas: 1973; arranged by Ian Fraser; Great Britain only, Embassy (CBS) 31237 or 31522 compact disc released in the United States as *Christmas With Julie Andrews*, Columbia CK 40857, 1982.

Julie Andrews (a reissue compilation from *Lass With the Delicate Air* and *Julie Andrews Sings*): 1975; RCA ANL-1-1098 Stereo; 1975 (U. K. RCA HY-1002). Not available on compact disc.

An Evening with Julie Andrews: 1977; (Japan only); Julie's only live concert recording. RCA SX-281(A-7). Not available on compact disc.

Julie Andrews Signature Album: 1978, Franklin Mint limited edition double-boxed set of red vinyl records. Not available on compact disc.

Victor/Victoria: 1982; soundtrack album; with Robert Preston and Lesley Ann Warren; MGM/PolyGram MG-1-5407; available on compact disc, GNP Crescendo 8038, with added material.

Love Me Tender: 1983; Peach River (Runaway). Available on vinyl and tape only.

Love, Julie; 1987; USA Music Group; with Bob Florence. Available on compact disc (USA 539; in United Kingdom: Success 135).

Julie Andrews: A Little Bit of Broadway: 1988; Available on compact disc, Columbia CK 44375.

The Sounds of Christmas—From Around the World: 1990; Hallmark (limited edition as a sales premium in Hallmark card stores). Available on compact disc and cassette only (Hallmark 9705).

The King and I: 1992; with Ben Kingsley, Marilyn Horne, Lea Salonga, and Peabo Bryson; John Mauceri and the Hollywood Bowl Orchestra, using the orchestrations from the 1956 movie version of *The King and I.* Grammy nomination. Philips 438 007-2.

Putting It Together: 1993; Original cast recording, with Stephen Collins, Christopher Durang, Michael Rupert, and Rachel York; musical direction by Scott Frankel; musical arrangements by Chris Walker; RCA Victor double compact disc (09026-61729) and cassette versions.

Julie Andrews: Broadway—The Music of Richard Rodgers: 1994; Philips CD 106250; arranged and conducted by Ian Fraser; lyrics by Lorenz Hart, Oscar Hammerstein II, Stephen Sondheim, and Richard Rodgers. Grammy nomination.

Victor/Victoria: Original cast album, 1995; music by Henry Mancini and Frank Wildhorn, lyrics by Leslie Bricusse; with Michael Nouri, Tony Roberts, Rachel York and Gregory Jhara. Philips 446919. Grammy nomination.

Broadway's Fair Julie (Spain only): "dos albumes clássicos en CD, Edición Limitada, Especial Coleccionistas: Heart-rending ballads and raucous ditties." CBS Sony 4809982 (two compact discs).

Thoroughly Modern Julie: The Best of Julie Andrews: 1996; Rhino 72281.

Julie Andrews: Broadway—Here I'll Stay—the Words of Alan Jay Lerner: 1996; with music by Frederick Loewe, Burton Lane, Kurt Weill, Leonard Bernstein, Charles Strouse, and André Previn. Philips 446 219-2.

The Sound of Julie Andrews: 22 Classic Songs: 1996; Time–Life Records (mail order only); Sony Special Products A26718.

INSTRUMENTAL SOUNDTRACKS FROM THE MOVIES OF JULIE ANDREWS

The Americanization of Emily: 1964; music by Johnny Mandel; Reprise RS-6151 Stereo. NOT available on compact disc.

Torn Curtain: 1966; music by John Addison; Decca DL-79155 Stereo. Available on compact disc (Varèse-Sarabande VSD-5296).

Hawaii: 1966; music by Elmer Bernstein; United Artists UA-LA283-G Stereo. Available on compact disc in Germany only (Tsunami TSU 0105).

The Pink Panther Strikes Again: 1976; music by Henry Mancini; Julie sings "Until You Love Me" in a man's voice on the sound-track, as a "drag" entertainer; United Artists. NOT available on compact disc.

10: 1979; composed and conducted by Henry Mancini (plus Ravel's "Bolero"), lyrics by Robert Wells; vocals by Andrews solo ("He Pleases Me"), in duet with Dudley Moore ("It's Easy to Say"), and by Max Showalter ("I Have an Ear for Love—The Reverend"); Warner Brothers BSK 3399 Stereo. Available on compact disc in Japan only, Warner Brothers (WPCR-785).

Tchin-Tchin: (A Fine Romance): 1991; compact disc, in France only, (Milan CH809; BMG, distributor).

SELECTED SINGLES AND EXTENDED PLAY RECORDINGS

"Polonaise" from *Mignon:* 1947; Columbia (U. K.). Julie's solo, introduced by Vic Oliver, is part of a two-disc 78-rpm recording of *Starlight Roof.*

"Je Veux Vivre" from Gounod's *Romeo and Juliet*/"Come to the Fair": 1948; Columbia (U. K.) 78 rpm. (The "B" side, a traditional English song, is a duet by Julie and her stepfather Ted Andrews, with Barbara Andrews on the piano.)

"Ah! Vous Dirai—Je Mama"/"The Wren": 1948; Columbia (U. K.) 78 rpm. With Ted Andrews conducting the orchestra, and Barbara Andrews on the piano.

Jack and the Beanstalk/"When We Grow Up": 1950; His Master's Voice (U. K.). A twelve-inch 78-rpm disc. Side One offers the cast of the radio show *Educating Archie,* including Julie, in a comic version of the fairy tale. On Side Two, Julie and the ventriloquist's dummy, Archie Andrews, chat and sing.

My Fair Lady, Volume 1: 1956; Columbia EP-5581, an extended play 45-rpm disc. Side A: "On the Street Where You Live"/"Wouldn't It Be Loverly?"; Side B: "I Could Have Danced All Night"/"With A Little Bit of Luck."

My Fair Lady, Volume 2: 1956; Columbia EP-5582, an extended play 45-rpm disc. Side A: "Get Me to the Church on Time"/"I'm an Ordinary Man"; Side B: "I've Grown Accustomed to Her Face"/"The Rain in Spain."

"Tom Pillibi"/"Lazy Afternoon" 1960; 45 rpm; United Kingdom, Decca 11230.

"Meantime" (Carol Burnett)/"You're So London" (duet with Carol Burnett): 1962; 45-rpm radio station promo copy only, from the album *Julie and Carol at Carnegie Hall*. Columbia JZSP 57713.

"He Loves Me"/"Dear Friend": 1964; 45 rpm; CBS DB 7252 (United Kingdom only).

"Supercalifragilisticexpialidocious" (with Dick Van Dyke)/"A Spoonful of Sugar": 1964; 45-rpm single; Buena Vista F-434.

"Jimmy"/"Thoroughly Modern Millie": 1967; arranged and conducted by André Previn; 45 rpm; Decca 32102.

"The Sound of Christmas"/"O Come All Ye Faithful": 1987; arranged by Ian Fraser, with chorus; USA Music Group, 45-rpm; 1987.

"Living in the Shadows," a compact-disc single produced to raise money for Broadway Cares/Equity Fights Aids. Philips SACD 1199.

APPENDIX 4

Major Television Shows and Appearances

High Tor: with Bing Crosby, Nancy Olson, Everett Sloane, Hans Conried, and Lloyd Corrigan; originating network, CBS, as part of its *Ford Star Jubilee* series; produced by Arthur Schwartz; directed by James Neilson; teleplay by Maxwell Anderson (based on his own stage play) and John Monks Jr.; music by Arthur Schwartz; lyrics by Maxwell Anderson, March 10, 1956. The first made-for-television movie according to the *Guinness Book of World Records*. The show was broadcast in black and white, though it had been announced as a color presentation.

Guest appearance on *The Ed Sullivan Show,* singing "I Could Have Danced All Night" and "Without You" from *My Fair Lady;* CBS; July 15, 1956; black and white. This was the first of four Andrews appearances on the Sullivan program.

Guest appearance on *The Ed Sullivan Show,* in a tribute to *Life* magazine, singing "Wouldn't It Be Loverly?" "I'll Follow My Secret Heart," and "Someone to Watch Over Me"; CBS; November 11, 1956; black and white.

Cinderella: with Edith (later Edie) Adams, Kaye Ballard, Alice Ghostley, Dorothy Stickney, Howard Lindsay, Jon Cypher, and Ilka

Chase; produced by Richard Lewine; directed by Ralph Nelson; music by Richard Rodgers, lyrics and libretto by Oscar Hammerstein II; sets and costumes by William and Jean Eckart; CBS; March 31, 1957. The show was telecast in color in the Eastern Standard Time zone only, in black and white in the rest of the United States. A record 107 million viewers watched. Julie received her first Emmy nomination.

Crescendo: a ninety-minute special starring Rex Harrison as a visiting Englishman entertained by a sampling of most styles of American music. Julie and Stanley Holloway did a medley from *My Fair Lady.* CBS; 1957. Black and white.

Guest appearance on *The Dinah Shore Show,* singing "Blue Moon" and "Whispering Hope" solo and, with Shore and Chita Rivera, "Life Upon the Wicked Stage" from *Showboat;* NBC, January 12, 1958; color.

Guest appearance on *The Big Record,* a live show from New York, hosted by Patti Page, with whom Julie sang a duet. Other guests on this eclectic musical episode included the Everly Brothers, Woody Herman and his jazz orchestra, "The Herd," and singer Roberta Sherwood. CBS, February 5, 1958. Black and white.

Guest appearance on *The Jack Benny Hour,* in which she sang "Summertime" from *Porgy and Bess,* a medley from *My Fair Lady,* "Ain't We Got Fun" and "I'm Just Wild About Harry"; CBS; May 23, 1959, repeated in 1963. Black and white.

The Julie Andrews Show, a four-week BBC series on which she hosted guest stars from her British vaudeville past, including Ted and Barbara Andrews, and Vic Oliver from *Starlight Roof.* Julie's new husband, Tony Walton, was the set designer for the programs. The British Broadcasting Corporation (BBC), November 12–December 24, 1959. Black and white.

The Fabulous Fifties, a two-hour special chronicling the outstanding theater, movies, books, and popular music of the decade; Julie sang "Just You Wait" after she and Rex Harrison had replicated the rehearsal process for *My Fair Lady,* which even included her working on her Cockney dialect with Alfred Dixon. CBS; January 31, 1960. Black and white.

Guest appearance on a segment of *The Bell Telephone Hour* titled "Portraits in Music," hosted by the poet Carl Sandburg. Julie sang in a medley of Sigmund Romberg operetta numbers, including "The Fireman's Bride" and "Lover Come Back to Me." NBC; February 12, 1960; color.

Guest appearance on *The Ed Sullivan Show*, in a special tribute to Lerner and Loewe on the fifth anniversary of *My Fair Lady*. Julie and Robert Goulet sang "Almost Like Being in Love" from *Brigadoon*, and she soloed on "Wouldn't It Be Loverly?" and "I Could Have Danced All Night." To promote their new Lerner and Loewe show, Andrews and Richard Burton sang "Camelot" and "What Do the Simple Folk Do?" CBS; March 19, 1961. Black and white.

Four guest appearances on *The Garry Moore Show*, a weekly variety series. CBS; May 2, 1961, September 26, 1961, December 19, 1961, and May 1, 1962. On the first show, Julie and Carol Burnett sang "Big D," from *The Most Happy Fella*, as part of a regular tribute segment "That Wonderful Year" [1956]. In her second appearance, Andrews sang "This Can't Be Love" from Rodgers and Hart's *The Boys From Syracuse* in tribute to the "wonderful year" 1939. The third program was a Christmas show, also featuring Gwen Verdon. On her last appearance, Julie sang part of a medley from *Finian's Rainbow*, saluting the year 1947. CBS; May 2, 1961, September 26, 1961, December 19, 1961 and May 1, 1962. Black and white.

The Broadway of Lerner and Loewe, an hour-long special on which Julie sang "With a Little Bit of Luck" and "Show Me," and joined Maurice Chevalier (from the movie *Gigi*), Richard Burton, Robert Goulet, and Stanley Holloway in the finale, "I Could Have Danced All Night." NBC; February 11, 1962. Color.

Julie and Carol at Carnegie Hall: With Carol Burnett; produced and directed by Joe Hamilton; special material by Mike Nichols and Ken Welch; choreography by Ernest Flatt. The special won an

Emmy Award, and the Rose d'Or from the Montreaux International Television Festival—the first ever awarded to an American program. CBS; June 11, 1962. Black and white.

Guest appearance on *The Andy Williams Show,* a weekly series. On this segment Julie promoted *The Americanization of Emily* by showing clips of love scenes from the movie as Williams counted her kisses with James Garner. Andy and she did a duet of "Where Is Love?" from *Oliver!* Julie sang "Supercalifragilisticexpialidocious" with series regulars the Osmond Brothers. NBC; November 30, 1964. She received an Emmy nomination for this guest spot. Color.

The Julie Andrews Show: an hour-long special with Gene Kelly and the New Christy Minstrels; produced by Alan Handley; musical direction by Irwin Kostal; NBC. The program received two Emmy Awards. November 28, 1965, repeated in 1968; color.

An Evening with Julie Andrews and Harry Belafonte: produced and directed by Gower Champion; musical direction by Michel Legrand; NBC; November 9, 1969. Color.

The Grand Opening of Walt Disney World: a promotional special for the new theme park in Florida, on which Julie sang "When You Wish Upon a Star" and "Zip-a-Dee-Doo-Dah." NBC; October 29, 1971. Color.

Julie and Carol at Lincoln Center: Produced by Joe Hamilton; directed by Dave Powers; special material by Ken and Mitzi Welch; choreography by Ernest Flatt; CBS; December 7, 1971. Color.

The Julie Andrews Hour (a series of twenty-four shows): produced by Lew Grade; directed by Bill Davis; with Alice Ghostley and Rich Little as regulars; guest stars included Angela Lansbury, Cass Elliot, Steve Lawrence, Peggy Lee, Joel Grey, Sid Caesar, Sammy Davis Jr., the Smothers Brothers, Robert Goulet, and Henry Mancini. Julie wrote the music to the program's theme song, "Time Is My Friend," with lyrics by Leslie Bricusse. The

series won seven Emmy Awards. ATV-ABC; September 13, 1972-
March 31, 1973.

Julie on Sesame Street: with Perry Como and the Muppets; she
sang "Bein' Green" with Kermit the Frog. ATV-ABC; November 23,
1973.

Julie's Christmas Special: With Peggy Lee and Peter Ustinov; Lee
and Andrews sang a medley including "Just in Time," "Swinging
on A Star" and "Sentimental Journey." ATV-ABC; December 14,
1973.

Julie and Dick at Covent Garden: with Dick Van Dyke and Carl
Reiner; produced and directed by Blake Edwards; ATV-ABC;
April 21, 1974.

Julie and Jackie—How Sweet It Is: with Jackie Gleason; Gary
Smith, producer; Dwight Hemion, director; ATV-ABC; May 22,
1974.

My Favorite Things: with Peter Sellers and the Muppets; produced
and directed by Blake Edwards; ATV-ABC; April 18, 1975.

Salute to Sir Lew Grade—The Master Showman: Julie was joined
by Tom Jones in a duet of "You Will Be My Music." To honor the
producer of *The Julie Andrews Hour* and many of her specials,
she also sang two golden oldies, "The Sound of Music" and
"Wouldn't It Be Loverly?" ABC; June 13, 1975.

The Puzzle Children: With Bill Bixby; a program about learning
disabilities among children. PBS, October 19, 1976.

America Salutes the Queen (in the United Kingdom, *Silver Jubilee
Royal Variety Gala*): with Bob Hope. NBC, November 29, 1977.

Julie Andrews—One Step into Spring: with Miss Piggy, Leslie
Uggams, and Leo Sayer; Julie sang "At the Ballet" from *A Chorus
Line.* CBS; March 9, 1978.

Guest appearance on *The Muppet Show:* Julie sang "The Lonely Goatherd" from *The Sound of Music.* ATV—syndicated in USA; 1978.

Julie Andrews' Invitation to the Dance: with Rudolph Nureyev, Ann Reinking, and the Green Grass Cloggers; directed by Tony Charmoli; written by Buzz Kohan; Julie sang "Shall We Dance?" from *The King and I,* and Nureyev sang "I've Got Your Number" from *Little Me* to her. CBS; November 30, 1980, repeated in 1981.

The 38th Annual Tony Awards: cohosted with Robert Preston. NBC; June 15, 1984.

Mancini & Friends: with Henry Mancini, Dudley Moore, Andy Williams, Johnny Mathis, Steve Allen, Sue Raney, Laurindo Almeida, and Gary Owens. A "Great Performances" special on PBS; March 21, 1987.

Julie Andrews: The Sound of Christmas; with John Denver and Placido Domingo. ABC, December 16, 1987.

American Film Institute Salute to Jack Lemmon: CBS, May 30, 1988.

Julie and Carol Together Again: ABC, December 13, 1989. Available on video (Live Home Video 69938).

Julie Andrews...in Concert: A solo autobiographical program taped at the Wiltern Theatre in Los Angeles in 1989 at the end of her cross-country concert tour; PBS, March 9, 1990. Available on video (Questar QV22780).

The 45th Annual Tony Awards: Cohosted with Jeremy Irons; CBS; June 2, 1991.

Our Sons: with Ann-Margret, Hugh Grant, Zelijko Ivanek; ABC made-for-television movie, May 19, 1991. Available on video (Atlantic).

Julie: five episodes of a situation comedy; directed by Blake Edwards; with James Farentino. ABC, May 30–July 4, 1992. A sixth episode was shot but never shown, nor was Edwards's 1991 pilot for the series, *Millie.*

Some Enchanted Evening: Celebrating Oscar Hammerstein II. PBS, March 6, 1995.

Julie Andrews: Back on Broadway. PBS, October 25, 1995.

Bibliography

BOOKS

Adams, Edie. *Sing A Pretty Song....* New York: William Morrow, 1990.

Arntz, James, and Wilson, Tom. *Julie Andrews.* Chicago: Contemporary Books, 1995.

Dunne, John Gregory. *The Studio.* New York: Farrar, Straus & Giroux, 1969.

Gottfried, Martin. *Nobody's Fool: The Lives of Danny Kaye.* New York: Simon & Schuster, 1994.

Harrison, Rex. *Rex, An Autobiography.* London: MacMillan, 1974.

Hart, Kitty Carlisle. *Kitty.* New York: Doubleday, 1988.

Hoare, Philip. *Noël Coward: A Biography.* New York: Simon & Schuster, 1996.

Lees, Gene. *Inventing Champagne: the Worlds of Lerner and Loewe.* New York: St. Martin's Press, 1990.

Lerner, Alan Jay. *On the Street Where I Live.* New York: W.W. Norton, 1978.

————. *The Musical Theater: A Celebration.* New York: McGraw-Hill, 1986.

Moseley, Roy (with Philip and Martin Masheter). *Rex Harrison: A Biography.* New York: St. Martin's Press, 1986.

Newquist, Roy. *Showcase.* New York: William Morrow, 1986.

The Noël Coward Diaries. Ed. by Graham Payn and Morley Sheridan. Boston: Little, Brown, 1982.

Shapiro, Doris. *We Danced All Night.* New York: William Morrow, 1990.

Spindle, Les. *Julie Andrews, a Bio-Bibliography.* New York: Greenwood Press, 1989.

Stevenson, Isabelle. *The Tony Award.* New York: Crown, 1987.

Wilson, Sandy. *I Could Be Happy.* New York: Stein & Day, 1975.

NEWSPAPERS AND MAGAZINES

Andrews, Julie, "All About Me," *Coronet* (September 1965), reprinted from *Women's Magazine.*

Covert, Colin, interviews with Andrews and Edwards, *Minneapolis Star-Tribune* (May 21, 1995).

Davis, Ivor, interview, *Los Angeles* magazine (December 1986).

Doten, Patti, interview, *Boston Globe* (July 1, 1989).

Ehrenstein, David, Blake Edwards interview, *The Advocate* (April 23, 1991).

Farley, Ellen, interview, *Los Angeles Times* (August 31, 1977).

Gittelson, Natalie, interview, *McCall's* (November 1986).

Houston Chronicle (December 16, 1994), story on postponed *Victor/Victoria.*

LeRoy, Bridget, interview, *The Independent*, Peconic, N.Y. (____ 1996).

Luhr, William, and Peter Lehman, profile of Blake Edwards, *DGA News* (August-September 1993).

Lyte, Charles, *Daily Mirror,* article on the Julie Andrews rose (May 19, 1992).

Meryman, Richard, interview, *Lear's* (September 1992).

Michaelson, Judith, interview, *Los Angeles Times* (August 9, 1984).

O'Conner, Patrick, review of Rodgers recording, *Gramophone* (January 1995).

Osborne, Robert, coverage of *Victor/Victoria* opening-night party, *Hollywood Reporter* (November 1, 1995).

Pacheco, Patrick, interview with Andrews, Edwards, and Stephen Sondheim, *Los Angeles Times* (March 14, 1993).

Sommers, Michael, account of Theater Hall of Fame induction, *Newark Star-Ledger* (February 5, 1997).

Sweeting, Adam, interview (for *The Guardian*), *Calgary Herald* (November 28, 1994).

Szymanski, Michael, Andrews interview, *The Advocate* (May 1991).

Tevlin, Jon, interview, *Minnesota Monthly* (May 1995).

White, Timothy, interview, *Cosmopolitan* (July 1982).

New Orleans Times–Picayune, October 9, 1989, account of BAFTA awards.

Newsday, February 10, 1997, Patrick Pacheco interview.

————, May 20, 1996, Jack Kroll coverage of Tony controversy.

————, October 4, 1996, Ward Morehouse III and Kyle Smith article on Liza Minelli.

The New York Times, January 26, 1997, Vincent Canby review of Liza Minnelli in *Victor/Victoria.*

————, May 31, 1996, Peter Marks backstage-with-Andrews article.

————, May 12, 1996, William Harris interview with Emma Walton.

————, May, 8, 1996, Peter Marks story on Tony controversy.

————, December 8, 1995, unsigned interview with Carol Burnett.

————. October 1, 1995, Philip Weiss, Sunday magazine cover story on the Andrews–Edwards marriage and return to Broadway.

————, November 17, 1987, Stephen Holden interview.

————, February 2, 1979, Aljean Harmetz piece on casting *Little Miss Marker*.

People, March 14, 1977, Barbara Wilkins interview with Andrews and Edwards.

————, May 27, 1996, unsigned coverage of Tony controversy.

Playbill, January 1997, Harry Haun interview with Liza Minnelli.

Prodigy Interactive Service, October 4, 1995, Mervyn Rothstein interview.

The Saturday Evening Post, June 1996, Earl L. Conn interview.

————, January/February 1980, George Haddad-García interview.

Show Music, Winter 1992/93, unsigned review of *The King and I* recording.

Sky, February 1988, Lidia De Leon interview.

Sunday Woman, September 30, 1979, Jane Ardmore interview with Barbara Andrews.

TheaterWeek, July 29–August 4, 1996, Ken Mandelbaum commentary on Julie's last-minute *Victor/Victoria* performance cancellations.

————, May 31, 1993, Christopher Durang interview.

Time, May 20, 1996, unsigned piece on Tony controversy.

TV Guide, May 18, 1991, Mary Murphy interview.

Newark Star–Ledger, February 5, 1997, Michael Somers account of Theater Hall of Fame induction.

New Orleans *Times-Picayune*, October 9, 1989, account of BAFTA awards.

Newsweek, December 7, 1987, unsigned review of concert tour.

———— May 20, 1996, Jack Kroll coverage of Tony controversy.

New York Post, October 19, 1995, Chip Deffea interview.

———— May 31, 1996, Peter Marks backstage with Andrews article.

———— May 12, 1996, William Harris interview with Emma Walton.

———— May 8, 1996, Peter Marks story on Tony controversy.

———— December 8, 1995, unsigned interview with Carol Burnett.

———— October 1, 1995, Philip Weiss, Sunday magazine cover story on the Andrews-Edwards marriage and return to Broadway.

———— November 17, 1987, Stephen Holden interview.

———— February 2, 1979, Aljean Harmetz piece on casting *Little Miss Marker*.

People, March 14, 1977, Barbara Wilkins interview with Andrews and Edwards.

———— May 27, 1996, unsigned coverage of Tony controversy.

Playbill, January, 1997, Harry Haun interview with Liza Minnelli.

Prodigy Interactive Service, October 4, 1995, Mervyn Rothstein interview.

The Saturday Evening Post, June, 1996, Earl L. Conn interview.

————, January/February, 1980, George Haddad-Garcia interview.

Show Music, Winter 1992/93, unsigned review of *The King and I* recording.

Sky, February, 1988, Lidia De Leon interview.

Sunday Woman, September 30, 1979, Jane Ardmore interview with Barbara Andrews

USA Today, October 28, 1994, David Patrick Stearns interview.

Vanity Fair, October, 1995, Jonathan Van Meter interview.

Variety, May 14, 1996, Army Archerd column quotes. Also, February 18, 1983; April 13, 1992, March 1, 1996, May 10, 1996.

TELEVISION PROGRAMS

Charlie Rose, PBS, November 20, 1996, Blake Edwards interview.

Good Morning America, ABC, September 29, 1995, Joel Siegel interview.

"Julie Andrews—Back on Broadway", *Great Performances*. PBS, October 25, 1995.

Late Night with David Letterman, CBS, February 20, 1997, interview.

Rosie O'Donnell Show, syndicated, January 31, 1997, interview.

"Showbiz Today," *CNN*, October 26, 1995, coverage of *Victor/Victoria* opening.

60 Minutes, CBS, October 22, 1995, Mike Wallace interview.

The Today Show, NBC, October 21, 1996, Katie Couric interview.

Index

257